Beyond
the
Ashes

Beyond the Ashes

Cases of Reincarnation from the Holocaust

Rabbi Yonassan Gershom

A.R.E. Press • Virginia Beach • Virginia

A.R.E. Press
Sixty-Eighth & Atlantic Avenue
P.O. Box 656
Virginia Beach, VA 23451-0656

Library of Congress Cataloging-in-Publication Data
Gershom, Yonassan, 1947-
Beyond the ashes: cases of reincarnation from the Holo-
caust / by Yonassan Gershom.
        p.   cm.
Includes bibliographical references and index.
ISBN 0-87604-293-0
1. Reincarnation—Case studies. 2. Reincarnation
therapy—United States—Case studies. 3. Transmigration—
Judaism. 4. Mysticism—Judaism. 5. Holocaust, Jewish
(1939-1945). 6. Kabbalah. 7. Gershom, Yonassan, 1947- . I.
Title
BL515.G375   1992
296.3'3-dc20   92-31485
                                                    CIP

Edgar Cayce Readings © 1971
by Edgar Cayce Foundation
Reprinted by Permission.

Dedicated to the memory of Michael Finley,
a true friend and brother on the spiritual path.

Contents

Foreword

This book is destined to be a classic. The author, Yonassan Gershom, is a neo-Hasidic rabbi who stands in the long tradition of authentic kabbalistic mystics and seers. The theme touches upon one of the most traumatic events of modern history, the Holocaust, and brings to it fresh esoteric insight, deep faith, and new meaning.

Belief in — and reliance upon — dreams, apparitions, visions, déjà-vu, past-life memories, reincarnation, channeling, angelic communications, post-mortem contacts with deceased relatives, saints and sages, spirit guides, prophecies, and spiritual healings have all been known within the kabbalistic tradition and at various times accepted as part of the natural instrumentality of divine revelation.

Here, Rabbi Gershom combines historical scholarship with his own professional experience as a spiritual counselor in this tradition to relate the fascinating story of his own odyssey to a startling conclusion: many souls who were victims of the Nazi Holocaust have reincarnated — both as Jews and as non-Jews—as part of a natural and divinely sanctioned process of healing and planetary spiritual transformation.

He came to this conclusion much in the same way that Drs. Raymond Moody and Elisabeth Kübler-Ross came to their conclusions about "life-after-life": through listening to many patients who had had significant near-death experiences (NDEs). In this case, Rabbi Gershom listened to over 200 people who contacted him for spiritual counseling after they had experienced specific flashbacks, spontaneous memories or dreams, or visions of themselves dying as victims of the Nazi Holocaust. Many were Jews, but some were not. Yet even these non-Jewish persons often had knowledge of, and/or an innate resonance for, Jewish beliefs, customs, or ritual practices to which they had never been exposed in their present lifetime.

Rabbi Gershom is careful to tell us that this is not a scientific study, but the story of his own living, existential encounter with human souls and their experiences, an encounter which he respects as a spiritual counselor and rabbi. He points out that he is neither a psychologist nor a psychical researcher, in any event. But it is refreshing to find one in his position who is, nevertheless, aware of the recent body of serious research on human psychic and mystical experience, spirit phenomena, and reincarnation. He is one of the few members of the clergy today, whether Jewish or Christian, who really understands the relevance of this kind of research to the future of academic studies in the human sciences and the history of religions.

It may come as a shock to many mainstream

Jews and Christians alike that the ancient Near Eastern metaphysical soil out of which both of their respective religious traditions arose once allowed for such beliefs, but it did. Historians of religion have discerned at least four major kinds of belief about the afterlife present in Jewish tradition from Biblical times through the Middle Ages:

1. Survival through one's descendants
2. Physical resurrection
3. An immortal soul in heaven
4. Reincarnation

Rabbi Gershom examines each of these in turn and finds that they are by no means mutually exclusive, but rather complementary beliefs. He would say that when correctly interpreted in the right context, they are consistent with the development of monotheistic tradition in ancient and medieval Judaism. He also takes note of the fact that belief in reincarnation was present in the Jewish community out of which Jesus came and is reflected in both the New Testament and in noncanonical sources of the same period (e.g., first century B.C.E. through first century C.E.).

Rabbi Gershom logically suggests that there are timeless human psychic and spiritual experiences, such as real spirit contacts in dreams and visions, apparitions, past-life flashbacks, out-of-body and/or near-death experiences, and "heavenly journeys" or "visits" to higher dimensions of psyche and spirit which may lie behind the early Jewish and Christian beliefs about the afterlife. Ancient patriarchs, matriarchs, prophets, and rabbis actually experienced such spiritual realities. These experiences were committed to oral and later written traditions in legends, myths, symbols, and finally doctrines. But frequently these accounts were taken out of context and interpreted in a crude fashion by persons who did not understand the nature of such sacred psychic and spiritual experiences.

One of the most important implications of Rabbi Gershom's work is that there is a "meta-cosmic insight" (the words here are mine, not his), which can emerge from our understanding of history and its worst tragedies—like the Holocaust—in the light of such experiences of the "other world" and an afterlife. This "meta-cosmic insight" is that there is a divine plan, an intelligent process working to bring victory out of tragedy, healing out of pain and despair, and light out of darkness. Although this view of history is central to Jewish thought, it is often overlooked in the modern world.

For all of the evil that human beings can perpetrate, there is, ultimately, a remedy built in by the Creator. That remedy involves the facing and repenting, by each of us, of all that we have done and become that is wrong, that does not reflect the love and compassion of God. That remedy or healing process can occur because, whether in this life or in another, whether in the afterlife or again on earth, we do have the chance to reprogram ourselves in the living Divine Law or Torah of the one God and come eventually to reflect the Divine Light.

There is thus a purpose to human history which is "meta-cosmic," as I have said, in Rabbi Gershom's view. It is a purpose which encompasses the commitment in faith and truth to an all-wise and compassionate Creator, the God of Abraham, Isaac, and Jacob, the God of the patriarchs, matriarchs, and prophets who leads, guides, and inspires His children in the Light—even in the midst of all the tragedies which history can know—to an ultimate victory.

This book is an answer of faith to the despair of our time. Its author invites you to share in the Divine Light of love, power, and wisdom, which he has found.

John Rossner, Ph.D., D.Lit.
Professor of Religion
Concordia University, Montreal

Preface

In writing this book, I have worn many hats: the fur streimel of Hasidic mysticism, the rainbow-colored yarmulke of cultural pluralism, and the plain black hat of Jewish tradition. In addition, there were many times when I needed a healthy dose of bare-headed secular scholarship. Balancing these many perspectives was not always easy, and if there are inconsistencies within these pages, I accept full responsibility.

Beyond the Ashes is not a scientific study, but rather an anecdotal collection of personal stories that were told to me over the past ten years by people who believe that they died in the Holocaust and have reincarnated. These people did not seek me out as a parapsychologist (which I am not) but as a religious counselor. The very nature of this relationship precludes the kind of detached scholarship necessary for a scientific study because, in order to be effective, I have to become personally involved with the client. I also freely admit that I believe in reincarnation, and it was this belief that made it possible for people to open up to me in the first place.

In many ways I am like the lone inventor who, while puttering away in the basement, has inadvertently stumbled upon something that works. In the process of telling their stories to me, people often experienced genuine healing and were able to get on with their lives. This was all the more surprising precisely because many of them had already been though more conventional therapy but with no apparent relief. There was something about the Holocaust memories that required a religious dimension as well as a psychological one. Therefore, in writing this book, I have chosen to openly include religious teachings, as well as my own personal beliefs, where I felt that they would be helpful to the reader.

My ministry is somewhat unusual in the American Jewish community, in that I do not have a regular congregation nor am I currently affiliated with any one branch of Judaism. My own personal path has been dubbed "neo-Hasidic," in that I adhere to most of the traditional ways but am also open to new ideas from the fields of psychology, sociology, and modern metaphysical philosophies. I received my ordination from Rabbi Zalman Schachter-Shalomi, well-known pioneer in Jewish spiritual renewal. Reb Zalman, as he is known to his students, is himself a Holocaust survivor and has spent his life being a "bridge" between the Old World and the New. His teachings have deeply influenced the Jewish world view that you will find in these pages.

As a storyteller, I was already familiar with reincarnation tales from past centuries, which formed an integral part of my belief system. Isaac

Luria, a sixteenth-century rabbi who is regarded as one of the greatest Jewish mystics of all time, not only taught reincarnation but was reputed to be an accurate past-life reader. The same has been said of Israel ben Eliezer, known as the Baal Shem Tov, founder of the Hasidic movement in the eighteenth century. Reincarnation stories from both of these teachers and their disciples abound in written and oral form.

Because these classical stories were already familiar to me, I was not surprised when people began sharing their own memories of past lives. If souls could reincarnate from the Spanish Inquisition in the 1500s or the Chemielnicki massacres in the 1600s, then why not from the Holocaust in this century? I viewed the stories told to me by modern seekers as a continuation of this tradition and interpreted them in a Jewish religious context, as journeys of the soul on its way back to God.

Eventually word got around that I was interested in Holocaust reincarnation cases, and I was contacted by secular counselors and hypnotherapists who were finding similar cases in a completely different context. In addition, as I traveled around the country, I began meeting reputable psychics who were also picking up this type of information. It was at this point that I saw my work as having an importance outside of the Jewish community. I then began reading about research on reincarnation and near-death experiences, and was amazed to find how similar the scientific findings were to the "folklore" of Jewish tradition.

I also discovered how few people were even

aware that Judaism has anything to say about reincarnation. Therefore, although this volume includes some cross-cultural comparisons of reincarnation beliefs, my focus remains distinctly Jewish. I feel this adds to the value of the book because very, very little is currently available in English about reincarnation from a Jewish perspective. (For the benefit of non-Jewish readers, I have tried to define all technical terms clearly in the text, and you will find a glossary of these terms at the end of the book.)

The vast majority of Reform and Conservative Jews (and even many of the Orthodox) have no idea that such teachings even exist. On the other hand, to my knowledge all sects of Hasidic Jews believe in reincarnation as a matter of course. Many Sephardic Jews also believe in it, which is not surprising, since kabbalah flourished among the Jews of Spain and Portugal before the expulsion by Ferdinand and Isabella in 1492. When these Sephardic Jews fled the Spanish Inquisition, they took kabbalah with them. The sixteenth-century mystical community in Safed, Israel, where Rabbi Isaac Luria resided, included a high percentage of Sephardic refugees. (See Appendix for a brief description of the different groups of Jews.)

In addition, there is currently a revival of interest in Jewish mysticism on both the popular and academic levels. Although some of the early scholars like Martin Buber tended to ignore the reincarnation teachings, more recent scholarship has not. The late Gershom Scholem, recognized in his lifetime as the foremost academic expert in the field of kabbalah, clearly stated in many places that reincarnation was an integral part of Lurianic kabbalah and Hasidism.

This book, then, has three main purposes: (1) to provide hypnotherapists, parapsychologists, and past-life readers with some theological and cultural context for these cases; (2) to empower individuals with Holocaust past-life memories to begin work on healing their personal karma; and (3) to provide the general public with an overview of Jewish teachings on reincarnation.

I make no claims that my work is definitive; quite the contrary. *Beyond the Ashes* is merely an attempt to break the ice about a subject which has been circulating for years among past-life readers and therapists, but which has seldom been openly discussed because of the fear of offending the Jewish community. Almost every time I have spoken on this topic at a spirituality conference, one or more counselors have told me that they, too, have found such cases. It is my hope that this book will encourage others, who are no doubt better equipped than I, to begin investigating this phenomenon with the seriousness that it deserves.

When I finally began recording the cases in a more organized fashion, I tried to ask questions about the subject's age, gender, physical description, place of birth, religious and cultural background, in addition to actual memories of a Holocaust past life. I admit that I was not always consistent in this. I also admit to making certain judgments about whether or not the story was really a past-life memory. In some cases it seemed to me that the person's description of "feeling Jewish" was so colored by Christian theology that their "past-life experience" was more likely an archetypal dream or fantasy. Such cases are not included here.

Also not included in the book, except in a very general way, are more than 100 stories that were shared under confidential circumstances where we agreed not to record them. While these cases definitely influenced my thinking, I respected the clients' wishes and did not write them down. I did, however, count them in the total. Altogether I have met more than 250 people who believe they are reincarnated from the Holocaust.

As of this writing, there are 78 people for whom I have some kind of written record: 56 women and 22 men. Of these, 16 were born Jewish, 7 converted to Judaism, and 55 were not Jewish in this life. Concerning their past lives in the Holocaust, 58 believed they were Jews, 15 believed they were non-Jews, and 5 were not sure. These figures do not include additional past lives, both Jewish and non-Jewish, which some people claimed to have experienced in other centuries. The subjects came from seventeen states, as well as New Zealand, Israel, France, Germany, and Canada.

There are also some stories which, although I have no written record, were, nevertheless, included because they impressed me so much that I remember them quite clearly. When I travel around the country, I often spend the Sabbath with informal groups of spiritually minded Jews who meet to share the Friday evening meal in somebody's living room. During the course of the evening, the subject of reincarnation invariably comes up because I am there, and people take this opportunity to tell their own stories. But because it is forbidden for traditional Jews to write or tape on the Sabbath, I do not have on-the-spot records of these discussions.

In retelling the stories I have naturally had to change some details in order to protect privacy. It goes without saying that all the names of clients are pseudonyms. In giving places of birth or residence I have retained the actual place, with the precaution that unless the client came from a large city, I named the state or country only. My purpose in doing this was to show how widespread this phenomenon is, without giving away the identity of somebody in a small town. In cases where the client remembered his or her name from the previous incarnation, I used the actual name because, presumably, that person is now dead.

For me to merely tell these stories as "tales of Holocaust reincarnations" would be blatant sensationalism. I have, therefore, tried to present the stories within a wider framework, to show how they are consistent with history, Jewish mystical thought, and reincarnation theory in general. Although I had neither the time nor the funds to verify the actual details in the stories, I did, whenever possible, try to include references to historical events that are similar to what the subject described. In addition, I have also shared a great deal of personal opinion about the impact of the Holocaust on world karma.

I have sometimes been asked what role my own psychic ability has played in this work. That is a difficult question to answer. I do not bill myself as a psychic or give "readings" as such, nor do I go into a trance or channel spirit guides. What does happen is that, in the course of ordinary activities, I sometimes get impressions that seem to be coming from another level of consciousness. Some of these experiences are visual or auditory, while others are more like a sense of "inner knowing." When this happens, I am still completely aware of my surroundings, so much so that people around me do not usually realize that anything "psychic" is happening. In a few of the stories I have described these intuitive experiences.

There are so many people who have contributed to this work that it would be impossible to list them all, but I do wish especially to thank: Reb Zalman, who validated my spiritual quest; my wife Caryl, who encouraged me throughout the writing process; Dan Weiss, who spent many hours listening to my theories; the Shevet Shalom network, who fed me during the lean years; Evenstar Bookstore, which provided classroom space for my early workshops; my editor, Jon Robertson, who helped make my writing clear to the general reader; and all the people who have shared their stories, without whom this book could not have been written. May you all continue to walk the spiritual path in beauty, joy, and peace.

Reb Yonassan Gershom
18 Elul, 5752
(Birthday of the Baal Shem Tov)

In the week when we read:
"And you shall rejoice in all the good
which YHVH your God has given you."

Chapter 1:

Strange Encounter on a Snowy Night

I had seen her many times in the audience as I lectured on kabbalah and Jewish esoteric teachings. It struck me as odd at the time that this young blonde Norwegian should have such a fascination with Jewish mysticism. Little did I know how deep her interest really was.

That snowy winter's night I had canceled the discussion group in my home, but she had not received the message and showed up anyway. "Well," I said, "since you made the effort to get here, why not come in out of the cold and have some coffee?"

She accepted the invitation. After serving coffee, I asked what she would like to talk about, fully expecting a question on kabbalah. Instead, she wanted to discuss the Holocaust!

Ever since childhood, she told me, the very mention of the Holocaust filled her with unexplainable dread. Now her sister was doing a research paper on the concentration camps and insisted on sharing the material, but she simply could not bear to discuss it.

As my guest talked, I saw the fear in her deep blue eyes. Then suddenly I felt myself slip into an altered state of consciousness, as I sometimes do when counseling. Superimposed over her beautiful face I saw another visage, thin and emaciated. At the same time I could hear the sound of many voices singing an old Hasidic tune. The effect, for me, was as if we were moving back and forth between two different periods in time. My guest, however, was apparently unaware of what was happening to me.

"I would like to try something," I said. "Let me hum a tune, and you tell me if you have ever heard it before." I began humming the song in my vision, and her eyes grew wide with terror. Then she broke down and cried, sobbing that she had "died" in the Holocaust. The tune was *Ani Maamin,* "I Believe," a hymn of faith sung by many thousands of Jews as they entered the gas chambers. She had never, in this life, heard the song before.

This encounter happened in 1981. Since then, I have talked with literally hundreds of people who believe that they died in the Holocaust and have returned. They have come to this conclusion through every possible means: dreams, visions, déjà vu, past-life readings, intuition, spirit guides, automatic writing, and hypnotherapy. Most are ordinary citizens from all walks of life—and more and more are coming forward every day. What is this phenomenon? Has the Holocaust become a universal archetype for human suffering, or are these people really victims who have reincarnated?

When I first began hearing these stories of Holocaust reincarnations, I kept them to myself, afraid of losing my credibility as a teacher. The Holocaust is a sensitive subject in the Jewish community, and I did not want to be accused of sensationalizing so great a tragedy. So for the next three years I did not say much about it in public, but began quietly to drop hints in small group discussions that I was open to the idea of Holocaust reincarnations.

One by one, people would call for an appointment, cautiously feeling me out over the phone before saying that they, too, believed they had died in the Holocaust. In most cases, I was the first person in whom they had ever confided. Perhaps because I was already known to be interested in the psychic, they felt safe and shared their stories.

Then in 1984 I was invited to speak on Jewish mysticism at the annual Spiritual Frontiers Fellowship (SFF) retreat at Carleton College in Northfield, Minnesota. SFF is an eclectic group of spiritually oriented people who are interested in psychic phenomena, and most believe in reincarnation. Here, I thought, would be a receptive audience for these case histories that I had been gathering. So I suggested "Cases of Holocaust Reincarnation" as my topic.

I was turned down flat. The SFF representative explained that the theme of the retreat would be "I Am the Light," and they wanted to focus on uplifting, positive material because that's what people expected. The Holocaust was just too heavy and depressing, and might upset people, even if I *were* talking about reincarnation. Couldn't I do something more inspiring, like a Sabbath liturgy?

I agreed to speak on "Embracing the Sabbath Light," and that Friday evening I led 500 people out of the auditorium into the sunset, chanting *shalom* in joyous ecstasy. I had given them the positive, uplifting experience they were paying me for, but the Holocaust issue would not be silenced. People at the retreat felt so comfortable with me after the chanting experience that they began seeking me out for private consultation about their spiritual lives. Several of these seekers cautiously asked whether I believed that Jews could reincarnate as non-Jews. When I said yes, they shared what they believed to be past-life memories.

The time was ripe for a workshop on this, but where to do it? Every time I suggested the topic to some metaphysically oriented group, they responded negatively. And the Jewish community, by and large, was not interested in mysticism, especially when it involved the Holocaust. The subject was just too hot to handle. Yet more and more people were coming to me with these accounts, relieved at last to find *somebody* who was willing to listen. As the word got around that I was open to this kind of thing, additional people were referred through a third party. I also began collecting stories secondhand from reliable sources, often clergy or therapists who wanted my opinion on behalf of a client.

Then in July of 1985, I attended a Jewish *Kallah* or retreat gathering where, for obvious reasons, the subject of the Holocaust was not taboo. The week-long *Kallah* was sponsored by a group known then as B'nai Or ("Children" or "Disciples" of Light), a network of spiritual seekers founded by Rabbi Zalman Schachter-Shalomi, well-known pioneer in Jewish spiritual renewal. Schachter-

Shalomi taught kabbalah and had been dialoguing with Eastern mystics for years, so he was thoroughly familiar with reincarnation teachings around the world. I was studying for ordination under Schachter-Shalomi's direction and was personally acquainted with many of the workshop leaders on the program. The *Kallah* would be home territory where, I hoped, I could find a receptive ear.

The 150 or so participants were mostly Jewish professionals and educators (both rabbis and laypersons) connected with Schachter-Shalomi's work—hardly a gathering of crackpots. I was officially scheduled to lead a "Jewish Vision Quest" experience, but was also hoping to find an opportunity to broach the subject of Holocaust reincarnation stories. After all, if I couldn't discuss it within the Jewish renewal movement, then where?

The opportunity came sooner than expected. On Monday evening after the program, some of us were sitting on the steps swapping stories about our home communities. I happened to mention that I knew a number of converts to Judaism who seemed to remember having lived during the Holocaust in another life. All of them were born between 1947 and 1953, and had grown up with very little contact with Jews. Yet each had felt an innate familiarity with Judaism from the moment they first entered a synagogue. And all believed that their conversion was a return to their "own people" from a previous incarnation.

Someone asked, "How many of these cases are there?" and I replied, "At this point there are maybe a dozen," which the group did not regard as a very conclusive sample. I agreed, but explained that I had not been collecting the stories in a very scientific way and that there could be a lot more that I did not know about. That's why I was mentioning it now—to find out if anyone else at the retreat had found similar cases.

While we were discussing this, I noticed a woman sitting at the edge of the group, listening intently. The next day she came up to me and said, "I really want to talk to you." She told how, the night before, she had been "drawn" to the steps where we were sitting. Our conversation had sent chills up her spine because she, too, was a convert to Judaism who remembered dying in the Holocaust.

It was now or never. The woman and I decided to offer an impromptu discussion group at the retreat. But how to do it without sensationalizing the subject and scaring off participants? In order to remain low-key and nonthreatening, we passed the announcement word-of-mouth, asking if anybody wanted to gather informally and share what they thought might be Holocaust past-life memories.

Nine people showed up, all of whom told reincarnation stories about themselves or other people. So it wasn't just a local Minnesota phenomenon. Here were Jewish professionals from across the country, independently discovering cases like mine—*and they seemed to fit a pattern.* Most had been born in the United States during the "baby-boom" generation and were experiencing similar nightmares and flashbacks. At that moment I realized I was on to something much bigger than I had previously imagined. From then on, I began taking notes and taping the interviews whenever possible.

In March of 1986 I completed my rabbinical thesis and was finally ordained by Rabbi Schachter-Shalomi. Now at last I had time to begin writing about my reincarnation findings. But once again I met with resistance. No Jewish publication would touch it, while publications on alternative spirituality still did not want to deal with the Holocaust. It seemed that reincarnation was a fine topic if you were discussing events that happened thousands of years ago. Everybody enjoyed being told that he or she might have been an Egyptian princess or a Tibetan monk, but the possibility of having died recently in a concentration camp was just too horrifying. And, quite frankly, some of the editors I contacted felt that combining the Holocaust with reincarnation would offend the Jewish community.

Then in November, 1986, *Venture Inward* magazine, published by the Association for Research and Enlightenment, Inc. (A.R.E.), ran an article on Jews who were studying the teachings of Edgar Cayce, a well-documented American psychic known as the "sleeping prophet." The article was entitled "The Dilemma of Christ-Oriented Readings" and dealt with the difficulties many Jews had experienced in studying the Cayce material because of his heavily Christian orientation. Nevertheless, in spite of this theological "language barrier," the Jewish members of A.R.E. had persevered in their studies because, they believed, the teachings of Cayce had universal applications that went beyond religious differences.[1]

In his own lifetime, Edgar Cayce's clairvoyance had been considered an amazing phenomenon. Although he had no medical training whatsoever, while in a deep trance he could correctly diagnose patients "at a distance" merely by knowing the person's name and location at the time of the consultation. Time after time he was proven correct, and the treatments which he suggested were often effective. Although Cayce was repeatedly investigated by skeptics during the forty-three years that he demonstrated this ability, no indications of fraud were ever found.

When Cayce died in 1945, he left behind over 14,000 stenographic records of clairvoyant consultations that he had given for over 6,000 different people. These "readings," as they are called, are preserved at the A.R.E. headquarters in Virginia Beach, Virginia, and are still studied today by both medical doctors and laypersons. In addition to diagnoses, many of the readings contain information about the spiritual growth of the clients. One of the central ideas in them is that, in almost every case, the person who received the reading had lived on earth many times before and that events in past lives were often affecting this life, both in the form of physical disease and in problems of daily living. In other words, Edgar Cayce taught reincarnation.[2]

The above-mentioned *Venture Inward* article had caught my eye because here was a publication produced by a reputable organization that was at least willing to discuss Jewish issues in the context of metaphysical studies. Could this be a place to publish my findings on reincarnation and the Holocaust?

I sent a query to editor A. Robert Smith and yes, he would definitely be interested. The article was somewhat long for their format, but Smith was so impressed with the case histories that he willingly gave me the space. Thus it was that *Venture Inward* officially broke the story when "Are Holocaust Victims Returning?" appeared in the November/December 1987 issue.

Neither Smith nor I was prepared for the enormous response. Within a week of publication, the *Venture Inward* office began receiving replies from readers, which they forwarded to me. Many of the letters were from people who had been deeply touched by the article because they felt that they, too, had been reincarnated after the Holocaust. And they gave fascinating details which further confirmed what I had already found. Some even sent tapes of their regressions under hypnosis.

At first I answered all the letters personally, but as the number grew and grew, I simply did not have time for more than a polite acknowledgment, if that. I was performing my rabbinical duties on a freelance basis without a regular congregation to support me, and there was no funding for what was rapidly becoming a full-blown reincarnation project. I did not even have a secretary to handle my correspondence. My apologies to those who never received answers, but I was simply overwhelmed.

In addition, people were now calling from as far away as New Zealand to unburden themselves of dreams, visions, nightmares, and phobias connected with a Holocaust past life. Words cannot describe the emotional healing that often took place during these phone calls. Although I could not see the faces of the callers, I could hear a distinct change in their voices as they bared their souls to me. Here were ordinary people who had been haunted by these reincarnation memories since childhood, but had never told anyone for fear of being called crazy. Now my article confirmed that others, too, had had the same experience. Given permission at last to talk about it, talk they did, and were then able to find peace of mind.

Nevertheless, it was still difficult for many callers to broach the subject. Some hung up two or three times before getting the courage to stay on the line, while others carefully tested me out before explaining why they had called. It was this sincere reticence, combined with the striking similarity among the stories, that convinced me the phenomenon must be real. Why else would hundreds of ordinary people from across the continent, who had never met each other, be coming up with the same experiences? Either they were telling the truth, or a huge network of liars was concocting an elaborate worldwide hoax just to make a fool out of me! But even if such a hoax were likely, what could possibly be the motive? It was more logical to believe that the callers were sincere.

A typical call would begin with a shy, hesitant voice on the other end which asked whether or not I was the rabbi who wrote about reincarnation. When I affirmed this, the caller would begin to tell me his or her story, sometimes choking up or even breaking into tears while describing childhood nightmares, frightening flashbacks, and years of feeling like the "odd one out" for no apparent reason.

My interaction with the callers varied. I wish I could say that I was able to systematically interview them and get consistent data based on age, sex, occupation, place of birth, etc. But that was not always possible. In some cases the callers remained anonymous, while in others they did not want to be bothered with "trivia." Quite often I was simply a compassionate listening ear.

The average call lasted at least half an hour, but many were much longer than that. Toward the end of the conversation I could frequently detect a new tone of calmness in their voices, as if telling me their story had been a kind of catharsis. Sometimes they would actually verbalize this, saying something like, "I feel so much better now" or "The terrible burden is finally gone." Then they would thank me and gently hang up the phone.

As I, too, put down the receiver, I would feel a sense of awe at what we had just shared. Although it is difficult to describe on paper, there was such a feeling of inner peace that I just "knew" a healing had taken place. Unfortunately very few of these people ever called back, so I did not get much opportunity for follow-up. Those who did call a second time usually reported that the horror of the Holocaust memories had faded, and they were now able to get on with their lives.

The fact that I was a rabbi also played a big role in establishing trust. Many of the callers were not Jewish and had felt that claiming a Jewish past life would somehow be offensive. Most had absolutely no idea that Judaism even taught anything about reincarnation. Although reincarnation is a fundamental part of Jewish mysticism and is widely believed among Hasidic and Sephardic Jews today, this fact is not generally known to the world at large. Nor is it known to the majority of American Jews, many of whom have rejected the more mystical aspects of Judaism in favor of an "ethical monotheism" which is often devoid of any esoteric teachings.

To find a rabbi who openly believed in reincarnation must have been very reassuring. In addition, there were sometimes details in the experiences which were meaningless to the callers, but which I immediately recognized as Jewish rituals or customs. For example, one Lutheran housewife described a desire to light candles on Friday night, a compulsion which had no basis in Lutheranism and meant nothing to her or her family. Yet for thousands of years, Jewish women the world over have kindled the Sabbath lights on Friday just before sundown. This ritual is so central to Jewish life that even under the most trying circumstances a religious Jew will still try to perform it. I have heard Holocaust survivors tell of women who, when arrested by the Nazis on a Friday afternoon, took the Sabbath candles along and lit them at sundown in the crowded boxcars.

Another non-Jewish caller told me that when his young son was first learning to eat by himself, he refused to drink milk if there was meat on the table. If the parents insisted, he would dump the milk on the floor. This behavior was exasperating to the boy's parents, who had no idea why he did this with milk but never with water or juice. Once again, I immediately recognized this as a possible carry-over from a Jewish past life. One of the basic fundamentals of the Jewish dietary laws is that meat and milk are never under any circumstances eaten at the same meal. On the other hand, it is perfectly kosher to eat meat with water or juice.

In return for my time, I asked all callers if they would allow me to use their story (with names changed, of course) in my research. Those who refused were counseled anyway, but most were more than willing to give permission. Several even urged me to write a book so that others like themselves might benefit. (Some of their stories are included in these pages.)

September 1988 brought an article about my work in *Omni* magazine,[3] which used both material from the *Venture Inward* article and a phone interview with me. *Omni* accurately quoted me as saying that a high percentage of these cases were blond-haired, blue-eyed non-Jews in this life, who died as terrified children fervently wishing that they weren't Jewish. I had explained that self-blame is very common among abuse victims and, in the case of reincarnation, might account for why some of those I had interviewed were reborn as blonds.

Because of the *Omni* article, however, the story was pirated and sensationalized by the tabloids. "Holocaust Victims Being Reincarnated in Blond Bodies!" read the *National Examiner*.[4] For the first time, I began receiving irate phone calls from members of the mainstream Jewish community, as well as accusations of racism—something I had never intended or expected. But because both the *Omni* and *Examiner* articles had focused on the idea of Jewish victims returning as non-Jewish blonds, some people thought that I was anti-Aryan, while others accused me of laying a "guilt trip" on blonds. Quite the opposite was the accusation by one black man that I was implying white bodies are somehow "better" than dark-skinned ones.

None of these ideas were anywhere near my intent. I had not focused on the non-Jewish cases because of any prejudice, but simply because these were the cases that most clearly supported a belief in reincarnation. When a rural child from a Protestant family, who has never met any Jews and knows nothing of Judaism, nevertheless has dreams and memories of a past life in Eastern Europe, the evidence is very convincing. Certainly there are also cases of Jews who reincarnated again as Jews, but these are more difficult to prove, since they have grown up in this life with a knowledge of things Jewish. In the limited space of one article, I had simply chosen to write about the most convincing cases.

Nevertheless, my entire ministry became suspect in some circles, with the result that I was refused hospitality on several occasions. Even though Judaism does contain teachings about reincarnation (see Chapter Three), the connection to the Holocaust was perceived by many as a piece of "new age" sensationalism. Plus, there were Jews in Hasidic circles who were deeply disturbed by my assertion that their ancestors may have reincarnated as non-Jews. Although there is disagreement in the Jewish source texts about whether or not this can happen, the majority of modern Hasidim follow the opinion of the sixteenth-century mystic Isaac Luria, who taught that Jews remain Jews for all incarnations. This did not fit the evidence as I found it, however, and I was not about to alter my theory just to conform with medieval dogma.

On the other hand, doors in many of the alternative spiritual communities began to open. I was now regularly presenting workshops and speaking on talk shows, while continuing to collect

material for the book. I had over 150 cases recorded, some of them quite detailed. Just as I was
feeling ready to begin writing, personal tragedy
struck. My wife Caryl had developed Environmental Illness, necessitating a complete change in life
style. For the time being, the book was on hold.

Environmental Illness has been called the "twen-
tieth-century disease," and consists of multiple
sensitivities to modern chemicals and pollutants.
The symptoms can be quite severe; in Caryl's case,
they included collapsing on the floor and loss of
muscle control in the presence of perfumes and
glues, as well as irritability, muscle aches, and
mental confusion brought on by exposure to various other chemicals. We were living in downtown
Minneapolis, right in the heart of the urban smog,
and things had gotten so bad that Caryl could
hardly leave the house without becoming ill. Even
a short walk with the dog left her confused and
uncoordinated from exposure to exhaust fumes.
There was no known cure except to avoid the
pollution. We would have to leave the city.

In the spring of 1988 we moved to a very small
town about 100 miles north of Minneapolis where,
I hoped, I would be able to continue my free-lance
ministry in the Twin Cities, as well as expand my
interfaith work among Christians in the northern
Minnesota area. Having a regular congregation
was now out of the question, both because Caryl
could never tolerate a synagogue full of people
wearing perfume and because there were simply
no Jews in rural Minnesota.

In order to understand why this lack of Jewish
contact was such a problem for us, it is necessary
to explain a little about what being Jewish really

means. Although many people think of Judaism as primarily a religion, in reality the phrase "of the Jewish faith" is totally foreign to the Jewish way of thinking. A word often used by Jews to describe the traditional way of life is *Yiddishkeit,* usually translated "Jewishness." But that does not really convey the meaning. There simply is no word in the English language that can express what *Yiddishkeit* really means, because it encompasses an entire way of life. The closest I can come is to say that "Jewishness" is like belonging to a tribal culture.

What I missed in rural Minnesota were the Jewish celebrations, with special foods, songs, stories, and an indefinable ambiance that says "we are a community." In Minneapolis our home had been a gathering place for Jews of all backgrounds, and on special occasions like Passover we would entertain twenty-five or thirty guests for a joyous ritual meal that lasted well into the night. But now that we lived so far from the city, all of that was gone. On Jewish holidays it was business as usual for everyone in town but us. And on the Sabbath, when it is customary for Jews to visit each others' homes, we felt totally isolated. There was no place for 100 miles where any *Yiddishkeit* could be found.

Nor was there any interest in interfaith work. In the Twin Cities I had frequently taught adult education classes on Jewish customs and beliefs to church groups, but here there was no market for such skills. The only Christians who sought us out seemed to be pamphlet-pushing missionaries bent on converting us. Not once was I ever invited to speak to a church group, even though it was well known in town that I was a religion scholar. People simply were not interested in learning about Jews; interfaith dialogue was so unknown that a local newspaper misspelled it "interface" in our ad!

And anything esoteric was immediately suspected of being connected with Satanism. After discussing reincarnation on a local TV talk show in 1989, I was banned from doing volunteer work at the nearby prison because of fundamentalist prejudices. Unable to prove discrimination, I had to wait until changes in the prison staff opened the door to me again.

Meanwhile, my ministry in the Twin Cities was winding down, while out-of-state speaking engagements became fewer and fewer. This, in turn, threw us into a cycle of grinding poverty, because I was so overeducated as to be totally unemployable in a rural area. Coping with my wife's illness, the cultural shock of being a religious Jew in a small town, and my long-term isolation from other Jews, all had taken their toll. I was, quite frankly, burned out. Feeling that my days as a rabbi were over, I began to turn my efforts toward secular writing and a new occupation.

But the reincarnation story refused to die. Copies of "Are Holocaust Victims Returning?" have continued to circulate, so that now, *five years* later, I am still receiving letters and phone calls from people asking for further information. Believe me, this is a very unusual response to a single magazine article! Even as I write this, the article is being translated into Japanese for inclusion in an anthology on Western mysticism, and I have received a request from Czechoslovakia for reprinting it there. So the story insists on being told, and, like it or not, I am apparently the chosen channel.

I have frequently asked myself why it fell to me to carry out this task. It has not been easy to listen to so many nightmares, visions, and vivid memories of torture and betrayal. Such counseling requires a deep level of empathy, and at times I have been so emotionally drained that I could scarcely go on. Many were the nights I went to bed extremely depressed, asking my Creator why I had been given this overwhelming sad burden.

One such night, I dreamed that I was a young Hasidic boy, about eight or nine years old, living in Eastern Europe. The Jews of the village had gathered together, and we could hear the sounds of battle in the distance. My father, who was the village rabbi, was trying to comfort the people. He explained that although they were about to die, they should not be afraid, because the body is only a garment. The soul, he said, lives forever, and will one day return to earth in a new garment.

But the rabbi explained sadly that there was a problem. For many, many incarnations, their souls had returned to this same village to be born as their children's children. This time, however, the village would be destroyed completely, and none would survive to provide new bodies for the souls. They could never again come back to this place and might, therefore, become separated from one another in the next life. How would they ever find each other again?

It was decided to draw straws. The person thus chosen would incarnate immediately and look for a new place for the villagers to return to. After preparing the way, he would serve as a psychic beacon for the other souls, who would seek him out. In this way, it was hoped, the villagers would not become lost to one another.

Solemnly the Jews said a prayer together, then each took a straw, while the sounds of battle drew closer and closer. Suddenly everyone gasped—I had drawn the short straw! Just as I was about to protest that I was too young and didn't know how, the Nazis entered the village and began shooting everyone. I woke up.

Whether or not this dream is literally true, I do not know. I certainly have a natural affinity for Hasidic Judaism, which I did not grow up with but adopted later in life. Hasidic music, stories, and teachings resonate with my soul in a way that modern American Judaism does not. On other occasions I have felt that I lived before in Eastern Europe, during a time before the Holocaust, when Hasidism was still mystical and had not yet succumbed to politics. Over the years, a number of people have confided that they believed me to have been their rabbi in another life. I am willing to accept the possibility.

But I am also inclined to believe that this particular dream is meant to be more symbolic. Like the boy in the dream, I have been entrusted with a responsibility that is not entirely of my own choosing. Perhaps it was only chance that brought a frightened woman to my home on that snowy night over ten years ago. Or perhaps I was chosen simply because I was willing to listen and take her story seriously. Whatever the reason, once I opened the door, the way was cleared for other wounded souls to find one another and begin to heal. This book is the story of that healing.

Chapter 2:

Flashbacks to Another Life

Beverly was a single mother in her thirties, whom I first met through a social service agency in 1984. Her father was non-Jewish, her mother Jewish, but very secretive about it. In fact, Beverly's parents did not even tell her that she was Jewish until adulthood. Therefore, neither she nor her teen-age daughter Susan had any training in Jewish customs, teachings, or beliefs.

Why would Beverly's mother have hidden her heritage from her? What many people today do not realize is that before the Civil Rights Act was passed in 1964, many of the same restrictions that were used against people of color in the United States were also directed against Jews. Being openly Jewish often meant being denied housing, employment, or admission into many colleges and universities. Beverly was born in 1950, and because of such discrimination, her mother had apparently decided that her child would have a better chance at life if she could pass for a Gentile.

But now that Beverly had found out about her background, she was eager to explore her heritage. She was a deeply spiritual person and had felt frustrated that her parents had never really practiced any religion. Nor had Beverly been able to study on her own, because she was functionally illiterate. This is important information, because not only had she never read the Bible, she also had not read books on psychic phenomena or the Holocaust.

Over the next few months, Beverly and I became friends, and she often came to our house for the Sabbath or Jewish holidays. One such Sabbath afternoon, after we had finished the traditional meal and were sharing personal stories, the subject turned to dreams. Cautiously at first, as if she were afraid that I might not believe her, Beverly told my wife Caryl and me about a recurring childhood nightmare.

In the dream she was a little boy about seven or eight years old, standing in a line with his mother. Beverly described how they got to a table where a man was telling some people to go to the left and others to the right. He pointed and they went through a door.

The scene shifted, and they were suddenly in a horrible place, where there was a terrible smell. Some men were throwing people into a fire alive, and then the little boy was thrown in, too. He kept patting himself trying to put out the flames, then he died.

At this point in Beverly's narrative, I suddenly began to smell burning flesh. Excusing myself from the table, I went to the kitchen, even though we are vegetarians and it was not logical to be looking for meat in our oven. Still, it was the natural place to check for something burning.

Everything was fine in the kitchen. But I could still smell smoke, so I decided to look outside. No sooner had I walked out the door onto the front porch, than the smell was gone! None of my neighbors were barbecuing, nor was there any other kind of fire that could account for what I had smelled. But when I came back inside, there it was again. Whatever the smell was, it was definitely inside the house and strongest in the living room, where Caryl and Beverly were beginning to wonder about my strange behavior.

"Is something wrong?" Caryl asked.

"I smell smoke," I said. "Don't you?"

Beverly and Caryl looked at me strangely and both shook their heads. My wife, who must have the most sensitive nose on earth because of her severe allergies, did not smell a thing!

A chill went up my spine as I suddenly realized that I was having an olfactory psychic experience. As Beverly was telling her story about being burned alive, I had apparently tuned in to her soul memory. As soon as I realized this, the smell went away.

I wasn't sure how Beverly was reacting to all of this, but I need not have worried. She felt reassured by my psychic experience, taking it as a sign that I really did believe her story. After refilling her coffee mug, she told us the rest of her dream.

The scene shifted again, with the little boy and his mother finding themselves standing once again in a long line of people. Up ahead were the most beautiful gates, and the little boy knew it was Heaven. Strangely, the men in the line were wearing hats, and Beverly remembered thinking it was odd that they didn't take off their hats to go into Heaven. Then the little boy grew tired of waiting and wandered off down to a lower level where he met a "male angel." The angel said, "Now that you have come down this far, you will have to go back to earth again." He didn't want to go and kept asking for his mother, but the angel said they would have to find him another mother. The boy was then shown a beam of light that he followed into the womb of a woman. And then "he" became Beverly.

This dream strikes me as authentic. It is recognizably a dream about the Holocaust, but it is not a stereotype—there are no cliches, no oft-repeated phrases or scenes that she might have picked up from radio or television. Beverly neither mentions gas chambers nor starving people. And her memories of being burned alive are historically accurate. Many Jews were burned alive in the early stages of the Holocaust, when they were herded into synagogues and the buildings were locked and set on fire.[1] There are also eyewitness accounts of Jews being soaked with gasoline and set on fire.[2] But these are not the images one usually associates with the Holocaust and would probably not show up in an "archetypal" dream about the camps.

In the public mind, the deaths of Jews in Nazi Germany are usually associated with concentration camps and gas chambers. But in reality the Nazis used many different methods of slaughter throughout their reign of terror from 1933 to 1945.

Even before Hitler came to power, gangs of Nazi ruffians were beating and terrorizing Jews in the streets. This behavior increased with government sanction and was soon followed by the Nuremberg Laws of 1935, which robbed the Jews of their civil rights, confiscated their property, and forced them to wear a yellow star to make them easily identifiable targets for abuse. Once this wedge was driven between the Jews and their German neighbors, the Nazis then proceeded to round up the Jews. Some were shot, some were hung, some were tortured to death, some were sent off to slave labor camps.

When Hitler invaded Poland in September 1939, special units of SS troops were assigned to round up and kill the Jews in each village that fell to the German army. At this stage, most of the victims were simply taken into the forest and shot. Sometimes, in a perverse kind of cruelty, they were marched to the Jewish cemetery and executed there. Religious Jews, anticipating their deaths, often put on their prayer shawls so that at least they would be properly dressed for burial. In response to this, some SS units began requiring the Jews to strip naked before they were shot. This policy of hunting down the Jews continued in each country conquered by the Nazis, often with the help of the local populace.[3]

The next technological "advance" in this human-made hell was to use panel trucks with the exhaust pipes re-routed into the cargo area. Contrary to popular conception, the Jews did not enter these death vans willingly. They often screamed and fought back, but were beaten into submission. Then the trucks were sealed and the engines started. When the screams stopped, the trucks were driven to the woods where the bodies were buried.[4]

Bodies were evidence, however, so eventually the Nazis decided to use crematoria instead. At this stage of the Holocaust, the death trucks were driven to the ovens. Sometimes the carbon dioxide did not do its work, and, when the van was opened, the fresh air revived the people inside. At least one eyewitness saw such victims thrown into the ovens alive.[5] The gas vans were, therefore, not "efficient" enough, and by 1942 the Nazis had begun building the infamous "showers" that were really gas chambers. At first these, too, used diesel fumes, but it was not long before the Nazis began experimenting to find a more toxic, faster-working gas.

I do not dwell on these details out of morbidity, but to point out that the popular conception of "six million Jews in gas chambers" does not reflect the many ways in which they were actually killed. Nor does it take into account the tens of thousands of Jews who died of starvation, overwork, disease, suicide, or forced marches. Jews were shot, stabbed, raped, hanged, drowned, disemboweled, dragged behind vehicles, burned, buried alive, and killed in medical experiments. One cannot help but be horrified by the fiendish imaginations of the Nazi death squads, who never seemed to lack for new ways to torment their victims.

If the people who contacted me with memories of a past life in the Holocaust were inventing the stories or simply having bad dreams, one would expect them all to claim that they had died in gas chambers. But this is not the case. In the chapters that follow, you will see that my subjects reported dying in a wide variety of ways that correspond with actual historical accounts. In addition, there are often significant details which can be verified.

Returning to Beverly's dream, recall the man at the table who points to the left or right. This is an authentic detail that is unlikely to occur in an ordinary child's dream. There is probably no Holocaust survivor alive who does not remember the "selections," where to go "right" meant life and "left" meant death. Children were separated from their mothers and often killed immediately. Thus, Beverly remembers the "terrible smell" of burning flesh and death (also described by survivors), but apparently did not live long enough to experience starvation.

Even more convincing to me is the fact that the men in the line to Heaven were all wearing hats. Nowadays the average American thinks of religious Jews as wearing yarmulkes (skullcaps) and this is how they are generally portrayed in the media. But in pre-Holocaust Europe, the yarmulke was an everyday, indoor head covering; on the Sabbath or other "dress" occasions, men wore a hat over the yarmulke. Hasidim, especially, would not have felt properly dressed wearing only a yarmulke in public and would no doubt have wanted to wear their best Sabbath hats when meeting their Maker. But how did Beverly come up with this image of Heaven when, as a child, she neither knew she was Jewish nor had any contact with Jews?

Nor were these hats the only "instinctive" Jewish imagery she possessed as a child. Little Beverly had also insisted on sprinkling salt on her bread, a custom at the Jewish Sabbath table but generally unknown elsewhere. And while playing house, she would often wind string down her arm "like a snake"—could this have been a memory of the *tefillin* straps worn on the arm by Jewish men during prayer?

Telling this dream to Caryl and me was a great catharsis for Beverly. Over the next year she began to exhibit a new self-confidence and was more able to tackle the problems of life. Not long after that, Beverly and Susan moved to another city and I lost track of them. But I firmly believe that the move itself was an act of independence which resulted from letting go of the pain of the past life and becoming more "grounded" in this one.

Beverly's recall was unusually clear, but others have also had fragments of such memories. Phobias are common; one teen-ager named Joan, who grew up on a Midwestern farm, had an unexplainable terror of barbed wire. There was nothing in Joan's current life that could account for this fear. She had never been tangled in barbed wire, which should have been nothing more than a normal part of keeping the cows in the pasture. Nevertheless, every time her father brought home a roll of wire in the pick-up, she would take one look and be filled with absolute terror.

Eventually Joan came to believe that this phobia was connected with a past life and, after having a dream about dying in a concentration camp, the fear lessened. Joan still does not like barbed wire, but at least now she can mend fences on the farm without having a panic attack.

Others have reported fears of police, uniforms, and sirens. Sometimes actual physical symptoms manifest—for example, asthma and other breathing problems—at the initial moment when such a memory awakens. In two cases, an asthma attack was actually triggered through contact with Jewish rituals, as if the very thought of being Jewish evoked a sudden inability to breathe.

In 1982 Frieda had traveled from Germany to the United States to convert to Judaism because the rabbis in her own country would not, after the Holocaust, do conversions. She went through the conversion ceremony on a Friday afternoon before the Sabbath, and not long after that began to feel ill. On Saturday night, during the *havdalah* ritual to end the Sabbath, she had a serious asthma attack and was hospitalized. The attack was diagnosed as an allergic reaction to incense burned at the *havdalah* ceremony. Upon being released from the hospital, Frieda returned immediately to Germany.

Months later, Frieda sent me a cassette describing how she had never really accepted the doctors' diagnosis. Strange as it sounded, she believed the asthma attack was triggered by a "concentration camp blanket" which her hostess had given her when she started feeling ill. (Whether it was really a blanket from the Holocaust or only looked like one, I do not know.) That Saturday night while in the hospital, she had dreamed of experiencing the Holocaust as a teen-age boy. The words "Never come home; you can never come home" reverberated in her consciousness, and the message carried over into the next day. All the way to the airport she heard these words, but believed that God was watching over her and guiding her, and that her faith brought her home.

Later Frieda's doctor in Germany told her that she had, in fact, come very close to dying. But Frieda felt that "coming home" meant far more than safely returning to Germany:

"Not 'to die'—what is 'to die'—that is nothing. But *never come home!* And this is something I found with this brown, horrible blanket . . . I can tell this to you, because I know you will understand me right, you'll know what I'm trying to say. I didn't know it, until I was home in my dreams, and I dreamed of the concentration camp and it comes all together."

For Frieda, becoming a Jew was "coming home," because she believes that is where her soul truly belongs. She has written to me a few more times and is very happy. And yes, the rabbis of Germany did accept her into the Jewish community.

Sometime during the mid-1980s, Nancy, an American college student, was also thinking about converting to Judaism. On the invitation of a guest rabbi at the college, she decided to attend her first synagogue service in nearby Philadelphia. The worship was in Hebrew, but she later said it seemed strangely familiar, as if she had experienced it all before. Although she did not understand a single word of the language, the rhythm of the chanting, so different from the hymns in her Protestant church, seemed to awaken distant memories.

When the congregation reached the "Shema" prayer, Nancy began to choke and cough. Unable to get her breath, she kept repeating *Adonai Echad* ("the Lord is One") from the first line of the prayer. She was helped from the room, and after about half an hour stopped coughing. "Oh, what a nightmare that was!" she gasped and described a vision of dying in the gas chamber.

The fact that she knew no Hebrew but could repeat the words is astonishing enough. But how could she have known that those same words are spoken by Jews on the deathbed, words that were doubtlessly gasped out by millions of Jews with their dying breaths?

These two stories bear an uncanny resemblance to the case of Patricia Farrier, cited in Noel Langley's book, *Edgar Cayce on Reincarnation*. Patricia had been told in a past-life reading by Cayce that she had spent her previous life near Fredericksburg, Virginia, and that records of that lifetime still existed. So she and her sister Emily went there to see if they could find the evidence. While on this search, the two women stayed at a small rural hotel. During the night, Emily was awakened by the sound of her sister choking. Patricia was in a deep coma and on the verge of death when the doctor arrived and brought her out of it.

A later Cayce reading revealed that in her previous life Patricia Farrier had died in a root cellar when the floor above her caved in, suffocating her under a pile of dirt and vegetables. Their present hotel was either on the same site or near enough to the site of her former life to have aroused the memory, causing her to physically replicate the death throes of another life.[6]

Some Holocaust reincarnates have also returned in this life to the scene of their deaths, and many of these experiences show startling evidence of the past-life connection. Judy, an American exchange student who spent her junior year of high school in Germany, is one such person. While there, she went on a tour which included a visit to the former site of the Dachau concentration camp.

As a sickening familiarity stirred within her, it was, she said, like being in two lives at the same time. Everything was frighteningly familiar, and she knew where all of the buildings had stood and what they were used for, even before the guide explained it. The building where she had died was long since torn down, but she knew exactly where it had been, and on the screen of her memory she saw her own death.

Throughout the tour, Judy kept having the sensation of walking in mud, although the weather was very dry and the path was graveled. (In fact, during the 1940s there had been no gravel, only endless mud.) Later, when she removed her shoes, the soles were dry, but somehow her feet and socks had gotten muddy. Was it perspiration? Or had she somehow "walked" into another life? And if so, what was the lesson for Judy that such a startling physical phenomenon had manifested in her life? Judy did not know.

Another curious "coincidence" to Judy's story is that, upon arrival in Germany, she started having very severe menstrual cramps, which she had never experienced before. These continued monthly until the concentration camp tour where she saw her own death. In the vision, Judy had been a sixteen- or seventeen-year-old girl in childbirth. Someone cut her open, took out the child, and killed it. In a soft, sad voice she described feeling herself die and then standing there in the spirit, watching them kill her newborn baby. After experiencing this vision, her menstrual cramps went away and did not return.

Jacob's experience was totally different from that of Nancy's, Frieda's, and Judy's. While they were seeking to become Jews, Jacob was running away from his Jewishness. Born in 1940, he grew up in a small Orthodox congregation in the South, where he received a traditional Jewish education. Sabbath rituals, prayers, the Hebrew language— all of this was very familiar to Jacob during his childhood. But after entering college he totally rejected Judaism and became, in his own words, "very rationalistic and skeptical." He went on to become a medical doctor.

Having lost his faith, Jacob no longer attended synagogue. But on one occasion, he did go to the bar mitzvah of a relative, more out of duty than devotion. During the service he "half fell asleep," then "smelled something" and saw himself as a small child between three and five years old. He was standing next to a man and knew that, if he looked up at him, he would have a gray beard and that this was his father studying Torah. The feeling was that of a *stetl* (Jewish village) in Eastern Europe, but the "father" in the vision did not resemble his father in his present life.

At the time, this experience did not mean anything to the rationalistic Jacob, who wrote it off as merely a nostalgic dream induced by the religious surroundings. Then in 1986 he began to go through some deep personal changes that made him more open to mystical ideas. A year later, someone gave him a copy of my *Venture Inward* article, "Are Holocaust Victims Returning?" and it "sent shivers" through his soul, enough for him to call me and talk for an hour long distance. Jacob believed that if he did die in the Holocaust, it was not in the camps, but by being shot in a field in Poland.

As was explained above, in the early days of the

Holocaust many Jews were taken out into the fields or forests and shot. In some cases they were forced to dig a mass grave, then line up at the edge so their bodies would fall into the pit. In other cases, they were forced to lie down in the pits like sardines, to be shot in the back. Many did not die immediately and were buried alive. A few of these Jews actually survived the ordeal and later lived to tell the tale.[7]

But what of those who did not escape and slowly suffocated under the crushing weight of dirt and bodies? Over and over, the theme of being buried alive in mass graves recurs in the past-life dreams and memories of many. Consider this letter from Cynthia, who wrote to me from New Jersey in response to the *Venture Inward* article in 1987. Cynthia is not Jewish and was born in 1954. At the age of twenty she developed asthma "out of the blue for no apparent reason" but believes it may be connected with her death in a past life:

"I have believed for several years that I was a Jew in the Holocaust and recently met someone who totally overwhelmed me [emotionally] . . . I regressed myself [with self-hypnosis], looking for where I had known this person before, and found myself being buried alive—no casket—dirt being thrown on my badly damaged body. I'm not sure how I was hurt, only that *I couldn't move*—dirt on my face in a pit with dead bodies or other badly hurt people, and somehow—looking up and seeing men with guns in hats and coats and this person [the one from this life] on some kind of rack or tree or something, I think being tortured. I'm not really clear on that part."

From Oklahoma came another letter, written by Barbara, who is a professional past-life reader and describes herself as a "blue-eyed blonde in a brunette family." Barbara was born on September 24, 1939, and at eighteen months of age almost died of whooping cough. She still has chronic sinusitis and bronchitis. Barbara has Bavarian Gypsy blood on her grandmother's side of the family and believes she might have been a Gypsy when she suffered death at the hands of Nazis in another life:

"I spent the first three years of my life in absolute terror. I had the same nightmares, night after night—of being buried alive with Nazis throwing dirt on me. In my childhood there was no color TV—just radio and black-and-white newsreels. I would go to pieces every time I saw a newsreel and I knew what color the Germans' uniforms were—I just 'knew.' I didn't have this terror with the Japanese—just the Germans. I KNEW about concentration camps before I knew the English words . . .

"I couldn't BE hypnotized by others. I learned to regress myself [into remembering a past life]. I found the answer in an extremely traumatic way—yet it brought me peace and released much frustration. I found myself as a five-year-old girl being buried alive by Nazis in the early winter of 1939. I remember the terror, the death, the confusion. The 'why me'

carried over into this lifetime. 'Why me . . . '
"The childhood memories were always the
same—over and over and over . . . It was so
cold and dark—a forest—I still see tall trees,
a mass grave, Germans. I especially remember their black boots. There was snow. I still
see blood. But not me bleeding. I was buried
alive and suffocated. The dirt was so heavy
and it seemed like there was wood—a tree—I
really don't know . . . "

These two similar accounts were from people
born many miles and years apart. We know today
that the Nazis often did not even bother to shoot
the children during these round-ups but simply
threw them into the pits alive, in order to save
ammunition.[8] This much of the above accounts is
clearly very accurate. But what intrigues me even
more is that both people mention a tree. Was there
really an incident like this, where Nazis tortured
someone on a tree while shooting Jews in a forest?
And if so, did both of these souls die together in the
same mass grave, or did they somehow psychically "tune in" on the same tragic event?

The fact that Barbara was born in September of
1939 but describes herself as dying in "early
winter" of the same year is puzzling. Granted that
winter snows could come early in a cold country
like Poland, she still would have come back ex-
ceedingly fast. This is not impossible, but there
could be another explanation.

According to Hazrat Inayat Khan, a great Sufi
master who came to the West in 1910 and whose
teachings are still studied today, it is possible for
a soul descending to earth to pick up memories

from another soul returning to the spiritual plane. He writes: "Souls which are passing through the sphere of the *jinns* towards the physical plane, and who do not stop in that sphere, meet with other travelers who are on their journey back home, and they learn from them a great many things."[9] Khan goes on to say that if the descending soul is deeply "impressed" with these memories, it will feel as if it had actually experienced them.

Edgar Cayce also taught that memories could be transferred from one soul to another:

> "*Q. Are not transferred memories misappropriated by individuals and considered to be personal experiences?*
>
> "A. Personal experiences have their influence upon the inner soul, while disincarnate entities (that may be earth-bound, or that may be heaven-bound) may influence the thought of an entity or a mind."[10]

Barbara could have gotten the information in her dream from another soul on its way back to Heaven. Or she might have reincarnated immediately after her brutal death. Or, since she is a psychic, she could have been receiving impressions of events taking place on the other side of the globe. In any case, telling her story was very therapeutic, and she began using her psychic abilities to help other people who believed that they had reincarnated from the Holocaust. In a follow-up letter she wrote, "So here I am, talking to people about the Holocaust, whereas before I couldn't deal with it. So it looks like great progress in internal healing . . . If there are five million of us back for world peace, we will be a FORCE!"

I am frequently asked how to determine whether or not a particular person's story is an actual case of reincarnation. My answer is that there are no positive ways to prove it. Could these people be making all this up? Yes, they could. They might also be having hallucinations or simply indulging in morbid fantasies. But even if these are only dreams or delusions, they still show how deeply the Holocaust has affected our collective consciousness. For the people experiencing these flashbacks, they are very real, and I believe it is my responsibility as a spiritual director to respect that and take them seriously.

While I do personally believe in reincarnation, I am also aware that my work is not a scientific study and that these anecdotal accounts will not be proof enough for the skeptic. Although there have been some very convincing studies of people with past-life recall,[11] there does not, at this time, seem to be a way to prove it beyond a doubt. This does not necessarily mean that reincarnation is false. It only means that we do not yet have proof. It frequently happens that mystical truths can later be investigated scientifically with the invention of better technology.

Consider the fact that from time immemorial, Eastern yogis have claimed to be able to control states of consciousness through the use of specific breathing techniques. Western medicine laughed at this, writing it off as so much quackery. Then came Swami Rama from the Himalayas, who demonstrated, under laboratory conditions at the Menninger Foundation,[12] that he could alter his brain waves at will and control bodily functions normally handled by the autonomic nervous system. Swami Rama was able to raise his skin temperature, lower his blood pressure, and stop his heart beat for fifteen seconds — through breath and throught control alone! Modern laboratory equipment had made it possible to verify the claims of the yogis. This research, in turn, opened the door for the development of biofeedback techniques widely used by the medical profession today.

A similar breakthrough has happened with the subject of near-death experiences. All cultures have stories about angels, demi-gods, deceased relatives, or other spirit beings who appear to guide dying people to the next world. Shamans worldwide have claimed to be able to enter the "other world" at will, often through a long tunnel with a spiritual light at the end. In some cultures, the shaman's initiation is actually called "the little death," and many spiritual healers have described how their powers were given to them by the spirits after a near-terminal illness or coma. But again, this was regarded by most anthropologists as just so much mythology.

With the invention of modern medical technology, it became possible to bring patients back from clinical death with relative frequency. And sure enough, many of these otherwise ordinary people described experiences that closely paralleled those of the tribal shamans. But although more and more nurses and doctors were hearing about near-death experiences from patients who had "died" on the operating table, the medical profession was reluctant to give credence to anything so mystical. Not until Dr. Raymond Moody broke the ice in his book *Life After Life*[13] in 1975 did people begin to talk openly about the phenomenon. Today it is the subject of serious research.

One of the reasons that these Holocaust reincarnation cases are so exciting is that they relate to a very recent historical event, and some details can, therefore, be verified. In addition, enough people are claiming similar experiences to provide an adequate sample for comparison. Thus far, there has not been a full-scale scientific investigation of this phenomenon. I hope that someday there will be, because this could be a great opportunity to prove that reincarnation does, in fact, exist.

Meanwhile, these cases keep cropping up with increasing frequency. As I have been acting as a spiritual director, not a psychologist or scientist, I try not to judge the experiences as true or false, but rather work with the individuals' personal growth within their own belief systems. Certainly I do not claim that every case who comes to me is actually reincarnated from the Holocaust. However, some stories strike me as more probable than others, especially those with a *combination* of the following criteria:

1. *Childhood nightmares, phobias, etc., with Holocaust themes.* As many of the examples in this book demonstrate, these dreams can be quite vivid, with details that seem out of place in the usual childhood nightmares. It is also possible that "Nazis" have become a kind of archetypal bogeyman in the collective unconscious and that some of these dreams may reflect ordinary fears and insecurities clothed in Holocaust imagery. To me, the most convincing reincarnation dreams are those which contain specific information that the

child would not normally know in his/her present lifetime.

If you have had nightmares like these, try keeping a journal, then checking in books on the Holocaust to see if there were actual events that resemble those in the dream. If your child has similar dreams, encourage him or her to talk about it and maybe draw pictures of the dream. I firmly believe that if children can talk about possible past-life memories and are taken seriously, any trauma that has carried over will be healed more quickly.

2. *A non-Jew who has had virtually no contact with Jews or Judaism, but who has compulsions, habits, or other behaviors that might be carry-overs from Jewish customs and rituals.* I am not speaking here of commonly known Jewish themes, like the Exodus from Egypt, but rather of customs and rituals which are not described in the Bible or commonly known outside the Jewish community. The Jews of Eastern Europe were not culturally the same as the "ancient Hebrews." Judaism has grown and evolved over the centuries, and the Bible does not specifically describe customs like lighting Sabbath candles, nor does it explain the details for making a prayer shawl or putting on *tefillin*.

In addition to the written Torah, which Christians know as the "Old Testament," there is a vast amount of oral tradition that can only be learned through actual contact with Jews. "Torah" means "teachings" in Hebrew, and in its broadest sense is used by Jews to refer to all of Jewish wisdom, both written and oral, over the past 5,000 years. Although much of this "oral Torah" is now published in books and even translated into English, in the non-Jewish world it is virtually unknown outside of academic circles. While theoretically someone could study up on this and concoct a convincing story, there is a certain "feel" to Jewishness that is very difficult to fake. One or two people might pull off such a hoax, but when this occurs in such large numbers, I am inclined to believe that people are telling the truth.

Again, journaling the memories and dreams is important here. Then, try to find verification. Remember that in the library, books about Judaism are not filed in the "Old Testament" section under Christianity, but in a separate "Judaism" category (look under "BM" in the Library of Congress system). Books on the Holocaust itself will be in the history department. Also try visiting a synagogue, listening to Jewish music, and talking to Jews who are sympathetic to reincarnation issues.

3. A Jew from a nonreligious background who seems to have an innate grasp of Jewish mysticism. Most Reform and Conservative synagogues do not teach kabbalah: a "feel" for it might indicate a Hasidic past life or perhaps an earlier incarnation among the medieval kabbalists in Spain, northern Germany, or Provence, France. (There may also be Holocaust victims reincarnating in the Orthodox and Hasidic communities of today, but because of their intensive Jewish education in this life, testimony from these individuals would not be evident under this criterion.)

In this category I would also include Jewish children who seem to be innately more religious than their parents. One little girl, when taken for the first time to a Jewish gift shop, immediately picked up a toy Torah scroll, hugged it to her heart, and began dancing with it. "Oh, Mommy, Mommy!" she shouted excitedly. "Please buy me this—it is the very best present I ever had!" This child had never been to a synagogue nor had she ever seen a Torah scroll before, and could not have known that Jews do dance with the Torah on certain holidays. Her parents were born Jewish but long ago had become Unitarians, and had not practiced any of the Jewish traditions since before the child was born.

Many Jews who are remembering a more spiritual past life as a Jew tend to feel frustrated with modern American Judaism. Sadly, the Holocaust has eclipsed much of the joy and beauty in Jewish practice. Notice that I said "eclipsed," not "extinguished." If you are in this category, rest assured that the spirituality you once knew is still there in your soul memory. Try to go within and access the deep understanding of Torah that you once had, then "bring it forward" into your present observance of the Sabbath, holidays, etc. Judaism is badly in need of spiritual renewal, and you can be a valuable part of that process.

4. *Feeling "out of place" in the family.* The psychic Edgar Cayce, who died in 1945, revealed a trend of children dying in World War II who were coming back too quickly and choosing incompatible families:

> "Towards the close of his life, as World War II loomed darker and darker, Edgar Cayce's concern for the children who would be innocently caught in its meshes became more and

more evident and urgent. He was not alone in the fear that the souls of children, bewildered by violent deaths, would wander in equal bewilderment in the lower astral planes, unable to proceed 'towards the Light,' and that they would tend in their confusion to return to earth too swiftly, merely for the sake of the temporary sanctuary of a womb. Joan Grant, the English psychic, was equally concerned, and her psychiatrist husband, Denys Kellsey, using the regression technique in hypnosis, came across many cases of these 'war children' reincarnating too soon, into uncongenial families, in search of makeshift shelter from the terrors of the bombing and extermination camps which had clung to them like malignant thought-forms after death." [14]

Under normal conditions, when death comes naturally through old age, there is a longer "waiting period" between incarnations, and souls tend to return within their karmic group. In times of war or other mass disasters, however, this process is sometimes upset, and souls can get "lost." If you feel that you are one of these lost souls, born into a family of "strangers," try to understand that both you and your parents are, in a sense, the innocent victims of war. While you were grabbing the first available body, your parents may well have been desperately wishing for a baby, any baby, to bring life into the world after so much death and destruction. As incompatible as you may be, on some level you did choose each other.

As much as possible, try to make peace between you and your family now, so that you will not have unresolved karma with each other in the next incarnation. If communications have broken down to the point where you simply cannot be with your family, then at least begin to let go of the anger on your end, again so that you will not be karmically tied to your parents. Resolve that, in future incarnations, you will learn from this experience and not be so hasty in choosing your next body.

5. *Birth during the "baby-boom" and/or almost dying at birth.* The vast majority of the cases cited in this book were born between 1946 and 1953 (although I have found some as early as 1939 and as late as the 1970s) and are now in their thirties and forties. This, of course, is the generation which later became active in the civil rights movement and gave birth to the peace movement of the sixties. Did those millions of souls come back as quickly as possible to work for peace on earth so that the horrors they had been through could never happen again?

Some undoubtedly did. But there seem to be others who were born against their wills, who even after birth did not really want to be here. A number of these people whom I interviewed almost died at birth or had had serious childhood illnesses, as if the soul, upon discovering it was incarnate again so soon, had tried unsuccessfully to leave. Many of these people report having difficulty being "grounded" in this world, as if on some level they are afraid to fully participate in life. If you are one of these, begin to offset this fear by immersing yourself in the beauty of nature, taking time to examine the wonders of God's creation. By surrounding yourself with beauty, you will begin to offset the horrors that may still be reverberating in your soul.

Once you have accepted the fact that you are incarnate again, try to use this life for as much learning experience as possible. Choose one activity where you can contribute toward healing the planet. This can be anything from working to save the rainforests to praying for peace to feeding the homeless to planting a flower garden. Open your heart and the Creator will guide you.

6. *Asthma, breathing problems, or prone to bronchitis. Also anorexia and other eating disorders.* In some of these cases involving medical symptoms, the individuals first sought help through conventional medicine or hypnotherapy and only later explored past-life memories. I wish to be very clear that it is not my intention to blame all breathing and eating disorders on a past life during the Holocaust. But in *combination* with other criteria listed here, these symptoms could be an indication.

For example, I know of one case in which a young man who converted to Judaism became a Hasidic rabbi with such spiritual insight that he attracted a considerable following. Shortly thereafter he developed anorexia and literally starved himself to death. While one could argue that this was merely a case of a fanatical ascetic going too far, it could also be that he was working out "unfinished business" from a previous life. If he had been a Rebbe (Jewish spiritual master) whose Hasidim starved to death in the camps while he had an "easier" death, he might have felt the need to gather the group together again and atone for what he saw as a failure to stand by his disciples in their time of need.

If you believe that a medical problem might be rooted in another incarnation, consider going to a reputable hypnotherapist *in addition* to consulting with a medical doctor. Following the advice of both together is the best policy; don't rely on hypnotherapy alone to cure a medical problem.

7. Light hair and eyes, especially if the only one in the family. Here I must caution that although about two-thirds of the people interviewed for this book have this coloration, this is not necessarily a hard-and-fast figure, because it only includes the people who have come to me. If we could count all of the unknown cases who may have returned as Jews with dark hair and eyes, as well as blacks or other races, the percentage would naturally be much smaller. Still, if light hair and eyes occur *in combination* with some of the other criteria, it does strengthen the case.

8. An extremely emotional response to the Holocaust, either during childhood or triggered by an event in adulthood. I am not referring to the normal reactions of horror that anyone might feel when reading about atrocities, but rather an overwhelming flashback experience accompanied by unexplained terror or even physical pain. One woman was literally convulsed into hours of sobbing by the motion picture *Sophie's Choice,* which is a very unusual reaction to any movie, even one about the Holocaust.

Here I also try to determine whether there is a background of child abuse in this life, which might lock in with the archetype of the Holocaust and trigger a flashback clothed in Holocaust imagery. If, for example, a person was starved or beaten during childhood, he or she might feel "like a Jew in a concentration camp," using that imagery to describe the experience of being abused. This does not necessarily rule out reincarnation, as the abuse could be a result of returning into an incompatible family (#4 above). However, if there has been abuse in this life, I recommend some standard therapy in addition to any psychic work.

9. *The sincerity of the client, the general "feel" of the interview and my own psychic and/or intuitive impressions.* This, of course, is very subjective, but some interviews just seem to click and send shivers through my soul, while others do not. Here I must also caution not to allow personal or cultural biases to color one's reaction to the material. In the beginning, I tended to discount stories of people who said that Jesus came to them in the gas chambers to guide their souls to Heaven. As a rabbi, I found it improbable that fellow Jews would see Jesus at their moment of death.

But somewhere along the line it suddenly clicked that many Christians, too, were gassed by the Nazis, and they certainly *would* expect to see Jesus. As Dr. Moody explained in *Life After Life,* the "being of light" which comes to guide the soul to the next world will often take on the appearance of whatever figure the soul expects to see. Buddhists see Buddha, Christians see Jesus, Jews see angels or Elijah. And atheists? They simply see a bright light!

These, then, are the criteria which I look for in

determining whether or not a person might have reincarnated from the Holocaust. If these reincarnation stories are true, then there are a lot of souls out there, both incarnate and on the spiritual plane, who are still suffering from this terrible tragedy. This, in turn, is affecting our world today. In future chapters we will explore some of the issues surrounding the Holocaust, as well as processes for karmic healing on both the individual and group levels. But first, let us examine what Judaism has to say about reincarnation.

Chapter 3:

The Afterlife in Jewish Teachings

Does Judaism really teach reincarnation? Surprising as it may seem, the answer is yes. This does not mean that all Jews believe in it, however, because Judaism does not have one definitive doctrine on the subject of life after death. Jews have long recognized that there is no scientific proof of the exact nature of the afterlife, and that, therefore, it is ridiculous to be dogmatic about it. Over the centuries a number of beliefs about life after death have evolved within Judaism, and these continue to exist side-by-side, with each individual Jew free to choose from among them.

These beliefs fall into four main categories: (1) survival through one's descendants; (2) physical resurrection; (3) an immortal soul in Heaven; and (4) reincarnation. The categories are not mutually exclusive, and many Jews believe in a combined version. Follow along with me as we explore what has come to be a fascinating evolution of thought. But first, a few words about Jewish source material.

Although the general public is familiar with the
Hebrew Scriptures (also known as the "Old Testament"), many people are not aware that the Biblical
writings make up only a small percentage of the
books which Jews hold sacred. Space does not
permit me to go into detail here, but I would like to
explain the main categories so that you will have
a general idea of what is available.

Let us begin with the Talmud, which is a vast,
many-volumed compilation that spans over seven
centuries, from approximately 200 B.C.E. to 500
C.E. (the time of the Greco-Roman Empire). Originally the Talmud was taught orally, and this is
reflected in the style of the text. Rather than
presenting the material in a linear, step-by-step
manner, the Talmud groups separate passages
with similar themes into sixty-four sections called
"tractates." This format uses association to aid
memory and allows for considerable digression
into topics that may seem only loosely connected
to the main theme.

For example, in the middle of a tractate on
marriage *(Ketubot)* one finds a discussion about
the afterlife, and in a tractate on ritual blessings
(Berachot) there are many pages of material about
dream interpretation. Because of this literary style,
the Talmud is not a "book" to be read in the usual
sense, but rather a resource to be carefully studied page by page. In fact, the very word *talmud* is
derived from the Hebrew verb "to study."

The Talmud contains two basic kinds of writings: (1) *halachah* or material on Jewish law and
ritual, and (2) *aggadah* or nonlegal material. It is
the second category which primarily concerns us
here, because it contains some of the teachings on

the afterlife which we are about to explore. While the legal material is considered authoritative and binding on all Jews, there is a wide variety of opinion as to how much weight is given to *aggadic* material. For some, these parts of the Talmud are nothing more than entertaining stories, while for others they are true accounts of the lives and teachings of enlightened masters.

In addition to the Talmud, there are many, many other books which fall into both the legal and nonlegal categories. One important body of literature is called *midrash*, a term derived from the Hebrew word "to search." For Jews, to "search the Scriptures" does not mean to look through the Bible but rather to expand on the meaning of the text through intellectual inquiry and "soul-searching." *Midrash* often takes the form of verse-by-verse commentary, with allegories, parables, analogies, and stories that illustrate a deeper meaning to the verse in question. The *Zohar,* a major classic of kabbalah, is written in this *midrashic* style, arranged as a running commentary on the first five books of the Bible.

To the modern reader who is accustomed to self-help books and how-to-do-it manuals, these classical texts can be frustrating, because they do not clearly spell out the mystical teachings. This is because of a longstanding tradition (mentioned in the Talmud itself) that kabbalah should only be taught through hints and allusions to those students who are already well-grounded in Jewish knowledge. The mystical texts, therefore, assume that the reader is conversant with the Bible, Talmud, and Midrash in the original languages (Hebrew and Aramaic) and will be able to pick up obscure references without footnotes. In addition, many very ordinary Hebrew words, phrases, even individual letters have "technical" meanings which, it is assumed, the reader will already have learned from a teacher. In other words, the books are written in code. Becoming conversant in this code takes years of study, as well as personal practice of the Jewish way of life. (This is one of the reasons why I feel that an "innate" understanding of kabbalah may indicate a past life as a Jewish mystic.)

Collectively this vast body of knowledge — Bible, Talmud, halachah, aggadah, mysticism, parables, stories, rituals, ethical literature, etc. — is referred to as *Torah*. This Hebrew word is often translated as "the law," but it literally means "teachings." Christians often assume that the Torah is limited to the scroll in the synagogue which contains the Five Books of Moses. But when a Jew speaks of "learning Torah," he or she does not mean just the "Old Testament." The word "Torah," in its broadest sense, includes all Jewish writings, teachings, insights, and practices over the past 5,000 years. Obviously we will not be able to cover all of that here, but I do hope the journey we are about to take will whet your appetite for further exploration.

A basic principle in studying this material is that "there is no before or after in Torah." This means that later commentaries do not negate older teachings, but merely build upon them with new interpretations that always potentially existed but had not yet been "revealed" to earlier scholars. A student of Jewish texts, therefore, tries to reconcile these conflicting opinions, rather than choosing one above the others. (Even within

the Bible and Talmud there were differing opinions about the afterlife, and these have been
preserved side-by-side.)

For the sake of this book, I have decided to
present the following material in a basically historical order, but please keep in mind that all of
these opinions about the afterlife can still be found
within the Jewish community today. As was stated
above, many Jews believe in a combination of the
four catergories which we will now explore.

1. *Survival through one's descendants.* Many
Jews do not believe in the individual survival of the
soul, but rather that the thread of life is perpetu-
ated through one's descendants or "seed." This
accounts for the strong stress on geneology in the
early Biblical stories, where teachings are not so
much passed from master to disciple as from
father to son and mother to daughter. Childless-
ness is seen as a deep tragedy, not only for the
nuclear family involved but also for the clan.
Without children, the line of the parents ends
forever, both spiritually and literally. Within this
world view there is no room for celibacy, which is
seen as both irresponsibility toward the tribe and
a kind of spiritual suicide.

The very beginnings of the Jewish people stress
this theme of survival through descendants. In the
story of Abraham and Sarah, Abraham laments
that he has no heir; therefore, his servant Eliezer
will inherit everything. But God reassures
Abraham, promising that his descendants will be
numberless as the stars. Sarah apparently takes
this to mean that she should use a "surrogate
mother," Hagar the Egyptian, who does in fact give

birth to a son named Ishmael. This allows
Abraham's "seed" to survive, but what about poor
Sarah, his wife?

The Bible goes on to say that God "remembered"
Sarah, too, and through angelic messengers, she
is told that she will conceive a child in her old age.
The miracle of Isaac's birth lies not only in the fact
that Sarah becomes pregnant at the age of 99, but
also that the line of Abraham and Sarah survives,
to eventually become the Jewish people.

There is some biological basis for this belief, in
that a "spark of life" from each parent survives in
the sperm and egg which unite to form the child.
We do not know exactly what this "spark of life" is,
but we do know that in all nature life is conceived
from other life. Theoretically this "spark of life" can
be traced all the way back to the very origins of life
itself. Something of the ancestors does indeed
survive in the descendants, if only through their
DNA. And conversely, if an individual is destroyed
before reproducing, then that particular "spark of
life" is removed from the gene pool forever. The
Talmudic teaching, "Whoever destroys a single
person destroys an entire world, and whoever
saves a single person saves an entire world"[1] is
traditionally explained in exactly this light.

One of the most common arguments against
reincarnation among scientists today is the idea
that these "memories" are somehow genetically
programmed into our DNA. In other words, instead of remembering something that happened to
our soul in another life, we could simply be acti-
vating our genes. But this does not explain how a
Caucasian subject, when regressed to another life
under hypnosis, could remember being a Negro

slave. Nor does it explain how some of my subjects could remember dying during the Holocaust—at a time when their current parents were still alive! According to Dr. Joel Whitton, author of *Life Between Life*, "there simply is not enough DNA to code even one life's memories, let alone several lifetimes."[2] While genetics certainly does play some role in our make-up, it does not provide all of the answers.

In medieval Jewish mysticism, the idea of a "primal spark of life" was developed into the teaching about Adam Kadmon, the First Human Being. This was Adam before the Fall, even before the creation of Eve. Adam Kadmon was a hermaphrodite, often pictured as having both breasts and male genitalia. He/she potentially contained all the souls of the entire human race within his/her "seed." Thus, all human beings today contain a "spark of the soul of Adam."

In addition, we each belong to a particular line of ancestors. In many Jewish stories, a saintly person is described as having "a spark of the soul of Moses" or some other archetypal figure. Whether this is meant literally or figuratively is not always clear in the tales, but no racism is implied. Converts to Judaism are symbolically "adopted" into the tribe and referred to as "sons and daughters of Abraham and Sarah." They and their descendants are considered Jews in every way, and consequently the modern community has members from all races and nationalities.

This belief in survival through descendants partially accounts for the lasting impact of the Holocaust on the Jewish community today. Not only were millions of Jews destroyed, but *six million potential worlds.* Each of those people was carrying a geneological line that is now gone forever. In many cases, entire families, even entire communities were completely snuffed out without a single survivor. Gone, too, are many of the family stories that were passed orally from parent to child through the generations.

For those few who did survive, it has become very, very important to permanently preserve the names of Holocaust martyrs, especially those who have no descendants to carry on their memory. Therefore, great stress is placed on building monuments and compiling records of the Holocaust and on those who died there, before the last witnesses are gone forever. At Yad Vashem, the Holocaust memorial in Jerusalem, a permanent list is kept of the names of every Jew known to have been killed by the Nazis.

2. *Physical resurrection.* Belief in a literal physical resurrection is not very common among Jews today, but during the Talmudic period it had a serious impact on Judaism, so much so that the concept became a central doctrine of Christianity, which sprang from Jewish roots at that time. It is not clear exactly when this teaching first entered Jewish thought. Moses was raised as an Egyptian prince in the court of Pharaoh, and the Egyptians clearly believed that the body must be preserved for the afterlife. Moses makes no direct reference to resurrection, but centuries later the prophet Daniel does: "And many of them that sleep in the dust of the earth shall awake, some to everlasting life and some to everlasting shame and contempt."[3]

Could teachings on physical resurrection have

been transmitted orally by Moses, to be written down many centuries later? Or were these teachings simply not revealed by God until the days of Daniel? We do not know. But what is clear is that there are some fundamental differences between Jewish and Egyptian concepts of resurrection, which will be explained here.

The ancient Egyptians conceived of the afterlife as being much like this life, with the same basic needs and desires. Although the Egyptians recognized the existence of a soul (the *ka*), they believed that it needed the earthly body in order to survive. Without the body, there was no afterlife, which accounts for the practice of mummification. Nor was the afterlife very democratic; mummification was a costly and time-consuming process, available only to the upper classes. The poor apparently ceased to exist when their bodies decomposed.

In addition to preserving the body, the Egyptians also furnished the tomb with all the earthly pleasures that the soul would need in the next world, including food, clothing, furniture, and servants, as well as handwritten texts to instruct the soul on its journey. From the Egyptian standpoint you *could* take it with you, and many Pharaohs spent their entire lives amassing wealth for their tombs. In some ways, preparing for the afterlife had become more important than fully experiencing this one.

It may have been in reaction to this Egyptian extravagance that the Jews opted for more simple funerals. They had, after all, been slaves in Egypt, and no doubt spent their lives working on tombs and other funerary projects for the Pharaoh. Having been "behind the scenes" as the artisans who

slaved to make the Pharaoh comfortable in the
next world, the Jews must have realized the futil-
ity of it all and rejected the Egyptian concept of the
afterlife.

The Bible clearly states in many places[4] that
dead bodies are dead, and do not eat, sleep, or
praise the Creator from their graves. This has been
interpreted by some Christians (especially
Jehovah's Witnesses) to mean that the Bible de-
nies the existence of an immortal soul.[5] What is
more likely is that these verses are meant to refute
the Egyptian idea that mummies can come back to
life and walk around in their tombs.

In Biblical times, Jewish dead were wrapped in
simple shrouds and laid in caves or crypts; nowadays, plain wooden coffins are used and the bodies
buried underground. In either case, the body is
allowed to decompose naturally without embalm-
ing. The only Biblical exception appears to have
been Jacob's son Joseph who, because he had
risen to a position of prominence in Egypt, was
accorded a state funeral and embalmed. Before
Joseph's death, however, he made his brothers
promise to carry his bones out of Egypt to the land
of his ancestors. This was done by Moses, who
took the bones at the time of the Exodus.

Whether or not a body was mummified, the
bones could survive for many centuries, even
millennia, under the right conditions. Preserving
the bones was deemed very important to those
who taught the resurrection idea, because they
would be needed in the Last Days, when the bones
would be fleshed out and given immortality. This
idea is most clearly stated in Ezekiel's vision of the
"Valley of Dry Bones."

The prophet Ezekiel, who was an exile among the Jews carried into captivity by the Babylonians around 550 B.C.E., was first shown a valley filled with sun-bleached human bones, presumably a battlefield where the Jews were slaughtered. Then, still in the vision, he saw the bones reassembled and once again covered with flesh. God then breathed life into them and said to Ezekiel: "O mortal, these bones are the whole house of Israel ... I am going to open your graves and lift you out of the graves, O my people, and bring you to the land of Israel. You shall know, O my people, that I am the Lord when I have opened your graves and lifted you out of your graves. I will put my breath into you and you shall live again, and I will set you on your own soil."[6]

Throughout the centuries many Jews (as well as Christians) have taken this prophecy literally, expecting a physical resurrection. Because of the phrase "I will set you on your own soil" cited above, as well as other references by Ezekiel to "the land of the living," some Talmudic sages taught that the resurrection could only happen in the land of Israel. This land was so holy, they felt, that even a nonbeliever would be resurrected simply by virtue of being buried there.[7] But what about pious Jews who were buried outside the land of Israel? Surely the righteous would not be denied eternal life simply because of the location of their graves! To solve this dilemma, a curious piece of folklore developed, first mentioned in the Talmud and later elaborated upon by numerous commentators through the centuries. The dead who were buried in other lands would have to tunnel underground and come up in the land of Israel. In some versions of the story, secret tunnels already existed, while in others, the dead would have to burrow to Israel like moles. The Talmud suggests that God Himself would open the tunnels, and the dead would "roll like bottles" to the site of the Resurrection.[8] But whatever the version of the story, it was always considered preferable to be buried in the Holy Land itself, in order to be spared the underground journey. Even those who did not believe these stories still wanted to be buried with their feet pointing toward Jerusalem, symbolizing their return at the time of the Resurrection. To this day a bit of earth from the Holy Land is placed in every Jewish coffin, to symbolically "connect" the body with its homeland.

Although these texts appear to be talking about literal, physical tunnels, there is a possibility that something more spiritual is meant. Traveling through a long tunnel that opens onto a beautiful landscape is one of the most common images described by people who have undergone near-death experiences (NDEs). It is tempting to suggest that one of the Talmudic sages had an NDE and described it to his colleagues as if it were a physical experience.

People in ancient times often spoke of dreams and visions in very concrete, literal terms, making no distinctions between psychic phenomena and waking reality. According to Princeton psychiatrist Julian Jaynes, this was because they did not always understand that these images were generated from within their own minds, but actually perceived them as something external.[9]

Some of the rabbis cited in the Talmud are known to have practiced a form of mysticism known as *Maaseh Merkavah* or "The Works of the Chariot," in which the practitioners meditated on a vision described in the first chapter of Ezekiel. *Merkavah* mystics claimed to "ascend" through seven "Heavenly Halls" and appear before the very "Throne of God." These journeys are always described quite literally, and only in later commentaries do we find statements like "the Patriarchs themselves are the Chariot."[10]

On the other hand, there are some clear rabbinical references to what appear to be out-of-body experiences. Perhaps the best-known example is related in the story of the "Ten Martyrs," which is read each year during the service on Yom Kippur, the Day of Atonement. In this story, the Roman Emperor Hadrian, in the year 135 C.E., called ten Jewish sages before him and, on trumped-up charges, ordered them executed. The sages asked for a three-day reprieve to "ascertain whether this was ordained from Heaven." Amazingly, Emperor Hadrian granted their request.

Rabbi Ishmael, who was also the High Priest, then ritually purified himself, pronounced the sacred Four-Letter Name of God, and "ascended" to find out if this persecution was indeed by divine decree. There he saw "one robed in linen" who said, "Submit, beloved saints, for I have heard from behind the Curtain [in the Heavenly Sanctuary] that this would be your fate."

Rabbi Ishmael then "descended" and told this message to his colleagues, who agreed to accept martyrdom. One of the rabbis executed was the saintly Akiba, who recited his prayers so fervently under torture that the executioner asked if he were a sorcerer, that he could overcome such pain.

Akiba replied that he was no sorcerer, but that he rejoiced at the opportunity to love God with all his life. He died while whispering the last words of the "Shema" prayer: *Adonai Echad*, "the Lord is One."[11] In doing so, he set the precedent for all Jews at the moment of death.

The obvious reason for including this story in the Yom Kippur liturgy is to inspire Jews to serve God with complete devotion. Yet it also contains what I feel is a clear reference to some kind of altered state which allowed the High Priest to "ascend" to Heaven while still alive on earth. As these are rabbis from the Talmudic period, this story does lend credence to my suggestion that the stories about the "tunnels" may have originated in descriptions of a near-death or out-of-body experience. This theory is further supported by the fact that the same Rabbi Ishmael mentioned in the story was the author of *Hekhalot Rabbati*, one of the texts describing ascents to the "Heavenly Halls" mentioned above.[12]

Belief in a literal physical resurrection has been abandoned by most modern Jews, again because of the Holocaust. If the physical body has been cremated and the ashes scattered, how can the now non-existent bones ever rise again? Perhaps the closest we can come to seeing this prophecy fulfilled is to regard it as a reference to the concentration camp survivors. When one looks at photographs of the emaciated "living skeletons" that were liberated by the Allies in 1945, it seems impossible that such "bones" could have remained alive. But not only did those survivors live and become fleshed out again, many of them also settled in the Holy Land and helped found the

State of Israel "on their own soil." Could this be the Resurrection that Ezekiel refers to—not a literal revival of corpses but a rekindling of the Jewish spirit after such a great tragedy?

③ *An immortal soul in Heaven.* Although the Bible does not clearly spell out the concept of an immortal soul, the existence of a soul is described in later Jewish writings recorded after the Bible was canonized. This has led some students of religion to believe that the idea of a soul is not really Jewish but was absorbed from other cultures—an assumption that I consider quite false. It is possible for a doctrine to exist orally for many centuries before finally being committed to writing. In ancient times, especially, esoteric teachings were kept secret, and because all books were handwritten, "publishing" frequently meant oral transmission rather than distributing many copies. Commentaries to texts such as the Bible were usually taught word-of-mouth and carefully memorized by repeating them at least a hundred times.

Nowadays we tend to distrust oral tradition, regarding it as akin to the children's game of "gossip." But before the invention of the printing press in the mid-1500s, the majority of teaching was done orally. Scholars would travel to where there was a copy of the book, memorize it, then move on to learn another text. Medieval troubadours were able to memorize several hundred lines of poetry after hearing them only three times, and university professors would show off to their students by repeating a hundred lines or more after hearing them only once.[13] Among medieval

Jews, the real scholar was the one who could pass a pin through several pages of the Talmud and tell you exactly which words it had pierced. In the world before the printing industry, oral tradition could be very accurate.

By the Middle Ages, Jewish teachings on the afterlife were appearing in both scholarly writings and folklore, and it is clear that the average Jew of that time believed in a soul. We read frequently of Jews praying at the grave of a saint or loved one, and of the soul of the deceased later appearing in a vision or dream. Although the soul had left the body, it was believed to be somehow attached to the earthly resting place and was, therefore, more accessible at the grave site.[14] This belief is still very common today. I recently heard a Holocaust survivor, upon being asked why she would ever want to return to the site of Auschwitz, reply, "That is where my mother's grave is. Where else can I be close to her?"

Maimonides, an important twelfth-century Jewish philosopher, sought to combine the belief in a soul with a physical resurrection. Although he accepted the Resurrection as an article of faith, he also had difficulty with the literalness of some of the texts. His solution was to say that although there would be a resurrection of the body in the time of the Messiah, that was not the end of the process. Eventually there would also be a spiritual state in which there is no death and no body. "For we believe," Maimonides said, "and it is the truth held by all those who have a mind, that the World to Come (Olam Ha-Ba) is souls without bodies, like angels."[15]

The term Olam Ha-Ba is Talmudic Hebrew and

seems to have originally referred to a purified, physical Planet Earth after Judgment Day—a literal "World to Come" similar to what many fundamentalist Christians still believe. Among modern Jews, however, the phrase "World to Come" can also mean the "other world" on a different plane of consciousness. In other words, Heaven.

The most common Jewish metaphor for Heaven is the Garden of Eden, where everything is in perfect harmony. There the greatest prophets, teachers, scholars, and saints gather under the Tree of Life, to share the secrets of Torah. The lion lies down with the lamb, and all is as it should have been before Adam and Eve ate the forbidden fruit on earth.

Another common image of Heaven, especially in Hasidic writings, is that of the Heavenly Academy (Yeshivat Hashamayim), also pictured as a great place of Torah learning, where the worthy souls study, feast, and sing around an eternal Sabbath table. (Jews sometimes refer to the Sabbath as "a taste of the World to Come.") The Heavenly Academy is also accessible to especially holy souls who are still on earth. In the stories about the Baal Shem Tov ("the Master of the Good Name"), eighteenth-century founder of Hasidism, it is said that he frequently left his body at night to ascend to the Heavenly realms. There he learned the secrets of kabbalah, which he brought back to his earthly disciples:

"He [the Baal Shem Tov's cantor] told of the hours in which the soul of the master rose to Heaven, while his body remained behind as if

dead, and that there his soul spoke with
whomever it would, with Moses the Faithful
Shepherd, with the Messiah, and asked and
was answered."[16]

But before the soul of the deceased can go on to
either the Heavenly Academy or the Garden of
Eden, it must first be judged by the Heavenly
Tribunal. This court is usually modeled on the
earthly *Bet Din* or rabbinical court, where Jews
settled their disputes during the centuries before
they were granted citizenship rights by secular
governments. There are still certain circumstances
in which a modern Jew will consult a *Bet Din* and,
therefore, the institution continues to function
today. The *Bet Din* consists of three Jewish scholars, at least one of whom must be an ordained
rabbi. In larger cities there is usually one rabbi
who permanently fills this role, while in smaller
communities a *Bet Din* is convened only when
needed. Any ordained rabbi can convene a *Bet Din*.
    An interesting parallel to this Heavenly Court
can be found in the research of Dr. Joel Whitton.
Whitton has regressed many subjects under hypnosis to what he calls the *bardo*, a Tibetan Buddhist
term referring to the spiritual state where the soul
spends its time between incarnations. A large
percentage of Whitton's subjects report having
had to appear before an etheric "board of judgment," usually made up of *three judges!* To my
knowledge, none of these people had ever heard of
the Jewish teaching about a Heavenly Tribunal. In
fact, although Whitton himself lists many cultures
which speak of a celestial triumvirate, he does not
even name Judaism among them. Nevertheless,

his research does suggest that there is some truth
to the imagery of the Heavenly Court so often
portrayed in Jewish stories.[17]

The one thing which souls do not have in the
World to Come is the opportunity to perform
mitzvot (commandments), because these require a
physical body. One cannot feed the poor or clothe
the naked in Heaven, where there is no hunger or
poverty. Nor can a Jew fulfill the ritual requirements of Judaism in the spiritual world, because
they, too, require specific physical objects. Only
on the material plane can one light the Sabbath
candles or enwrap oneself in a prayer shawl. And
while it is true that these outwardly physical
rituals also have a deep spiritual meaning, nevertheless it is not possible to perform them without
using the physical world.

The good deeds which we do while on earth are
forever recorded in the Book of Life and are counted
as merits in the World to Come. It is, therefore,
considered very important to fulfill as many of the
mitzvot as possible here on earth, while we have
the opportunity, because the more merits one has
and the more spiritual lessons one has learned,
the higher one's level will be in the next world. In
popular terminology, this is the same as accumu-
lating "good karma."

But what about those souls who have accumulated bad karma? For them there is Gehenna, a
kind of purgatory, where they will be purified of
their sins before entering into the Garden of Eden.
The "sentence" varies according to the quality of
one's life but is generally believed to be no longer
than a year. Judaism has no concept of an eternal
hell, because every person, no matter how evil, has

done some good in the world somewhere and that good must eventually be rewarded. Many Hasidic tales are built on the theme of some poor soul being saved from oblivion because of a seemingly insignificant act of kindness here on earth.

Still, if Gehenna lasts only a year, it is not clear what happens to a soul like that of Adolf Hitler. Whitton's research, cited above, suggests that in the next world the soul will experience all the pain and suffering it has caused others as if it were inflicted on itself.[18] If this is true, then perhaps a year of such an experience for a Hitler would indeed be sufficient. Most esoteric traditions agree that time as we know it does not really exist in the next world, so who knows what a "year" feels like there?

According to some Jewish mystics, the spiritual world has a number of levels, likened to the rungs of the ladder in Jacob's dream. Thus, there is a "lower Gehenna" for purifying the emotions and an "upper Gehenna" for purifying the mind. Similarly, the "lower Garden of Eden" is filled with emotional pleasure, while the "upper Garden of Eden" satisfies the mind also. At various times, when moving from one level to another, the soul is dipped in the "River of Light." Souls on higher levels can descend to help souls on lower levels while, in turn, being helped from higher up. Only God, the Creator of the Universe, is perfect; everything else continues to grow. Enlightenment, in this model, is a process, not a static state of being. [19]

As was mentioned above, souls in the other world cannot perform the physical commandments, but they can benefit from *mitzvot* done in their name here on earth. This explains the Jewish custom of dedicating a work of charity to the memory of a departed loved one. Non-Jewish visitors to a synagogue are often puzzled by the fact that so many objects—pews, books, lecterns, Torah scrolls, even the rooms themselves—are prominently inscribed in somebody's memory. In addition to physically preserving the name of a loved one through the inscription, the departed souls are also helped to progess in the next world. Every time someone reads from "their" Torah scroll or uses "their" cup for the wine blessing, it is counted as if they themselves had lent the object to the user.

It is also possible for a living Jew to specifically assign the merit of his or her own deeds to the departed. For example, one might specify at the beginning of a study session that the learning about to take place will be for the merit of so-and-so. The soul then receives credit for the Torah learning, which, in turn, helps the soul progress in the next world. This is also one of the reasons for reciting *kaddish*, the prayer for the dead, at the synagogue morning and evening. Most souls, it is believed, spend some time being purified in Gehenna immediately after death. And because nobody wants to imply that their loved ones received a full year's sentence, *kaddish* is only said for eleven months after death.

One other custom that should be mentioned in connection with this is *Yahrzeit*, the commemoration of the anniversary of a death. Until recently Jews did not customarily observe birthdays; instead, the "day of remembrance" is the *Yahrzeit*, regarded by Jewish mystics as a birth into the next world. But even ordinary Jews light a twenty-four-hour candle on the evening of the *Yahrzeit*, and many have the custom of sponsoring a religious feast on that day or on the nearest Sabbath. Again, the merit of the Torah taught, of the stories told, and of the songs sung at such a feast is counted as "good karma" for the departed soul.

It is tempting to interpret this world view as an attempt to "buy" one's way into Heaven, and at its worst it could certainly be that. However, we must remember that all of this is symbolism for a spiritual process, taught in the context of Jewish tradition, which we do not fully understand. What I interpret these customs to mean is that there is a reciprocal relationship between this world and the next, and that the veil between them is really very thin. Both worlds are interconnected and must help each other to grow. In the words of Reb Zalman, one of my teachers: "It is a reciprocal relationship. We give them what we have much of on earth—capacities for good actions and loving remembrances. They give us what they have much of in Heaven—love, awe, joy, trembling, generosity, and devotion to God."

4. Reincarnation. As was already stated above, there is no clear description of life after death in the "Old Testament," so obviously we are not going to find reincarnation explained there, either. However, there are some Biblical verses which were taken by later commentators as "hints" referring to reincarnation. But in order to understand these references, it is necessary to know the "code" by which Jews often read Biblical texts.

One of these "code words" is explained in the *Bahir*, a book traditionally ascribed to the second-century Talmudic sage, Rabbi Nehuniah ben Ha-Kana. Rabbi Nehuniah was the foremost mystic of his time and the undisputed master of *Merkavah*, the mysticism of the "Chariot" and "Palaces" mentioned earlier. Scholars dispute whether or not Rabbi Nehuniah actually wrote the *Bahir*, as it did not appear in its present form until the twelfth century. It is possible that the *Bahir* contains oral teachings of Rabbi Nehuniah that were not committed to writing until the Middle Ages. Be that as it may, the *Bahir* was and still is accepted as an authentic kabbalistic text.

In the *Bahir* we find the following cryptic exchange:

> What is the meaning of [the phrase] "generation to generation"?
> Rabbi Papas said [quoting Ecclesiastes 1:4]: "A generation goes and a generation comes."
> Rabbi Akiba said: "The generation came" — it already came.[20]

This is a very important passage, because it tells us that the *Bahir* reads "generations" as "incarnations"; that is, that the generation which "goes" is the same one that "comes." The practice of reading one word for another is common in rabbinic literature. Sometimes the alternative reading is based on "puns" in the structure of the Hebrew language, while in other cases it simply represents a way to reinterpret an older text in the light of new information. How long this reading of "incarnations" for "generations" was used before it was written in the *Bahir* is not known. But it was apparently an accepted interpretation, at least among mystics, because the same practice is also found in the *Zohar*, a better-known kabbalistic text that appeared in its present form about a century after the *Bahir*.

In addition to the "generations" section cited above, the *Bahir* makes reference to reincarnation in several other places. For example:

> Why is there a righteous person who has good, and [another] righteous person who has evil?
>
> This is because the [second] righteous person was wicked previously, and is now being punished.
>
> Is one then punished for his childhood deeds? Did not Rabbi Simon say [in the Talmud, Shabbat 89b] that in the Tribunal on High, no punishment is meted out until one is twenty years old or older?
>
> He [Rabbi Rahumai] said: I am not speaking of his present lifetime. I am speaking about what he has already been, previously.[21]

This passage bears a striking resemblance to a question asked of Jesus in the Gospel of John: "Rabbi, who sinned, this man or his parents, that he was born blind?" The question implies a belief in reincarnation, as there is no other way that the blind man himself could have sinned before birth! Jesus' answer differs from the *Bahir*: "It was not this man who sinned, or his parents, but that the works of God might be manifest in him."[22]

Just what this answer means is still debated among Christians. Some see it as a denial of reincarnation in general. Others say that it does not disprove reincarnation per se but merely explains the case of this particular man, who was born blind in order for Jesus to perform the healing miracle described in the next verses. Either way, the story does indicate a belief in reincarnation among Jews during the Roman period. Jesus and Rabbi Nehuniah were almost contemporaries; could they have independently drawn on the same esoteric teachings?

The practice of reading "generations" as "incarnations" also helps illuminate another Biblical passage that is sometimes used by Jews as a reference to reincarnation. This verse occurs in the Book of Deuteronomy, where Moses is explaining the Covenant at Sinai to the new generation of Jews that is about to cross the Jordan into the Holy Land: "YHVH God made a Covenant with us at Horeb [Sinai]. It was not only with our ancestors that YHVH made this Covenant, but with us, the living, every one of us here today."[23] The verse then goes on to repeat the Ten Commandments. In order to understand how this could possibly be read as a reference to reincarnation, it is necessary to first understand what took place at Mt. Sinai.

A "covenant" is a treaty or agreement between two or more parties for mutual benefit. The format of the Covenant outlined in the Torah closely follows the conventional style of suzerain treaties between rulers and vassal states in the ancient Middle East. First, the ruler offering the treaty identifies himself ("I am the Lord your God"), then he states the terms of the treaty (the Commandments). This is followed by a list of benefits and rewards for keeping the agreement (the blessings

in Deuteronomy 27) and a list of severe consequences for breaking it (the curses which follow in
the same chapter).[24] This treaty format would have
been completely familiar to the generation of Jews
standing at Sinai.

But in order for a suzerain treaty to be valid, it
had to be ratified by the subjects. According to the
Bible, this happened when "all the people answered as one, saying, all that YHVH has spoken
we will do."[25] The God of the Jews is not some
angry dictator in the sky who arbitrarily imposes
His will on His subjects. Rather He has spelled out
a specific agreement with His people, which they,
in turn, have freely chosen to accept. The idea that
Jews have a covenant relationship with God is so
central to Jewish theology that it is usually taken
for granted.

But there is a serious problem with the
Deuteronomy text cited above (footnote 23). Only
three of the adults who were present at Mt. Sinai
(Moses, Joshua, and Caleb) were still alive when
Moses spoke these words. The rest of that generation had died off during the forty years in the
wilderness. Granted, a few children might still be
alive who remembered the Revelation at Sinai, but
they were minors at the time and, therefore, could
not be parties to a contract. How, then, could
Moses say that the Covenant was binding on
"every one of us [who is] here today"? Wouldn't
that deny the free will of new generations?

From very early on, the oral *midrashic* tradition
dealt with this question by saying that the covenant was retroactive, including Jews who had
died before the Revelation at Sinai in the phrase
"with our ancestors." Future generations, on the

other hand, were covered by the phrase "those who are not here this day," found in another passage concerning the Covenant.[26] Therefore, all of the souls of all of the Jews who ever were or would be born were present, as well as those who were physically incarnate. Even before birth every Jew had already freely chosen—and was obligated to uphold—the Covenant at Sinai. This idea that all the generations of souls were present at Sinai is so well accepted among Jews today that even the modern Torah commentary produced by the Reform movement cites this *midrash* without bothering to footnote it.[27]

The kabbalists, however, took this teaching one step further. Based on reading "generations" as "incarnations," the mystics taught that not only were all the souls present, but *the very same souls* who had stood at Sinai and later died in the wilderness were now incarnate again, listening to the last words of Moses. Therefore, it was "not only with our ancestors" but also "with us, the living" that God made this Covenant, because the current generation is the reincarnation of its ancestors.

The Covenant at Sinai, according to this teaching, is not like some earthly agreement that ends with the bodily death of one of the parties. Rather it is *l'dorotam li'vrit olam*, "an eternal covenant throughout the generations/incarnations,"[28] and, therefore, it carries over from one life to the next. This is a very important concept in Jewish thought, which we will return to in Chapter Four.

Although the earlier kabbalistic texts alluded to reincarnation with obscure references recognizable only to the initiated, by the fourteenth century explicit and detailed writings on the subject had appeared. At first reincarnation was referred to in Hebrew as *ha'takah* ("transference") or *ibbur* ("impregnation"). The *Zohar*, a major thirteenth-century work which has been called the "bible" of kabbalah, called reincarnation *gilgul*, which became the standard Hebrew term still used today.

Originally *gilgul* and *ibbur* meant the same thing. But by the end of the fourteenth century, the two were differentiated. *Ibbur* came to mean the entry of another soul into the body of a living person as a kind of "benign possession." An *ibbur* usually occurred for a good purpose, with the visiting soul staying for only a short while to perform specific deeds. For example, a saintly soul which has fulfilled all but one of the 613 commandments in the Torah might be temporarily "channeled" as an *ibbur* for the purpose of doing this one *mitzvah*. Having completed its mission, the *ibbur* then left of its own accord to return to the spiritual realm. (This is different from possession by a *dybbuk*, which is an evil soul that takes over a living person's body and must be exorcised.)[29]

Gilgul, on the other hand, has come to mean the rebirth of a soul into a new body, that is, reincarnation. As was mentioned above, the kabbalists have differed widely in their interpretation of *gilgul*, unable to agree on who comes back or how many times. In the *Bahir* it is stated that reincarnation may continue for a thousand generations, which, as we have seen, really means a "thousand incarnations."[30] On the other hand, Rabbi Isaac Luria, the sixteenth-century mystic, believed that a soul usually returns only three or four times.[31] In future chapters we will explore some of these teachings further, as we see how they apply to cases of reincarnation from the Holocaust.

By now you may be asking, just how widespread were these kabbalistic beliefs? Is reincarnation a legitimate Jewish doctrine or the musings of some fringe group? And for that matter, what, exactly, is kabbalah?

The Hebrew word *kabbalah* is often translated as "tradition," but it literally means "that which has been received." *Kabbalah* is derived from the same Hebrew verb used in "Moses received *(kibel)* the Torah at Sinai" and for "receiving the Sabbath" *(kabbalat shabbat)* in the Friday evening synagogue service. Kabbalah, then, is not so much a written tradition passed down by scholars as a spiritual process of receiving inner wisdom.

How widespread was kabbalah in the Middle Ages? It is difficult to know, because in practice kabbalah was integrated into the outward forms of Orthodox Judaism. A kabbalist and a non-kabbalist could each be chanting the same exact liturgy but experiencing it completely differently — and who could tell the difference? The Jewish mystics were not iconoclasts out to destroy tradition. Quite the opposite. They saw kabbalah as the inner reason for scrupulously observing the Commandments, because every action on earth was seen as having serious consequences "On High."

But the teachings of the mystics were not necessarily the beliefs of the average Jew. Kabbalah was regarded as a secret esoteric doctrine, accessible only to the most scholarly rabbis. It was considered dangerous to teach kabbalah to the masses, both because its esoteric symbolism might lead the ignorant to heresy, and because the common people had a tendency to try to use it for magic or theurgy. Although the rabbis recognized the validity of theurgy, they believed that only the highest, most saintly persons were qualified to actually practice it. Entrance requirements to the mystical circles were rigorous, and in many cases the students were required to take an oath of secrecy.[32] Not until the sixteenth century, when the invention of the printing press made it possible to publish books in large quantities, would kabbalah be openly studied and practiced.

In the eighteenth century, the Baal Shem Tov, founder of Hasidism, "popularized" kabbalah and made many of the concepts accessible to laypeople. To my knowledge, all sects of Hasidic Jews still believe in reincarnation today. It comes as a surprise to many people that Hasidim, who are usually pictured as "ultra-orthodox" reactionaries, can possibly believe in something as mystical as reincarnation. Yet it is their very resistance to change which has preserved these teachings among the Hasidim. The Lubovitcher version of the Hasidic prayerbook even contains a bedtime prayer in which the supplicant forgives "anyone who has angered or vexed me . . . in this incarnation or any other."[33]

At the other end of the spectrum, Reform and Conservative Jews tend to be very skeptical about reincarnation. More than one seeker has told me that his or her rabbi said, "There is no such thing in Judaism." In most cases, this answer was merely a reflection of the rabbi's own ignorance because, until recently, kabbalah and mysticism were scarcely mentioned in Jewish seminary studies. Mainstream Judaism in the U.S. has gone out of its way to be "scientific," outrightly rejecting anything that seems to hint of "Old World super-stition." Thus, while the Orthodox ancestors of those same rabbis may well have believed in reincarnation, their modern descendants often do not know such teachings exist. This is changing, however. During the past three decades many Jewish mystical source texts have been translated into English, making "secret" teachings accessible to the layperson for the first time. For example, the *Tanya*, an important Hasidic text by Rabbi Schneur Zalman of Liady (the first Lubovitcher Rebbe), was translated into English in 1973. Rabbi Aryeh Kaplan, a respected Breslover Hasid, made the first translation of the *Bahir* in 1979 and included the entire text of *Hekhalot Rabati* in his excellent work, *Meditation and Kabbalah*, published in 1982. Raphael Patai has collected and translated hundreds of Jewish references to the Messiah and the World to Come into one volume, *The Messiah Texts*. And so it continues. (The interested reader is referred to the bibliography for information on these and other books about Jewish spirituality.)

In addition, many Jews who have studied Eastern religions, where reincarnation is openly discussed, are now returning to their own roots for a "second look" at Judaism. But in so doing, they do not necessarily reject what they have found in other traditions. Rather, they actively seek out authentic Jewish equivalents of concepts like meditation, spiritual healing, and reincarnation. In the process, such seekers often rediscover "lost" techniques and help shed light on formerly obscure teachings described in Jewish texts. This process of comparative philosophy has created a

movement that might be termed "neo-Hasidic,"
which seeks to combine the mysticism of Hasidic
teachings with a more personalized holistic consciousness. (I consider myself to be among this
group.)

As we have seen, there are vastly diverging
opinions about the afterlife within Judaism, ranging from genetic survival to physical resurrection
to eternal Heaven to reincarnation. It may well be
that all four of these viewpoints contain truth and
that different souls experience more than one of
these states at various stages of their spiritual
growth. Be that as it may, teachings about reincarnation do exist within Judaism, and while they
may not be mainstream, they are valid. Now let us
see how these teachings can be applied to cases of
reincarnation from the Holocaust.

Chapter 4:

Jewish Souls in Gentile Bodies

On September 2, 1939, as Hitler's troops moved through Poland, they occupied the town of Zaviercie, where 7,000 Jews lived. All Jewish men between the ages of 17 and 50 were rounded up in the marketplace and publicly tortured. During the week that followed, as the Nazis rolled across Poland, similar scenes were repeated again and again.[1]

On that same day in 1939, Martha was born to a Catholic family in the United States. During her childhood, blonde-haired Martha had no contact with Jews. Her father was an anti-Semite, who sent her to private boarding schools, where she was taught that "the Jews killed Christ." Martha did not hear about the Holocaust until she attended college. There she was ridiculed by the other students for intellectual pursuits and religiousness, at a time when women who attended college were expected to be looking for husbands.

In 1987, at the age of 48, Martha met a rabbi and developed an interest in Judaism. The first time she went to a Sabbath service, she cried with tears of uncontrollable joy. During other synagogue services she also had deeply emotional experiences. The liturgical Hebrew chants on Yom Kippur, the holiest day of the Jewish year, sent her into an "incredible state" of higher consciousness.

Martha eventually decided to convert to Judaism. During the *mikveh* (ritual immersion) ceremony, she began to tremble at the vow to be loyal to the Jewish people. The rabbis present remarked at her "religious fervor," but what Martha was actually experiencing was an overwhelming fear that seemed to have no explanation. Why, at this supposedly joyous moment in her life, was she so terrified?

That same year, Martha also decided to study Transcendental Meditation. She took the introductory classes and, on the appointed day, dutifully showed up with her gifts of fruit and flowers for her initiation. But instead of experiencing transcendental bliss, Martha suddenly began to "speak in tongues," in a Slavic-like language. She also found herself in excruciating physical pain. Neither she nor the meditation instructor had any explanation for this. A few weeks later, Martha watched a documentary on the Holocaust and had another extreme reaction, rolling on the floor in absolute terror.

While it is unlikely that Martha actually died in Poland on the same day she was born in America, it is certainly possible that she could have been tortured to death by the Nazis. As was explained in Chapter Two, the Nazi atrocities against the Jews began as soon as Hitler came to power in 1933 and were well under way before the invasion of Poland. Kristallnacht, the "Night of Broken Glass," when synagogues, chapels, cemeteries, and Jewish shops were destroyed and set on fire throughout Germany and Austria, took place on November 9-10, 1938, almost a year before Martha was born. The day after Kristallnacht, 35,000 Jews were arrested and sent to the Dachau, Sachsenhausen, and Buchenwald concentration camps in Germany.[2]

Martha's story fits a pattern that frequently occurs in these interviews. Over and over, Gentiles who grew up with absolutely no contact with Judaism have experienced déjà vu during their first exposure to Jewish customs and rituals. One might argue that while these people have not personally met any Jews during childhood, they were familiar with the Bible and could simply be identifying with Old Testament archetypes. But Judaism has changed and evolved over the centuries, and the customs of Eastern Europe have a "flavor" that cannot be gleaned from Bible texts alone. Christians and Jews read these texts very differently, and there is such a great gap between the two cultures that it would be virtually impossible for a Gentile to pass as a Jew simply on the basis of Christian Sunday school lessons.

Nevertheless, Martha did seem to have an innate "feel" for Judaism even though she was not raised Jewish. She is not really that unusual, because many of the people I have met with Holocaust past-life memories are not Jewish in this life. Interestingly, of those who have had some type of psychic reading and shared the material with me, very few believe they were religious Jews in their previous lives. Rather, the majority seem to have been marginal Jews, people for whom

Judaism was only an occasional affair and not central to their daily routine. If this was the case, it is quite likely that their very first experience of being Jewish was when they were forced by the Nazis to wear yellow stars and undergo all kinds of humiliation and torture before being put to death. Without previous experiences of the beautiful things about Judaism—the festivals, holidays, prayers, and rituals—such a soul might have become imprinted by the terrible suffering in the Holocaust and formed a negative association between "being Jewish" and "suffering." This, in turn, could have influenced the soul's decision to choose a non-Jewish body in this life.

Even today, the association of "Jewish" with "suffering" is more common than many people realize. When I do workshops on Jewish history and culture for interfaith groups, I sometimes ask the participants to write word associations on 3" x 5" cards, which are then passed forward and read aloud. In answer to the question, "What does it mean to be Jewish?" I frequently get "a lot of suffering" or "a lot of persecution." The question, "What does it mean to be chosen?" will sometimes elicit the same response. What this says to me is that, although the level of knowledge about Judaism may vary from person to person, the one thing everybody seems to know is that Jews have often suffered simply for being Jews.

When an adult knowingly suffers for a cause, that suffering can sometimes be a source of renewed strength and determination. But when a child suffers without understanding why, the experience is often felt as punishment and can result in harmful self-blame. Consider the following childhood nightmare, told to me by a middle-aged housewife who was born in Chicago:

"... I had my coat on with my yellow star, and I was told to take off my coat. So I took off my coat, and even on my dress I had my yellow star. I started to go through the line, and they started writing numbers on us. I remember asking my mother, 'Why are they doing this to me? But I've been a good girl.'

"[Later in the dream] . . . a soldier came in, and he just said that the children were going to be taken the next day, and we were . . . We got in a truck and they drove us halfway there, and I remember barbed wire was just about everywhere. And I still didn't know what was going on. This time I was closer to seven [years old]. It didn't really seem like we were there long, but it was too long . . . They had furnaces, I remember there were some furnaces that were in buildings, and they were brick, and they were tying some people down, strapping them down, just sticking them in. They opened up this door of the furnace, and they just started throwing the children in, one after another, and I kept on looking around to see if I could find my brother. I wanted him to hold onto. I couldn't find him anywhere. Soon it came my turn. I kept telling them, 'Well, I'll tell you what—I won't be a Jew.' I didn't understand what was wrong with being a Jew, but apparently it wasn't good. Didn't help at all."

Judaism teaches that one's focus at the time of

death is very important. The deathbed ritual includes the confession of sins from the Yom Kippur liturgy, and the faithful Jew is admonished to follow the example of Rabbi Akiba, who died, saying: "Hear, O Israel, the Lord is our God, the Lord is One!" But for a frightened child like the girl in the dream above, death does not come with such high consciousness. It is possible that she had never even heard of the "Shema" prayer, let alone of saying it at the moment of death.

We can imagine her growing up as a normal child in a German neighborhood, going to school with the other kids on the block. Then suddenly all of that is changed; she is now a "dirty Jew," forbidden to attend her former school and to romp with her playmates. She cannot go to the movies, play in the park, or even be seen on the streets. Eventually her home and possessions are confiscated, and she is torn from her mother's arms by brutal soldiers. Everything that she once knew and loved has been stripped from her simply because she is a Jew.

We know historically that some Jewish families in Europe were so assimilated into the non-Jewish world that their children did not even know that they were Jews until forced to put on the yellow star. It is not hard to imagine that such a child might see Jewishness as a punishment ("But I've been a good girl") and wish that she could somehow shed the "horrible stigma" of being Jewish. With this thought in mind, she could easily have become attracted to a non-Jewish body in the next life.

This idea is supported by another curious fact: about two-thirds of the cases I interviewed for this book are people with light hair and blue or hazel eyes. At first I attributed this to the high percentage of Scandinavians in Minnesota. But as I have traveled around the country, I found that this held true in other populations as well. A number of individuals said that they were the only person in the family with this coloration. The rest of the relatives had dark eyes and hair. While we know from genetics that both blond hair and blue eyes are recessive characteristics and can skip many generations before showing up, it is still strange that this occurs so frequently among people who believe that they died in the Holocaust.

The Nazis, as we know, placed great stress on their pseudo-theories of racial superiority, holding up the blond-haired, blue-eyed "Aryan" as their ideal. The vast majority of European Jews (and many non-Jews as well) were darker people, and we might imagine a soul beginning to identify with the oppressor, desperately wishing that he or she had been born with more "Aryan" features. If this thought were firmly embedded in the consciousness, the soul might well have been attracted to a light-haired body or perhaps even somehow produced it, believing that it would be a safe haven from further persecution.

The idea that one's previous life can affect the physical body in this one has been documented by Ian Stevenson in *Twenty Cases Suggestive of Reincarnation*. Stevenson has spent over thirty-five years studying children who remember their previous lives and in many cases has actually been able to locate living members of the family from the former incarnation. Stevenson has found examples in which birthmarks or deformities in this life correspond to wounds inflicted on the body in the previous life.[3]

Of course, it is also possible that some of my cases represent a psychological phenomenon from this life. According to University of Oregon psychologist Ray Hyman, who does not believe in reincarnation, these cases are based on internalized guilt. "Fair-haired, non-Jewish people," says Hyman, "may fantasize that they are reincarnated Holocaust victims to relieve the guilt they feel in being identified with the Nazi ideal—the Aryan race."[4]

No doubt, there are some cases who do fit Hyman's theory. Had they been living in Nazi Germany, they reason, they might have been among the oppressors. This thought so horrifies them that they want to identify with the Jews and other victims and, therefore, come to believe that they, too, died in the camps in their previous life.

I have never claimed that every blond who comes to me is an actual case of reincarnation from the time of the Holocaust. There have been some stories that I have recognized as being rooted in problems from this life. In such cases, I suggested standard therapy. But the very fact that these "fantasies" came clothed in Holocaust imagery is interesting in itself and shows how deeply the Holocaust has affected our consciousness.

I should also make it clear that blonds are not the only people with these past-life memories. Regina is black, with dark hair and eyes, who describes her skin color as "coffee with cream." She contacted me by phone after reading my article in *Venture Inward*. Not only did Regina have intuitive memories about the Holocaust, she had also undergone several hypnotic regression sessions to explore that lifetime and agreed to share the tapes of those sessions with me.

Born in 1950, Regina was not close to her family of birth and remembered thinking that she must be adopted because she simply did not fit in. She frequently had nightmares about her house being invaded by soldiers, whom she knew to be SS troops. Even as a child, she knew who they were, because they wore uniforms with swastikas on the armbands. More recently, she had also begun dreaming about hiding in the woods behind a *broken brick wall.*

Once, while sitting in a restaurant, Regina had a psychic impression of a child's composition book written in German. She could read it: the name at the top was Friederich, and he lived in Austerlitz, Czechoslovakia. Later, when Regina looked up Austerlitz in the library, she found a map that indicated a *brickworks* outside the town. Could this experience be related to her recent dreams?

Determined to solve the mystery, Regina sought out a hypnotherapist and underwent several past-life regressions. The regressions revealed that she had indeed been a Jewish boy named Friederich, who lived on Bergasstrasse in Austerlitz during the 1930s. His mother was named Esther, his father Johann. Under hypnosis Regina, as Friederich, wrote left-handed, although in the waking state she is right-handed. During one of the regressions, Regina described how Friederich's father came in one day with a sad, sickened look on his face, saying that "they've given Czechoslovakia to Hitler." The date, revealed during the session, was September 30, 1938.

This date meant nothing to Regina, who later looked it up in the library. She learned that throughout the summer of 1938, Hitler had been demanding control of the Sudetenland, the German-speaking region of Czechoslovakia. On September 30 at Munich, the triumvirate powers—Britain, France, and Italy—agreed to Hitler's demands. Germany would get the Sudetenland and, as a consequence, Czechoslovakia would lose its natural mountain defenses. Almost immediately, the SS began rounding up the Jews. Regina's past-life memory was historically accurate.

Gradually, over several sessions, the rest of the story revealed itself. When the Nazis came to get the family, Friederich went for his father's rifle, but the soldiers took it away from him and shot his parents before his eyes. His sister ran out the door and tried to hide but was captured, raped, and hung by the Nazis.

Friederich was taken alive but eventually was killed at the age of fifteen. Regina told the therapist that "after the gassing or whatever they did, the body looked ugly and greenish." She then described how, after Friederich died, he could hear his sister's voice calling and he saw "lights." Then the sister appeared in a "light body" to Friederich, who was now happy, feeling, in Regina's words, that "this is the part I've been waiting for."

Skeptics might point out that 1938 was too early for Friederich to have been gassed, because the Nazis did not build gas chambers until the 1940s. But this is not entirely accurate. As early as 1926, Hitler made reference to plans for poison gas in *Mein Kampf*. By 1941, Nazi experiments were already under way to find a "more efficient" way of killing besides the then-current practice of gassing people in panel trucks by re-routing the exhaust pipes into the cargo area. Friederich was taken alive, so it is entirely possible that he was sent first to a slave labor camp and then to one of the death camps. By 1942 the gas chambers at Belzec, Chelmno, Treblinka, and Sobibor were operative, but the gas used was still exhaust fumes from diesel engines.[5] Carbon monoxide poisoning does indeed turn the body blue or greenish.

It is these little details, often unknown to the people themselves, that convince me that these stories are valid and deserving of study. There have even been times that I have discounted aspects of a story because they did not "sound right," only to learn later that such an event could be historically documented.

For example, when Beverly (see Chapter Two) told her dream to Caryl and me, she described being thrown alive into the "ovens"—something that did not sound right to me. There is a Talmudic dictum that says, "It is impossible to have a dream that does not contain some worthless information,"[6] and I felt that this principle obviously applied here. So when I wrote up her story in my original article, I accepted the account of being burned alive, but made no mention of ovens, conjecturing instead that she might have died among those Jews who were burned alive in buildings.

Not long after that, a second woman made reference to people burning. When she was two-and-a-half, her brother had frightened her with a mask, so her mother took the mask and threw it into the fire. She watched it burn, but this did not help the fear, because somehow seeing the mask burn in the fireplace had flipped her back to past-life memories of seeing people thrown into a fire.

Years later as an adult, she went to see the
Holocaust documentary *Shoah* and just "knew"
that people had been thrown alive into the furnaces. She kept waiting for them to say this in the
movie and, sure enough, they did.[7]

How could a toddler know such details in 1954
that were not available to the general public until
the 1980s? Coincidence? Perhaps. But when hundreds of people have similar coincidences, one can
build a pretty good argument that there is something to their claims.

Consider the story of a Minnesota woman named
Irene, who was anything but a publicity-seeker.
Not only was she afraid of being labeled crazy, she
would not even give her name at our face-to-face
meeting in 1986, although she did consent to let
me use the material. I was the very first person
who had ever heard her story.

Irene was not Jewish nor did she seem to know
very much about Judaism. She had seen a flyer
announcing my workshop on "Reincarnation and
the Holocaust" at Evenstar, a "new age" bookstore
in Minneapolis. The subject sent chills up her
spine, but she was not about to be seen at such a
workshop, let alone tell her story there. So she
contacted me later. In the privacy of my living
room, Irene told how she had been driving down
the road one day, when something inexplicably
triggered memories of the Holocaust. So she
pulled off the road near some railroad tracks and
cried for about two hours. Irene could psychically
see crowds of people by the tracks—there were real
tracks there, but she was soon reeling back and
forth between the two time periods, and she could
see people being herded and separated from one

another. During this vision she had a strong sense of being a teen-age boy, overwhelmed with all of this fear, all this terror.

Then an old man appeared in the vision, and she felt like he was her father from another life, or maybe a spirit guide. He was telling her, as the teen-age boy in the vision, "not to forget, not to forget that this happened." The old man lovingly called her "Yosef, Yosef, Yosef."

I asked Irene if there was any way in this life that she might have known that name—did she know German or Hebrew? No, she did not. She had spelled it "Y-O-S-E-F" when she wrote the story down but had never heard this pronunciation before. ("Yosef" is the Hebrew for "Joseph." In German, too, "Joseph" would be pronounced with a "Y" sound.)

This was the beginning of a lot of these kinds of memories for Irene. In one vision she saw all of these people being herded into a shower room. She did not know why, but they were being told to take off all their clothes and go into the shower room. The door was then shut and the room was "full of death." Irene had no sense of these showers being gas chambers—if she had made up the story, she probably would have said "they were being herded into the gas chambers," but this isn't how she recorded it. They were simply being herded in, the doors closed, and the room was "full of death."

Irene was not married but always had a sense that, if she ever wore a wedding ring, she should wear it on the right hand rather than the left. Irene did not know that in a Jewish wedding ceremony, the groom first places the ring on the bride's *right index finger*, not the left-hand "ring finger." The

Jewish bride may, if she wishes, move the ring to another finger later, but there is no requirement to wear it on the left hand or even to wear it at all. In Europe, some Jewish women did wear it on the right hand.

I have dwelt at length on these stories of Jews in Gentile bodies because I feel that they are the most convincing evidence that this reincarnation phenomenon is real. This is not to say that no Jewish clients have ever told similar stories. They have. In fact, there are probably just as many—if not more—Jews with such memories. As was mentioned in the previous chapter, Hasidim not only believe in reincarnation, they expect that Jews will return again as Jews. So if a Hasidic child remembers dying as a Jew in the Holocaust, this is accepted as a matter of course. Such a person is not likely to seek me out for advice!

The idea that a religious or ethnic identity can carry over from one life to the next may seem foreign to many readers, who are probably accustomed to reincarnation literature with a more "universalist" approach. But within Hasidic circles there is a longstanding belief that Jewish and Gentile souls are somehow different. This idea is so widespread among Hasidim that almost every time I have mentioned these cases, I have been told that these people cannot "really" be Jews in Gentile bodies, because that "just doesn't happen." As one Lubovitcher Hasid told me, "Right after the Holocaust somebody asked the Rebbe if a Jew could come back as a non-Jew. The Rebbe said, 'No; once a Jew, always a Jew.' "

The exact nature of this difference between Jews and Gentiles varies, depending on the commentator. Some see it as primarily a matter of heredity and behavior, while others attribute it to the very "roots" of the soul. But one thread which runs consistently throughout the commentaries is that the Jews accepted the Torah at Sinai and the Gentiles did not, and this constitutes a major difference in spiritual responsibilities. In order to understand how this could be seen as something which affects reincarnation, we must first understand that, for many Jews, the Torah is not merely a written scroll, nor is it limited to the earth plane.

According to kabbalistic belief, which has been absorbed into Hasidism as well as other Jewish circles, the Torah transcends space and time. In addition to the written Torah as we know it, there is an esoteric Cosmic Torah that is written by God with letters of "black fire on white fire." As this Primal Torah is emanated from the Mind of God, it takes on denser and denser forms until it finally becomes the scroll which we know on earth. But even here, the Torah text which appears to be a mere Biblical narrative is, in reality, one long mystical Name of God.[8] Therefore, according to this model, the Torah exists, in one form or another, in all of the worlds and levels of consciousness throughout God's creation.[9] And, by corollary, if it exists in all worlds, it must be valid in all worlds.

The question of whether or not Jewish and Gentile souls are innately different cannot be answered in a work of this type. However, I do believe it is possible for a soul to decide to commit itself to a covenant that will be binding over many incarnations and in many worlds. According to Dr. Joel Whitton, author of *Life Between Life*, the "more advanced souls" do make plans "for several lives to come," spending the time in between lives in some type of study.[10] Many Jews believe that the souls of the righteous study Torah with the sages in the World to Come. Then, when the time comes for a soul to return to earth, it seeks out a life that will provide opportunities to do as many *mitzvot* as possible.

It is a common belief among religious Jews today that the consciousness of the parents at the time of conception will determine the nature of the soul which will come to incarnate. It is for this reason that many kabbalists considered Friday night (the Sabbath) as the very best time to have intercourse, because the husband and wife would be in a happy and peaceful mood. Reb Gedaliah Fleer, a highly respected teacher among the Breslover Hasidim, has written: "The soul conceived in purity and holiness will, in most cases, be more attuned and sensitive to the holy and Godly aspects of life. And so, purity of thought during conception is as vital, if not more so, than love."[11]

Jewish parents-to-be have often told me that they are praying for a child who will love Torah and *mitzvot*. Strange as it may seem, the children born into such families frequently do have an innate feel for *Yiddishkeit*, that untranslatable word which encompasses the whole Jewish way of life. Whether this childhood devotion is from "nature" or "nurture" would be difficult to prove. I personally believe that the parents' love of Torah on earth attracts a Torah-loving soul from the other world, so that religious Jews often do reincarnate as Jews once more.

I have also met Jews from the Conservative,

Reform, and secular communities who have Holocaust past-life memories, but their concerns are usually quite different from those of my non-Jewish clients. Most "progressive" Jews have no idea that there are teachings about reincarnation within Judaism and are often convinced that it is somehow "un-Jewish" to believe in it. They come to me, not to talk about their Holocaust nightmares, but to be reassured that it is O.K. for a Jew to believe in reincarnation! Their flashbacks, dreams, and visions are just as convincing as those of Gentile clients but, because the Holocaust permeates Jewish culture, it is more difficult to prove that these are due to reincarnation. The skeptical reader will ask whether these Jews are really remembering a past life or simply recalling something that was learned long ago in this life and buried in the subconscious.

Most non-Jews, on the other hand, are not saturated with the Holocaust. Many have even told me that they never heard of it until adulthood. This is not so impossible. The majority of these people are "baby-boomers," born in the 1940s and '50s. But until the mid-1970s, "Holocaust studies" was not a subject included in most curricula, even on the college level. Incredible as it may seem, several Ph.D. candidates who proposed Holocaust topics during the 1950s were turned down with the explanation that "nobody is interested in that."[12]

This "lack of interest" was, in fact, a form of emotional denial on the part of people, both Jews and Gentiles, who wanted to simply forget what had happened during the war and get back to "normal" as soon as possible. Nobody was talking

about the Holocaust much during the post-war
years. Even Elie Wiesel, that prolific writer who
has been called "the prophet of the Holocaust,"
was so traumatized by the experience that it took
ten years before he could bring himself to put pen
to paper. Wiesel's was a lone voice for over two
decades; for most other survivors, the experience
was still too close and painful to talk about.

Even in Israel, the Holocaust was hardly mentioned in the public schools until after the trial of
Adolf Eichmann in 1961. Ruth Firer, a researcher
at the Hebrew University School of Education and
a specialist on teaching about the Holocaust,
recalls that during the 1950s the Holocaust was "a
family secret—a shame." Everyone tried to cover it
up. The schools taught the heroism of the Warsaw
ghetto uprising, but that was it.[13] Not until the
1970s did large numbers of survivors come "out of
the closet" and tell what they had seen, at last
giving names and faces to the cold historical figure
of "six million Jews dead."

During the 1950s in the United States, not only
was there little talk of the Holocaust, there was
also very little social contact between Jews and
Gentiles. Some of my subjects who grew up in
isolated rural areas were not even very clear about
what Jews are. One woman from Arkansas told me
that she was an adult in her forties before she
realized that Jews do not celebrate Christmas or
Easter. Yet the past-life memories that these people
describe often fit Holocaust facts and Eastern
European Jewish customs. As has already been
pointed out, the clients themselves are frequently
puzzled by seemingly strange details, like wearing
a hat in Heaven or a wedding ring on the "wrong"

hand. In such cases, it is easier to recognize the reincarnation phenomenon because what they are describing is not consistent with their own culture in this life.

But there are other reasons why more Gentiles than Jews seek me out. People who died as Jews and returned as Jews may be having flashbacks, but their identity is rarely in question. On the other hand, non-Jews who remember having been Jewish in another life are often disturbed by this fact, feeling that they are somehow "deserters" from their own people—which, in a sense, they are. On some level, even if it was only through being confused after death and grabbing the first available body, these souls did choose not to be Jewish anymore.

This does not necessarily mean that they consciously said, "I want to be a blond-haired German." In some cases they simply wished to be something else besides Jewish, and this desire set the pattern for the next life. After a horrible death at the hands of the Nazis, it probably seemed safer to be born into the dominant culture, without fear of being singled out for persecution. Yet now that these souls are living in a relatively open society where outright persecution is not as likely, they find that Jewish memories are coming back to haunt them. Had they "stuck with it," they might now be participating in the current rebirth of Jewish religion, culture, and spirituality. Many of those I have interviewed, therefore, feel that they somehow failed, that at a crucial moment they may have denied their faith and are now in exile.

If this is true, then it gives a new meaning to the Biblical phrase to be "cut off from his people." The first time this phrase appears in the Torah is in connection with circumcision, where Abraham is told by God that an uncircumcised male shall be "cut off from his people; he has broken my Covenant."[14] In Hebrew, the word for "circumcision," *brit*, is the same as for "covenant," so the association with "cutting off" has a double meaning that is much stronger than in English: if a Jew cuts off his foreskin, he is part of the Covenant; if not, then he himself will be "cut off."

In later Biblical verses where "cut off from his people" appears, it is almost always used in connection with breaking ritual commandments that are specifically connected with being Jewish, such as the laws of Passover or the Sabbath.[15] For this reason, in later Jewish law, the Hebrew word used for "cut off," *karet,* came to have the technical meaning of "excommunication," which in practice meant ostracism. Could it be that *karet* also has another meaning on the spiritual level, namely, to be literally separated from the Jewish people in the next incarnation?

In my opinion, whether or not this is true would depend on the motivations of the individual soul. As was explained in Chapter Three, there is indeed a concept of "group karma" within Judaism, namely, the Covenant at Sinai. Ideally, all Jews should keep this Covenant, and I believe, as have many Jews throughout the centuries, that this obligation is valid from incarnation to incarnation. A Jew who consciously, deliberately chooses to break the Covenant by renouncing Judaism may eventually get what he or she has asked for, namely, to be reborn as a non-Jew. In such a case, this "exile" could be considered a type of *karet.*

But there may be other times when a particular soul needs to learn something from another culture. Such an incarnation can then become a learning experience. Using myself as an example, I was once told by a psychic that I have had more Jewish incarnations than anyone else she had read. This confirmed my own experience of a strong, inner "knowing" that I have lived many, many lives throughout Jewish history. But at the same time, not *all* of my incarnations have been Jewish. I have a strong sense that some of my lives were spent in other cultures in order to gain experiences that were not possible within the Jewish world at that time.

While I seem to be a soul which has returned again and again as a Jew, there are other souls which apparently return again and again as Hindus, Buddhists, or Christians. In addition, some individual souls seem to prefer wandering from place to place and culture to culture, often changing spiritual paths from one incarnation to the next. There must certainly be groups of souls who also journey this way together. For them, the karmic tie is not any particular religion, tribe, or nationality, but rather the personal relationships among the souls themselves. We can speculate that in God's infinite wisdom, there are many different kinds of situations by which karma is healed. All serve a purpose in the overall evolution of planetary consciousness and spiritual growth.

I believe that those souls who are not tied to a particular culture can sometimes serve as bridges among karmic groups, carrying inner knowledge from one time and place to another. This is a very important function, because it helps to break the

barriers that can develop among groups of people
if they are too isolated. At the same time, such
wandering souls also gain a wide range of experience for their own growth. Like honey bees, they
gather nectar from many flowers during many
lifetimes. Some of these souls, however, remain
shallow and find their energy dissipated by having
to learn the same things over and over in different
forms, without progressing beyond their personal
stumbling blocks.

For this reason, I believe that there also need to
be some souls who remain firmly anchored in the
various spiritual traditions long enough to progress
into more advanced levels of their particular paths.
A bridge without firm foundations on both banks
of the river is soon washed away. Those souls
which remain within the same framework life after
life serve as the pillars supporting the spiritual
bridge here on earth. They are able to become
highly specialized, drawing on the memories and
experiences of many lifetimes to master knowledge that could not be learned in one incarnation.
Using another analogy, souls who attain such
mastery are like lighthouses, remaining firmly
anchored in one place while guiding travelers on
the spiritual sea.

The soul of the Dalai Lama, for example, has
been the head of Tibetan Buddhism for fourteen
incarnations. Many of his close associates have
also been together over many lifetimes. Because
they are reborn each time into the familiar framework of Tibetan Buddhism, they are able to pick
up where they left off in the previous incarnation.
This does not mean that such souls are all prodi-
gies at birth, although that does sometimes happen.

But more often, there is simply an innate familiarity with the symbols, rituals, and language of the religion, so that knowledge from previous lives can be accessed more easily. This, in turn, has enabled this particular karmic group to develop an amazing level of detachment and spirituality.

Crossing cultural lines from one incarnation to another is neither good nor bad in and of itself. Rather, it depends on the spiritual needs of the individual and, at times, on the needs of society. It may be that because of the terrible hatred toward Jews that spawned the Holocaust, it was necessary for some souls to cross cultural lines in order to build mutual understanding.

For many centuries, prejudice on both sides has kept Jews and Christians so separated that each knows only a negative stereotype of the other. By "inter-incarnating," these souls may be helping to break down that wall of prejudice. A non-Jew with inner empathy for Judaism can more easily help foster respect for Jewish teachings within his or her own cultural circle. Conversely, a Jew who has spent some lifetimes practicing other spiritual paths can use the universal aspects of those experiences to help revitalize modern Judaism, which in many ways has become bogged down in fear and mistrust because of centuries of devastating effects from experiences like the Holocaust.

This is why, when some of these seekers have asked whether they should convert to Judaism in order to rejoin their karmic group, I have counseled caution. Being Jewish is not easy in this imperfect world, and there may be things that a non-Jew can more easily accomplish for the good of the planet, especially in places where Jews are still barred from full participation in society. For example, it would be impossible for a known Jew to enter certain Middle Eastern countries, even for humanitarian projects or peace work. And in rural America, where Saturday is the big business day and everything still closes on Sunday, it can be very difficult for a Sabbath-observing Jew to find employment.

Most rabbis, including myself, will discourage people from converting to Judaism. Traditionally, a seeker must be turned away three times before being accepted as a prospective convert. This is not because of chauvinism, but because we do not have the same kind of exclusive teachings as do most Christian churches. We believe that non-Jews, too, can serve God without becoming Jews. We also believe that any Gentile can get to Heaven if he or she obeys the Seven Laws of Noah to be "saved" (Jews don't usually use that terminology), so there is no need for the individual to convert to Judaism unless specifically attracted to serving God through the Covenant at Sinai.

The Seven Laws of Noah are: (1) not to worship idols; (2) not to profane the name of God; (3) not to murder; (4) not to steal; (5) not to eat blood or flesh cut from an animal while it is still alive, (6) not to commit adultery or incest; (7) not to take the law into one's own hands, but to settle disputes in courts of justice.

Note that these laws are similar to the Ten Commandments, but not exactly the same. The Sabbath, for example, is regarded as a specifically Jewish commandment that is not binding on non-Jews. This does not mean that Gentiles cannot have a day off, but rather that they are not religiously required to do it on Saturday like Jews. A Gentile may, of course, do more than obey just the Seven Laws; people who are attracted to Jewish prayers and holidays can participate in these, if they wish, without actually becoming Jewish, and many do. These Seven Laws simply represent the "bottom line" of what the Creator asks of all human beings, Jewish or not.

All people can serve the Creator from wherever they are. However, souls who have joined the Covenant at Sinai in the past will probably reconnect with the Jewish people in a future incarnation and should, therefore, spend some time exploring the joyful aspects of Judaism — our beautiful songs, prayers, stories, dances, and customs — to offset the painful memories of the Holocaust and replace any shame with healthy self-esteem. In this way, "Jewish" will have a positive connotation instead of being associated only with torture and pain.

For all of us, Jewish or not, the karma of the Holocaust has had a powerful impact. "Why did it happen?" I am often asked. There are no easy answers. It may well be that we are still too close to the event to understand its full implications. However, we can begin to work toward healing the deep wounds and helping individuals, both incarnate and on the "other side," who were traumatized by their experiences. For not only did these souls die a horrible death, but many of them went through that experience as helpless children. In the next chapter, we shall hear the stories of some of these children and explore what happens when a person's life is cut short before his or her work on earth has been completed.

Chapter 5:

The Souls of a Million Children

When Steve was born in 1955, he was unable to digest food and spent the first year of his life in the hospital. He was "officially allergic to everything." In addition, Steve had frequent childhood nightmares about trying to climb the walls of his bedroom. In these dreams he was always a woman and, upon awakening, would find himself repeating a seemingly meaningless word that sounded like *vendorswagens*. In school he wrote accounts about escaping from camp and being wrongly accused, stories which caused serious concern among his teachers.

At the age of sixteen, Steve's digestive problems began to subside, while at the same time he "miraculously" started playing quality piano without ever having been trained! But there was a dark side to this musical talent. Every time Steve sat down at the piano, he had nightmarish visions of playing for many thin, starving children. He would try to make the children laugh but could only cry inside because he knew they were dying. These impressions were so overwhelming that sometimes Steve could not go on playing.

But it was a mysterious phobia which finally drove Steve to consult a hypnotherapist. For some unknown reason, Steve's neck was always extremely sensitive, and he could not stand to have anyone even touch it. The very thought was terrifying. He knew this fear was not logical, but it simply would not go away. Eventually with the help of the hypnotherapist, the following story unfolded:

In another life, Steve had been a Belgian woman named Elaine Ader (pronounced ah-DAY), who was born into a family of traveling entertainers. Her father had died when she was only a child, and when she was fourteen her mother went into a sanitarium. Alone in the world, Elaine journeyed to Paris and lied about her age to get a job as a nightclub dancer.

The owner of the club was a Polish Jew named Balinchinski. Although he was considerably older than Elaine, they fell in love and were married two years later. Elaine remained Balinchinski's wife until he died. She inherited his nightclubs but was unable to keep them, so she went on the road again as a performer and talent scout.

Eventually Elaine remarried, this time to a Prussian. In 1943 her second husband was reported as "missing," so she traveled to Prussia to look for him. There she had an argument with her influential father-in-law. He accused her of stealing his son and wanted to break up the marriage. The next thing Elaine knew, she was being deported to Poland as a Jew. Her father-in-law had apparently convinced the authorities that Balinchinski was really her father, not her first husband.

Elaine was not sent to a concentration camp at first, but to "a part of town where we were all crowded together—starving, dirty" (the Warsaw ghetto?). Every morning Poles would come with carts to carry away the dead—carts that were called *vendorswagens*, the strange word in Steve's childhood dreams. But although the ghetto was a terrible place, surprisingly this was the first time that Elaine had really felt "at home," as if she now had a family. She took care of the children and the orphans, often performing shows to entertain them, and became very protective of their welfare. Once, when the children were sick and needed medicine, she slept with the supply officer in order to get it. This caused a big scandal, and soon after that Elaine was put on a train to the camps.

Because Elaine spoke so many languages, she was given preferential treatment and used as an interpreter for questioning the Jews as they arrived on the trucks and trains. But even as a privileged prisoner, Elaine saw so much pain and suffering that she began to lose her will to live. About that time, a fellow prisoner convinced her to join him in an escape. She could serve as his interpreter and maybe, just maybe, they would get help.

The plan was for them to escape separately, then rendezvous on the outside. Elaine escaped in a truckload of human hair and was found by peasants, who took her to the barn where she was to meet her friend. But he was not so lucky. German soldiers had tracked him to the hiding place, and they were both recaptured, taken back to camp, and hung. At the moment of death, Elaine felt ashamed to face anyone, as if she had somehow let them down by failing to escape and get help. This feeling, along with the choking sensation of hanging, had apparently carried over into the next life, which accounted for Steve's sensitive neck and his illness at birth.

As Steve himself explained it, "I did not want to come back again (to the earth plane), but it was my job. The children were coming back en masse. They had seen hell and they had seen heaven. Now they were ready to use their great potential. I had to be here for them. That was my job."

Although it may sound bizarre for a woman to be playing piano for starving children in ghettos and concentration camps, such things did actually happen. During the early years of the Holocaust, especially, the Jews in the ghettos tried to maintain a semblance of normalcy in their lives. They organized lectures, classes, concerts, and Torah study groups for both adults and children. In the Theresienstadt camp, where the Nazis tried to maintain a facade of "humane conditions" for propaganda purposes, there were also cultural activities for children, including concerts and plays. Of course, all of this was a cruel deception, because this "model" camp was nothing but a transfer station to Auschwitz.

Was there really an Elaine Ader who played music for starving children in the ghetto? Perhaps someone out there can verify this incredibly detailed story. Meanwhile, I can say that Steve is accurate about one thing—the children are indeed returning en masse. Of all the people who have contacted me thus far, only one claimed to have died as an elderly person. The majority were in their twenties or younger, and many remember dying as small children.

Why did these souls come back so soon? According to many teachings on reincarnation, there is usually a considerable waiting period between lifetimes. Ancient sources like Plato, Virgil, and the *Bhagavad Gita* refer to intervals of a thousand years or more.[1]

Among Dr. Whitton's subjects in *Life Between Life,* the interval ranged from ten months to more than 800 years, with the average being around forty years. According to Whitton, the length of time between incarnations has been getting steadily shorter in this century. He, too, found cases of souls who died in World War II and returned in the "baby-boom" generation.[2]

One of the reasons that has been suggested for this shorter timespan between incarnations is the rapid pace of change in the modern world.[3] Life in ancient Egypt remained basically the same for many centuries at a time, so there would have been little for a soul to learn by returning immediately. The same was true in many other cultures around the world. Even into the late Middle Ages, one life every few centuries was probably enough.

But during the past 500 years there has been a steady increase in the pace of social change and new technology. James Burke, author of *The Day the Universe Changed,* has pointed out how many basic discoveries which we now take for granted — the printing press, the telescope, and the microscope, to name a few — have had far-reaching effects on the world and how we experience it. This pace of scientific discovery is now so rapid that, in Burke's words, "We live with such a high rate of change that we have come to expect obsolescence."[4]

In my work as a nursing home chaplain, I am constantly amazed at how many times "the universe changed" during the current century. Many of the residents at the home remember the horse-and-buggy days and the first time they saw an automobile. I myself can remember our family's first television set, an invention which my sister, who is five years younger than I, took for granted. I also clearly recall that day in 1959 when my father showed me the headlines about the successful launching of a Sputnik satellite. During my teen years, computers were huge tangles of wire that took up whole rooms and were far less efficient than my grandson's video games! In a world which changes so rapidly, I can understand perfectly why souls might choose to spend less time in the *bardo* between incarnations.

Let us take a few moments to examine what many students of metaphysics believe happens between lives. Although the symbolism differs from culture to culture, the basic scenario is the same. At the moment of death, the soul is met by a deceased relative or other spirit, who guides it across the barrier to the next world. There the soul is helped to evaluate its life on earth and is cleansed or purged (the original meaning of *purgatory*) of its sins. This purging also removes the emotional pain associated with its experiences, so that the life can be incorporated into the soul's higher consciousness. Once this is accomplished, the soul remains in the other world until it is ready to descend to earth again for another round of spiritual lessons.

All of this is assuming that death comes naturally, at the appointed time. Elderly people or those with long-term illnesses have time to prepare for their deaths and usually go peacefully when the moment finally comes. But in cases of sudden or violent death this process can be upset, and the soul leaves the body without proper preparation. It can even happen that the soul is not aware of being dead and remains an earthbound "ghost" until it finally realizes that it is no longer incarnate—a subject we will return to in Chapter Eight. In other cases, the soul may feel that its life was not yet complete and will return to earth as soon as possible. Without the purification and healing period between incarnations, the soul often retains intense, frightening emotions carried over from its previous life.

Janet, who wrote to me from Vermont, described a number of symptoms that she believed were past-life related, including an obsession with food. She always felt that she must eat her food immediately, out of fear that it would not be there anymore, even though there was no basis for this. She wrote, "I feel that I was an eyewitness to the Holocaust (in another life) for quite a few reasons . . . My earliest memory is of my parents wondering at the intensity of my childhood nightmares in which I would awaken with a cold feeling of death that seeps through me . . . Although my parents were anti-Semitic, I have always had a fascination with Jewish ritual and have avidly read books about Jews."

Interestingly, Janet felt that she might also have lived during the time of the Spanish Inquisition and believed that one of her college professors, with whom she is now a personal friend, might have been someone she knew from that life:

"One of them (the professors) I feel I knew in Spain or Portugal in the 1400s. One day (in this life) we were all arguing about some point or other, when I flashed on a picture of me as a child in a boat. This professor and many other people were there, and he told me not to be afraid. This was so vivid. I never told him (about the vision), but (another friend in the same circle) had looked into these things and readily understood what I was talking about. She also felt that there was a strong bond among all of us and that we had all known each other forever."

Three other clients who contacted me believed they had been martyred during both the Inquisition and the Holocaust. What many people do not realize is that a very high percentage of the "heretics" and "witches" tortured by the Spanish Inquisition were *marranos* or "secret Jews" who had been forced to convert to Roman Catholicism but were secretly practicing the faith of their ancestors. Throughout the Middle Ages, Jews were often accused of being sorcerers by the Roman Catholic church and were burned at the stake.[5] This is another reason why kabbalah, often associated with "magic," was not taught publicly during this period.

When Sandra was born in 1944, she had a severe immune disorder, and the doctors did not expect her to live until adulthood. But in spite of a lifelong struggle with medical problems, she has indeed survived and is now a professional psychic consultant in Alaska. Sandra believes that she once died by burning and wrote: "Throughout

childhood I had nightmares of burning to death
and remember my mother telling me that in in-
fancy I'd scream in terror at the sight of a uniform.
I even cringed from my father when he wore his
peaked truck driver's cap." Sandra describes herself as having "a definite affinity for kabbalah" but
is more attracted to Tarot cards and the "occult"
than to Jewish practices. Could Sandra have been
a Gypsy during the Holocaust, burned to death by
Nazis in uniforms? The hats of the SS "death
squads" were indeed peaked as can easily be seen
in historical photographs.

The parents of children with these innate fears
are often puzzled by their behavior, because there
does not seem to be anything in their son's or
daughter's present life that could account for such
terror. One woman, born in 1950 in Michigan,
wrote that "my mother tells strange incidents of
my childhood. For example, one year I hid all of my
Halloween candy and that of my sister's. I would
tell the hiding place to no one. Months later, my
mother found the candy and asked why I had done
such a thing. I answered, 'There will be a war and
we will starve.'"

Bob from Colorado, who is not Jewish, described how he had suddenly gotten a psychic
impression that his girlfriend Alice had been in the
Holocaust during a previous lifetime. Because she
was open to the idea of reincarnation, Bob shared
this karmic insight. Alice stared at him open-
mouthed. She then related how once, when she
was five years old, she was crying and her father
asked her why. She said, "Why do people hate us
just because we're Jews?" Her father actually was
Jewish but had been so successful in "passing" for

a Gentile that even Alice's mother did not know. Later in her childhood, before the family watched a documentary about Auschwitz, Alice described it to them in detail, including where all the buildings were.

It has been estimated that over a million Jewish children were killed by the Nazis. Add to this the unknown numbers of other children from all backgrounds who died in the war itself, and we are faced with the possibility that a very large percentage of the "baby-boom" generation is composed of people who have reincarnated from World War II. The karmic implications of this are staggering.

There is an old Jewish saying that "once the sword is let loose in the land, it does not distinguish between the innocent and the guilty." Nowhere is this more true than in the case of children killed in a war. Some may be tempted to argue that these children were meant to die young because of karma from previous lives. But if this were really the case, they should have remained on the other side after their "preordained" deaths. The very fact that they returned so soon suggests that these deaths were not some kind of karmic payback but unplanned casualties of war. In fact, two people describe memories of having died twice as children or young adults in this century and are now back for the third time!

Although many people believe that we carefully plan out every detail of our earth lives while in Other World, this is not always the case. In fact, the research of Dr. Whitton seems to indicate that it is only the less-developed souls who have a detailed "karmic script" planned out in advance, often with very strong suggestions from the Heavenly Tribunal. The more advanced souls, however, decide only the main outlines of their next lives, leaving possibilities open for unexpected challenges.[6] It is, therefore, quite possible to die through no fault of one's own but simply by being in the wrong place at the wrong time. From a Jewish perspective, there is indeed such a thing as "bad luck."

Because their lives were cut short, these souls often have "unfinished business" which draws them back to reincarnate almost immediately. In many cases they seem to have simply grabbed the first available body, regardless of whether or not the family would be compatible. Over and over, my subjects have told me that they were the "odd one" in the family for one reason or another. Many felt like total strangers in an otherwise happy home.

Occasionally the parents have also recognized this "strangeness" on some level. Frieda, the German woman in Chapter Two, described her father as a Nazi who had never really accepted her. He frequently said that "this is not my child," although there was never any question that he was Frieda's biological father.

While some souls came back because of a burning desire to finish out their allotted lifespans, others returned because of specific commitments they had made at the time of death. Joe and Sarah, a middle-aged couple from Florida, are typical. It was love at first sight in this life, and both felt as if they had known each other forever. Sometimes they even joked about having met in a previous life. Their relationship developed quickly and soon they were married, but not happily ever after. Within a very short time things went sour, and eventually they divorced. At the time I met Sarah,

they were hardly speaking to one another.
Sarah was puzzled by all this. Why had she and
Joe been so comfortable together at first, only to
have the marriage end in such bitterness? If they
were really soul mates, why didn't it last? And if
not, then how could she explain their instant
attraction to each other? Eventually Sarah found
the answer in a past-life reading.

Joe and Sarah had been teen-age lovers during
the Holocaust and had made a solemn pledge to
always be together. It was puppy love, really, the
first time for both of them. Under normal circumstances they would eventually have discovered
that they were incompatible and broken up the
relationship. But these were not normal times. At
the height of their adolescent romance, Joe and
Sarah were killed, each dying with the promise of
"forever" in their last thoughts. This pledge was so
strong that it brought them back to earth almost
immediately, where they found each other and
picked up where they had left off. Now their
relationship was ending, as it no doubt would have
in their previous life if they had lived longer.

Learning about this "puppy love" from another
life made sense to Sarah. It explained their "instant attraction," as well as much of the
"immaturity" and "childishness" that had emerged
during the divorce process. Sarah was now able to
forgive Joe and get on with her own life. By doing
so, she no doubt saved herself from yet another
unhappy encounter with Joe in a future incarnation.

One of the most curious things about these
cases is that the memories connected with a past-
life trauma frequently surface when the person

reaches the same chronological age in this life. Steve, for example, began spontaneously playing piano at sixteen, corresponding to the age when he married Balinchinski in his life as Elaine. While the wedding itself was not traumatic, it was this marriage which eventually served as the excuse to deport Elaine as a Jew and set into motion the events which led to her death.

Exactly why these memories surface at a particular time is not clear. It may be that something in the development of the body itself triggers the past-life recall, causing a kind of inter-incarnational déjà vu. If the soul has returned to "pick up where it left off" in the previous life, it would make sense that the memories of that life would surface around the same age as when the death or other trauma occurred. Many of these people describe the onset of a specific period of very intense past-life recall, which in turn can trigger a personal crisis.

The following two stories were told to me by friends of the people involved:

"(My friend's) anorexia began in her teen years. She began to embrace the faith of Judaism in her twenties. It was during this time she also had flashbacks of the camps. Although she is now divorced, the very first night of the honeymoon she felt murderous rage, to the extent that she refuses intercourse to this day. Both parents love Germany and have been there twice or more."

(Connecticut)

"She had had Holocaust memories emerging during a period of mental illness and was convinced that the cause of the illness itself was due to past-life trauma, but was never able to discuss it with the doctors. She made the interesting statement that 'schizophrenics are people who are not fully incarnated on the earth plane,' and described how she had been afraid to fully commit herself to being in this world because of the Holocaust past life. She is recovered now and said that the mental illness was 'a great cleansing' for her."

(Minnesota)

Sometimes the "trigger" for the déjà vu is not chronological age but rather a particular time of year. Becky's story is an interesting example. Born in Tennesee in 1946, Becky never really knew her father because he left when she was only three months old. Her mother raised her as a Southern Baptist. When Becky was twelve years old, her mother explained that her father had been Jewish, adding that it was "nothing to be ashamed of."

Far from feeling ashamed of her Jewish roots, Becky decided to learn more. She wrote:

"I have always been drawn to the Holocaust since early teen years. I read (Leon Uris's) *Exodus* several times and could almost feel a part of that culture . . . For the last few years *in the fall of each year* I'm drawn to books about the death camps, mostly about Poland. So *for a couple weeks* I read, and at the time it seems as if a part of me is in another time and place. This is a feeling, not a memory or vision . . . The thing that made me *feel* that being Jewish goes much deeper than just

faith is when I crossed into Israel while with
a group of friends. I felt as though my bones
had come home, not that I actually *remembered* anything, once again it is a *feeling* . . .
In a very deep part of my being I find it hard
to believe (that) to be a Jew is a faith instead
of something much more profound."

On the Jewish calendar, "the fall of the year" is
the High Holy Day cycle, which begins with Rosh
Hashanah (the New Year) and is followed ten days
later by Yom Kippur (the Day of Atonement). The
High Holy Days are a time when Jews everywhere
focus on repentence, which in Hebrew is called
tshuvah, literally "returning" to God and the ways
of the Torah. These two weeks are the most solemn, serious time of year for Jews, and even those
who do not normally attend synagogue usually go
to services then. But why would a Southern Baptist feel obsessed by the Holocaust at this particular
time? Does her soul somehow "tune in" to the cycle
of the Jewish calendar?

Whatever the event that triggers these memories, the healing process is usually quite similar to
dealing with abuse issues in this life. As a matter
of fact, some skeptics have suggested that these
are not really memories of other lives, but simply
fantasies expressing long-forgotten abusive incidents from childhood. I tend to disagree with that
opinion, because although some of these people
come from dysfunctional families, not all of them
do. Many describe normal backgrounds that show
no logical reason for their fears and nightmares,
yet their stories are quite consistent with the
others.

But even if some of these memories are due to sublimated childhood traumas, the important thing is to help the person get beyond the pain and begin to find inner peace. In many cases, supportive listening may be enough. When the possibility of reincarnation is openly explored, it usually doesn't take very long for the fear and pain to subside. Apparently once the "unfinished business" is dealt with, either by completing the task or by consciously letting it go, the soul becomes fully "grounded" in this life. The memories of a previous existence are still there, but they fade into the past and no longer dominate the waking consciousness. Again, this process is not much different from treatment for abuse in this life.

Telling one's story and, most important, *being believed* also have a very powerful healing effect. Over and over, people have thanked me for opening the door and taking them seriously. Just about everyone quoted in this book expressed immense relief at finally being able to talk about something that had bothered them since childhood. My only regret is that they had to wait so many years to be able to do it. If they had been living in cultures which support a belief in reincarnation, they might have been spared many years of frustration.

We can, however, learn from their experiences, and be more open to children of the present generation who may have memories from another life. The sooner a soul can move beyond the trauma of a violent death, the sooner it can begin to progress in this incarnation. Therefore, if our children tell us about dreams which do not seem to fit into their present family experiences, we should take them seriously and encourage them

to talk about it. This should be done in a gentle,
loving way, always reassuring them that these
dreams are not happening now and that the
children are safe and loved.

As was already mentioned in Chapter Two,
Edgar Cayce was very concerned about these "war
children" who were coming back too soon. In
1943, the mother of a four-year-old girl from New
York consulted Cayce as to why her daughter had
such a terror of city life. The Cayce reading revealed that "here we have a quick return to earth,
from fear, back to fear, through fear."

In her previous life, the child had been a little
girl named Theresa Schwalendal. When Theresa
was only about five years old (in 1936 or '37) she
was killed by Nazis near the border of Lorraine and
Germany. She had reincarnated almost immediately and was born into the present body less than
nine months from her death. Therefore, the past
and present were locked together in her mind, so
that she could not distinguish between the normal
sounds of New York City and the din of sirens,
shouts, and other terrifying noises surrounding
her death.

Cayce counseled that this child must be gently
nurtured and sheltered from loud noises, sirens,
and other things which might remind her of Nazi
Germany. "Be patient, do not scold," Cayce said,
"Do not fret or condemn the body-mind . . . Never
tell her those stories of witches, never those of
fearfulness, or any great punishment, only of love,
patience."[7]

Cayce's "war children" were born into the generation we now know as the "baby-boomers." I find
it fascinating that this is the very generation which

has largely discarded *Grimm's Fairy Tales* and is producing happier, more life-affirming children's literature. In addition, this same generation is now openly discussing child abuse and exploring ways to prevent it. Before World War II, it was generally considered "normal" in Western societies for parents to beat their children, and "punishment" was seen as the best way to enforce discipline. But no more. Could it be that the souls of this generation, having seen and experienced such horrors in their previous incarnations, have decided once and for all to break the cycles of abuse which produce holocausts and wars in the first place?

The story of Steve, which opened this chapter, ended with his statement that "The children were coming back en masse. They had seen hell and they had seen heaven. Now they were ready to use their great potential." I believe that, as this post-war generation is maturing and coming into its own in so many fields, we are beginning to see this "great potential" manifest itself.

Cayce's advice not to frighten children with stories of "punishment" is wise for all families to follow. I believe this includes "religious stories" about hellfire as well as fairy tales about witches who live in gingerbread houses and eat children. Children everywhere tend to blame themselves when things go wrong, and this, in turn, creates a poor self-image which can carry over from one incarnation to another. There is deep wisdom in the teaching, common to many religions, that a child is not really responsible for his or her sins until a certain age, usually somewhere around puberty. This does not mean that children should be allowed to run wild or that they can do no wrong. What it does mean is that childhood mistakes do not generate lasting karma.

The Talmud states that one is not judged "On High" for one's sins until age twenty.[8] Mistakes made before that may carry immmediate consequences, but one will not necessarily have to answer for them in the "World to Come." For example, if a small child steals something, he or she should certainly be held responsible for that action in the here and now. But, according to the Talmud, the theft is not really considered a "sin" to be judged "On High" (by the Heavenly Tribunal), because the child is still too young to have really internalized the difference between right and wrong.

This teaching seems to be supported by modern research on near-death experiences (NDEs). According to Nancy Evans Bush, who has analyzed data at the International Association for Near-Death Studies, childhood NDEs are very similar to those of adults. Both groups describe the core experience of going down a tunnel, being in a void, and emerging into a light. The one striking difference is that although 25% of adult NDEs include some type of "life review," very, very few children report having a "life review." Of the seventeen cases of childhood NDEs which Bush examined, not one described any kind of "accounting" of their deeds.[9] Dr. Melvin Morse, who has also worked with childhood NDEs, believes this is because "they don't yet have much of a life."[10] But I believe the Talmud is right. Children's NDEs do not include a "life review" because they are not yet karmically responsible.

Long ago the teachers of many religions recognized that children need a "practice period" to learn how to behave among other human beings. They also realized that children can be almost neurotic in their self-criticism and will tend to become little perfectionists if judged by adult standards. Therefore, most cultures allow some leeway for children and usually provide some type of distinct ceremony for the transition from childhood to adulthood.

A well-known example of this is the Jewish *bar mitzvah* or *bat mitzvah*, which literally means "son or daughter of the Commandments." Before a Jewish child reaches the age of religious seniority (twelve for girls and thirteen for boys), the child's parents are karmically responsible for seeing that he or she keeps the Commandments. After entering adulthood, every Jew becomes responsible for his or her own religious karma, with or without an actual ceremony. In the very traditional form of the bar/bat mitzvah, the father of the child actually says: "Praised be to God Who releases me from the responsibility of this one."[11]

Therefore, from a Jewish standpoint at least, a small child who dies in a war or other disaster is not held karmically responsible for what happened. There is simply no crime that a child could commit which deserves dying in a Holocaust! For that matter, there is no crime committed by anyone, child or adult, which ever deserves torture, either in this life or a future one. The oft-quoted "new age" platitude that "you create your own reality" does not mean that victims of crimes or atrocities somehow "created" or "asked for" such a situation.

I have dwelt on this point because many of those

"war children" who reincarnated in the 1940s and '50s are now adults who still carry deeply internalized negative self-images that were put on them by the Nazis. There was nothing "wrong" with being Jewish, Gypsy, gay, lesbian, or whatever. What was wrong was the Holocaust and the war itself. The karma for misusing technology to build concentration camps belongs to the Nazis, not to their victims.

There is a Hasidic teaching which says that a coat has two pockets, containing two kinds of teachings about the world. In the right-hand pocket is the *midrash* where God took the first (androgynous) Adam on a tour of the Garden of Eden, saying, "All of this was created for you."[12] In the left-hand pocket are the words of Abraham, who pleaded with God, saying, "I am but dust and ashes."[13]

When we are feeling smug about our technological accomplishments, literally lording it over each other and the rest of creation, then we must take from the left-hand pocket of Abraham, reminding ourselves that we come from the dust of the earth and to the dust we shall return. But when we are feeling depressed and life seems meaningless, then we need the right-hand pocket of Adam. We must raise our self-esteem by saying, "God made this whole world for human beings, so there must be a reason to be here." At such times we reaffirm that we are the "crown of creation," the finishing touch of God's universe. In our Creator's eyes, we are loved, cherished, and of great importance.

It is by balancing these two "pockets" that we progress spiritually. If we only believe that "all this was made for us," then we risk becoming like the

Nazis, who had no feelings or empathy for anyone else but themselves. But on the other hand, if we constantly tell ourselves that we are nothing but "dust and ashes," we can become totally paralyzed with self-hate and insecurity. Only by balancing the left hand of justice with the right hand of mercy can we walk the spiritual path in beauty and truth.

Chapter 6:

Black Boots and Barbed Wire

Mary had been a beautiful dark-eyed baby with wavy brown hair, born into an Italian-Catholic family in the Midwest. During the day she was usually happy and smiling, but at night she would scream in terror for no apparent reason. As soon as Mary learned how to talk, she described nightmares of being bombed. And from earliest childhood, she was absolutely terrified of sirens.

When little Mary started school, she had a recurring "fantasy" that she had to walk and walk a long way to get home. This impression would often come to her on the way back from school or a friend's house, and she was always relieved to arrive and find that her mother was still alive. Once when Mary was acting out this fantasy, a real siren went off, and she began to scream in terror. Running into the street, she stopped a car and shouted, "We're going to be bombed, we're going to be bombed!"

The woman in the car tried in vain to calm her down and ended up giving her a ride home. Mary's parents had no explanation for their daughter's strange behavior. They thought she had simply "listened to too much radio as a baby." She was, after all, born in 1944, when reports about the war were still being broadcast daily.

But Mary knew even then that it went much deeper than that. As a child, she would lie on her back and see herself getting smaller and smaller, until she would "disappear." Sometimes she could see herself as a young woman, perhaps in her early twenties, very gaunt, wide-eyed, and frightened, asking, "Why, why, how can this be?" To this day, Mary has a deep fear of starving to death, even though she has never really known hunger in this life.

In 1969, at the age of twenty-five, Mary traveled to Germany with a friend, and together they boarded a train at Heidelberg. As the sliding doors closed, however, Mary suddenly began to hyperventilate and screamed in panic, "I've been here before, I've been here before! I died here!" Apparently the sliding doors had triggered a flashback to the moment in another life when the door was closed on the crowded boxcar that had carried her to the death camps. She tried to explain this to her friend, who could not deal with the idea of reincarnation and "did not want to hear about these things." That was the last time Mary tried to talk about it until she met me nineteen years later.

During the interview, Mary told me that when she had read the phrase, "Rachel weeping for her children and would not be comforted"[1] in the Bible, she had unexplainably burst into tears. This phrase from the Book of Jeremiah is frequently used by Jews as a metaphor for suffering in exile. The full text reads:

Thus says the Lord (YHVH): A voice was heard in Ramah, (a voice of) lamentation and bitter weeping; Rachel weeping for her children, and she would not be comforted, because they were not.

Thus says the Lord (YHVH): Refrain thy voice from weeping, and thine eyes from tears; for thy work shall be rewarded, says the Lord, and they (the children) shall come again from the land of the enemy.

Thus says the Lord (YHVH): And there is hope in thine end, says the Lord (YHVH), and thy children shall come again to their own border.

These words of hope were first spoken by Jeremiah during the Babylonian Captivity (circa 550 B.C.E.). He acknowledges the bitter exile of the Jews (Rachel's children) from their homeland but also promises them that God will one day bring them back from Babylon to the Holy Land. This theme of exile and redemption is used in a Jewish prayer called *tikkun chatzot*, which is recited at midnight, lamenting the sufferings of the exiles and praying for the coming of the Messiah. Part of this prayer specifically uses the metaphor of Rachel (favorite wife of Jacob) weeping for her children (their descendants, the Jews). Although *tikkun chatzot* has fallen into disuse in recent years, it was well known and used in pre-Holocaust Eastern Europe.

But Mary had never heard of *tikkun chatzot*, nor was she aware of the Jewish symbolism connected with Rachel's weeping. She had been raised Catholic and even at the interview did not seem to realize that "Rachel" was originally a Jewish name. Why, then, had this one Biblical phrase triggered such an emotional reaction?

Mary is not the only person with strange phobias and emotional reactions that seem to come from nowhere. For some people, ordinary objects invoke a terror that has no logical explanation in this life. But when put into the context of reincarnation, these fears suddenly begin to make sense. For example, three different people, born and raised many miles apart, have described a similar phobia connected with black boots. Donnie Ducharme, from Raleigh, North Carolina, wrote the following in a letter to *Venture Inward* magazine:

> "I was born in June 1948 into a Southern Baptist family in North Carolina. As a child, I was very sickly until age six. During the early years I was petrified of black boots—the shiny kind that go up to the knees. My grandfather had a rubber pair and I exhibited great fear about those boots. My mother would set them near the wood stove so that I wouldn't touch it and get burned. I never went near the stove because of the boots. I remember going around the perimeter of the room with my back against the wall—to get as far away from those boots as possible. I never understood why I was afraid of the boots until I watched a movie about Hitler and saw the goose-steppers. There were those boots! I felt then that I had been there. I have generally avoided Holocaust movies. I don't feel that I have deep-seated hangups about them—I just

would rather not see them. The realization about the black boots was a sort of catharsis.

"At age eleven my Sunday school class attended a service at a synagogue. I felt as if I were on holy ground. It was a monumental experience that is still clear in my memory. I have always been very sympathetic to the Hebrew nation. I also have an affinity for the turn of the century through the late 1930s."[2]

Donnie also sent a copy of her letter to me, which contained another interesting detail that was unfortunately omitted by the editors of *Venture Inward.* Immediately after the part about the Sunday school trip, Donnie wrote: "I also have an unusual habit. I look at magazines from the back to the front. Unless I am reading a book I always flip from back to front."

Both Hebrew and Yiddish books open from "back to front," opposite of English ones. But Donnie does not know either language. In fact, her contact with Jews is apparently so limited that she is unaware that Jews never call themselves "the Hebrew nation."

The second reference to a phobia about black boots came from Barbara in Oklahoma, whose story was already told in Chapter Two. Barbara wrote to me:

"As I sit here right now, something else just came to me. As a child, in this life, I was always afraid of black boots. Shortly before my mother died, she was laughing about sitting black boots at the top of the cellar stairs and at the bottom of the upstairs (to keep the child from going there) and how terrorized I was of black boots, when I wasn't afraid of horses, thunder and lightning, things children normally fear."

These two stories are so similar—even to the fact that in both cases an adult had utilized the strange phobia to prevent the child from getting hurt—that if I did not know better, I would say Donnie and Barbara had concocted their tales together. But to my knowledge, these two women have never met, and Barbara had already sent me her story months before Donnie's letter was published.

While writing the first draft of this book, a strange incident occurred which brought yet a third case of black boot phobia to my attention. As I explained in Chapter One, I received a great deal of mail in response to the *Venture Inward* article. Among these letters was a booklet of "channeled" poetry about the Holocaust which I had briefly perused but had not read cover to cover. I must admit that this was due to my own prejudice, because I tend to be very skeptical about things which are supposedly "channeled." Nevertheless, I did have the booklet on my desk in a pile of papers when I typed the above two stories.

I was about to move on to the next section of the chapter when something inexplicably startled me and I stood up, knocking the pile of papers to the floor. As I bent over to pick up the mess, my eyes fell upon the words "Black Boots." There, in the back of the poetry booklet, was an appendix which I had not read before—with yet another case of this phobia! Was this a coincidence, or did somebody

on the "other side" want Marsha's story to be told
here? Either way, I took the hint.

Marsha, too, was obsessed by black boots,
which stomped relentlessly through her childhood dreams. "The Black Boots were after me," she
wrote, "tall, shiny storm trooper boots, combing
the forests, flashlights turned on, off, stomping
through the mud, always searching."

But in Marsha's waking reality, there were no
black boots. She was born and raised in America,
nurtured by a loving family, and surrounded with
affection, kindness, and safety. Growing up was
fun and almost painless—except for the headaches.

No doctor was ever really able to diagnose them.
Terms like sinusitis, toothache, and eyestrain
became household words. But although medication after medication was tried, the headaches
always came back. Over the years there would be
new surroundings, new faces, new interests—but
always the same horrible headaches.

One day Marsha met Rita Rudow, a quiet,
sensitive woman who was developing her talent to
write "psychic poetry" which seemed to flow from
an unknown source. Rita had already published
two volumes of her channeled poetry and was
working on a third, *Voices from the Holocaust.*
Each poem had a number for a title and told the
story of a Holocaust victim whose soul was now on
the "other side."[3]

The two women became friends, each pursuing
her own interests but aware of the other's talents.
Marsha began to delve into her past-life history,
and regression placed her in Germany at the time
of the Holocaust. Little by little the memories came:

survival impossible . . . a murdered child . . .

Meanwhile, Rita continued to channel poetry. While writing the poem entitled "#61425," she broke out in a cold sweat and goose bumps. The poem was about a child who had died violently by having her head bashed to the ground by the Nazis. Suddenly Rita realized that this was Marsha's past-life story! The reason for the headaches now became obvious. When Marsha read the poem about her previous death, the headaches began to subside.

Marsha's case of healing is not unusual. Many people report that once they have recognized the source of the problem as coming from another life, the phobias and other symptoms disappear. This should not be taken as a prescription to stop regular medication. But if one is plagued by chronic symptoms that seem to have no organic cause, it might be worthwhile to investigate reincarnation as a possibility *in addition* to following your doctor's advice.

One area where past-life recall frequently does have curative results is in the treatment of phobias. As was briefly mentioned before, the same types of phobias occur over and over in these cases: fears of gas, sirens, explosions, airplanes, police, guns, barbed wire, and uniforms are common. Many people also have unexplainable fears of starvation, suffocation, asphyxiation, and being buried alive. Several also reported a deep-seated fear of burning to death, although they had never been in a fire. All of these phobias have Holocaust themes, and when one or more of them occur in combination with some of the other factors mentioned in this book, they serve to strengthen the case for reincarnation. These five samples, all told to me by "baby-boomers" living in widely separated locations across the United States, are typical:

> "My phobias are of loud noises, especially guns, jackhammers, buzz saws, etc. . . . I am pretty much obsessed by fresh air and am very uncomfortable in a sealed room, even though I grew up in the cold Northwest.
>
> "At age twelve my dad sent me to the NRA rifle course. I didn't care for it, but the .22s were tolerable. When Dad got out his larger rifles, I would cry. He told me to fire the 30.06 and I couldn't. I stood there, gun on shoulder, for twenty minutes but could not fire it."
>
> (Hawaii)

> "And now while you were leading the prayer, I suddenly saw myself as a young girl, maybe fourteen tops, a Gypsy family. We were Romanies, and I saw my two brothers. They're both back now (i.e., reincarnated). They are not my brothers now, but they were in that life. Then we were all taken and, speaking of asthma, all my life I had a fear of suffocation. I cannot stand being closed in without air. I get very panicky. So it's like all of a sudden I could see, we were taken from the camp with all the Jews and put in the trucks and driven off. I was torn from my brother, and my parents didn't seem to be there."
>
> (Minnesota)

> "One day a formation of planes flew overhead. Mother says that I was about four years

of age. All my playmates were jumping up and down in glee, pointing to the sky. Mother came outside to see what the commotion was about and found me cowering in the bushes because I was afraid of the planes. But she said I couldn't tell her why I was afraid of the planes or wouldn't." (Michigan)

"I'm finding more and more that it (the Holocaust past life) causes me upsets in this life. For instance, (the idea of) installing gas heat in our home had me upset and I didn't know why. Finally, three days before the installation it hit me, 'I'm afraid of the gas.' After I admit and release it (the fear), I am O.K., but it sure takes a lot out of me." (Tennessee)

"I have always had an obsessive attitude toward food. I am terrified that it will not be there, so I feel I must eat it immediately.
"Also, although my parents were anti-Semitic, I have always had a fascination with Jewish ritual and have avidly read books about Jews." (Vermont)

I am often asked if these stories might not simply be rationalizations to try to explain away the unknown. After all, don't these people already believe in reincarnation? What is to prevent the power of suggestion from taking over?

Certainly that is possible. But for many of them, belief in reincarnation did not come until *after* the memories began to surface. In fact, many of these cases come from conventional religious back-

grounds—Roman Catholic, Southern Baptist,
Lutheran, to name a few—where reincarnation is
not part of the dogma. Sometimes people have
started out by consulting a hypnotherapist simply
to get rid of a bad habit or a phobia, fully expecting
it to be rooted in some long-forgotten incident from
their childhood. At the time, they had no thoughts
about reincarnation and only came to believe in it
after hypnosis put them in touch with another life.
For some, the whole idea came as a shock. The
following story was told to me by a woman whose
childhood was as far from "new age" as anyone
could possibly imagine:

> "I was born in 1948 in Tennessee, the
> youngest of eighteen children. My family was
> poor, and only three of us graduated from
> high school. There's no reason for me to have
> memories of a life in Germany, as I've always
> lived in Tennessee and have no interest in
> foreign countries. I was raised in a strict
> Protestant church and have no knowledge of
> anything Jewish. I seem to identify more
> strongly with the German race and have the
> painful feeling of being one of them and still
> having to suffer the injustice (of the Holo-
> caust).
>
> "In this memory I was a child who was torn
> from her family. I have never connected it with
> war until a psychic channeled that life for me.
> I was told a story that fit my feelings. After-
> wards I went to our local library and just
> happened to look through *The Auschwitz
> Album*. In that book I came face-to-face with
> another me, a child of Hungarian Jews in

1944. Now I am wondering how many times I went through that horrible experience. (Author's note: She could have died twice, once as a German in World War I and again as a Jew during World War II.)

The following story was told to me by Paul, a Christian of Danish background who called from New Zealand. Paul did not originally believe in reincarnation but came to accept the idea after hypnotic regression, which he sought for medical reasons. His story is particularly interesting because he seems to remember the *bardo* period between his past life and this one. Paul specifically described choosing his current father, who was involved in smuggling Jews out of Denmark.

This is historically accurate. When Denmark was occupied by Germany in 1940, the Danes steadfastly refused to turn in their Jewish neighbors. For the next three years, the Danish underground aided Jews to escape from Germany, Austria, and Czechoslovakia into neutral Sweden. Then, on August 28, 1943, the Nazis declared martial law in Denmark, intending to use this opportunity to round up the Jews as they had done in so many other countries.

But the Danes, who had already been increasing their resistance to German occupation, got word of the Nazi plans. On the night before the deportation date (which was also Rosh Hashanah, the Jewish New Year), Danish sea captains and fishermen smuggled by sea 5,919 Jews, 1,301 "part-Jews," and 686 Christians married to Jews, into Sweden. Because of this heroism, only 500 Danish Jews were seized by the Nazis.[4] The Danish underground continued to smuggle Jews to safety throughout the rest of the war.

It was apparently this heroism on behalf of Jews which had attracted Paul, who had been a Jewish woman in his previous life, to his present Danish father. In a follow-up letter he wrote:

"There were many aspects to my thinking as a youth, which really came together when I had over a hundred hours of intensive regression around 1974 . . . While it was some shock to me to learn that I had been a Jewish woman in my previous lifetime, I gradually, through recall of successive incidents, developed a fuller and more certain picture of the considerations present in that life and how they are still with me or have affected this lifetime. The recall is as real as though I were remembering my first year at school.

"On losing my body, I moved north (in the spirit) and sought out my (present) father, who was sympathetic and active in helping the Jews out of and through Denmark, as was the manner at that time. I 'hovered' around my father, waiting a few years to claim the first (available) body.

"Something that may be of interest is that in my last lifetime I had a son, who I believe studied medicine in Berlin but emigrated to New York about 1933. I am not able to recall the surname but I believe that this doctor may still be alive in your country today. He would be about 77 to 83 years old. I consider that it would be possible to identify this person through a number of circumstances in his life. His father pre-deceased his mother (me) by quite a few years and probably died around the 1920s. His home was well-to-do in a smaller town south of Berlin. And, of course, he would have lost his mother (me) around 1944. She had sold or lost the lovely family house and was living in a smallish apartment-type situation during those last few dangerous years of the war. He was probably an only child. His mother was probably brunette, kind and thoughtful."

Paul was so convinced of the truth of these memories that he asked if I could help locate his still-living son from another life. Unfortunately there are so many elderly Jews in New York City that it would be virtually impossible for me to try to track him down without a surname. However, I did promise to print the story on the slim chance that someone might recognize it.

Thus far we have been talking about specific, Holocaust-related phobias and medical conditions which have occurred in the lives of people who are not Jewish in this life. But in addition to specific phobias, many of my subjects exhibit a more generalized kind of fear that could be carried over from previous incarnations. I see this especially in the Jewish community, where simply living in a Gentile world can be a source of uneasiness.

Although Jews of past centuries had an inner religious life and a personal relationship with God in spite of persecution, I have observed that their descendants today are often very reluctant to go beyond the surface levels of religion. How much of this is due to reincarnation and how much to modern history is very difficult to determine. But whatever the source, this fear must be confronted if we are ever to begin healing the karma.

In my work as a spiritual director, I have met privately with Jews of just about every background—Orthodox, Conservative, Reform, Reconstructionist, the *havurah* movement, unaffiliated and secular; American, Israeli, African, or European; young and old, male and female, rich and poor, warriors and peacemakers. These people come to me seeking personal guidance, and they bare their hearts in a way that never happens in public.

During these private encounters, one theme emerges over and over again. Jews today live with an enormous amount of fear, and the primary source of that fear is the Holocaust. Many feel as if another Holocaust could happen any day and that, no matter how happy and successful their lives may be right now, all of it could be taken away in the future. It is as if the entire Jewish community suffers from a collective case of post-traumatic stress disorder, with the slightest anti-Semitic incident triggering a major group flashback. This explains why some Jews react to current events as if they were still living during the Holocaust. Aside from the havoc that this fear wreaks on the Middle East peace process, it also paralyzes individual spiritual growth. No matter what your religion, if you are filled with fear, a true inner life is impossible.

As many psychologists have already pointed out, where there is fear there can be no real love. It has even been said that fear, not hate, is the

opposite of love. Nobody can love their enemies—
or even their friends—while living in constant
fear.

We all know that whenever fear is invoked, it
arouses the "fight or flight" syndrome. Most animals, including humans, would rather avoid
conflict and under normal circumstances will
prefer to flee from danger. But even very gentle,
domestic animals, when cornered or frightened,
will often turn and viciously fight to the death.
Whenever survival is threatened, the adrenaline
level rises and jungle instinct takes over.

By and large, the Jews of past centuries were
nonviolent people who generally chose to flee from
danger rather that fight it. In previous generations, there was always somewhere to run
to—through the mountains, over the border, or
across the ocean to another country where life
would be safer and one could start over. But the
Holocaust changed all that. In the mid-twentieth
century, the world suddenly shrank to a global
village—a village that largely slammed its doors in
the faces of Jews fleeing the Nazi death camps.

The gentle Jews died quickly, many of them as
martyrs who faced death as bravely as any Christian entering the lion's den. Survivors have told
how entire villages of Hasidim purified themselves
through ritual immersion, donned their prayer
shawls, and calmly chanted the deathbed confessional as the Nazis shot them down. Others went
to their deaths dancing and singing, knowing that
the Germans could kill the body but not the soul.
They refused to "fight back" not as cowards, but as
witnesses to the nonviolence which they believed
was central to their faith.

But there were other Jews who, when backed into a corner with no escape, decided to abandon nonviolence in favor of fighting to the death. Those resistance fighters who managed to survive had no choice but to believe that the world apparently did not like Jews, would not protect Jews, and, therefore, Jews could trust nobody but themselves. This bitter world view was not entirely true, because there were Gentiles who risked their own lives to save Jews, such as the Danish sea captains mentioned above. But by and large, the world did close its doors, and the bitterness of this experience continues to affect the Jewish community to this day.

I believe that it is this fear and bitterness which currently prevent Jews, even those in the so-called "new age," from expressing their spirituality within a Jewish context. Many times when I have spoken at multicultural spiritual gatherings, the Jews who were practicing other paths have gone out of their way to avoid talking to me, as if the mere presence of a rabbi would somehow "spoil" their present tranquillity.

Rabbi Shlomo Carlebach, well-known Hasidic singer and storyteller who has performed on the spiritual speaking circuit since the days of the "flower children," also sees this reluctance on the part of Jewish seekers. In 1985 Carlebach observed: "Nobody minds saying, 'Excuse me, I have to meditate.' But to say, 'Excuse me, I have to *daven mincha* (say the afternoon prayers)' is embarrassing . . . There never was such a generation of self-hating Jews as there is now. The majority of Jews think they have to excuse themselves for being Jewish."[5]

Whenever these "closet Jews" do meet with me, they often use words like "trapped," "limited," "separated," "confined," "rigid," "painful," "empty," and "depressing" to describe their perceptions of Judaism. Yet the vast majority of these seekers come from Reform or secularized backgrounds and have never, in this life at least, actually lived by the daily disciplines of traditional Judaism. Nor have most Jewish "baby-boomers" experienced the social barriers of their parents' generation. Although every Jew encounters anti-Semitism at one time or another, by and large American society is currently open toward Jews. Why, then, do these people feel "trapped"? Could this feeling be a carry-over from former lives?

California psychologist Morris Netherton has developed a technique for past-life therapy which utilizes word association to get in touch with previous incarnations. During the course of therapy, the counselor who is trained in the Netherton method pays careful attention to specific words, phrases, or expressions which recur in the patient's use of language. After isolating a specific phrase, the patient is asked to lie down and concentrate on this word or words, using it like a mantra, until another phrase or a mental picture comes to mind. Working from there, the patient then uses this image to get in touch with an incident from a past life.[6]

Although I have not specifically used the Netherton method, I have asked Jewish seekers to meditate on their mental pictures of Judaism. In many cases, when they do this, images of fear, pain, and persecution come to mind. This happens even with Jews who have had very little

religious education and who have grown up with
just about every comfort that a suburbanite could
ever want. Yet something has "spoiled" their inner
associations with Judaism. I believe that, in some
cases at least, this "something" is connected with
past-life memories from the Holocaust.

Nowadays there is a tendency among "globally
minded" people toward "universalizing" the Holocaust, to play down the specifically anti-Jewish
content of Nazi actions. Just about every time I
speak on this topic, somebody in the audience will
make the statement that "Jews were not the only
people killed, you know." This is usually said in an
accusatory manner, as if the Jews are trying to
deny that others have suffered. The statement is
often followed by a listing of all the other groups
who were also rounded up by the Nazis.

Jews have never denied that Gentiles were also
killed in the Holocaust. But what many people
today do not realize is that the Nazis not only killed
Jews, they went out of their way to use the Jewish
holidays and religious practices as targets for
"special treatment." Jews were rounded up and
families torn apart on the Sabbath, transforming
a day of joy into one of mourning. Humiliation of
rabbis in the streets was a daily occurrence, and
sacred objects were routinely collected and publicly desecrated. Prayer shawls were made into
women's dresses and sold in "fashionable" German shops. Torah scrolls were burned. Headstones
from Jewish cemeteries were used to pave the
floors of latrines, and horses were stabled in
synagogues. When the library of the world's greatest Talmudic Academy in Lublin, Poland, was
burned, the fire lasted twenty hours, and the Nazis

brought in an orchestra to celebrate.[7]

In the camps it was even worse. Everything about Judaism was publicly shamed and held up to ridicule. Work loads were purposely doubled on the Sabbath, and anyone who refused would be shot. On Yom Kippur, a holy fast day, the Nazis would force the Jews to stand at attention in front of tables filled with delicious foods such as they had not seen in months. Sometimes the Germans would taunt the hungry Jews by offering them a plate full of the delicacies, if only they would publicly desecrate the holy day by eating.

The concentration camps were designed not only to kill the body but to break the Jewish spirit. In many cases, they succeeded. Eyewitness Chaim Kaplan wrote in his diary on November 18, 1939, "The details of Nazi cruelty are enough to drive you crazy. Sometimes we are ashamed to look at one another. And worse than this, we have begun to look upon ourselves as 'inferior beings,' lacking God's image."[8]

Could it be that the Nazis did their dirty work so well that some reincarnated souls have carried negative feelings about Jewish traditions into this life? Is this why Judaism makes some souls feel trapped? The following story is a composite of three similar incidents which strongly suggest this possibility:

I was leading a roundtable discussion at a Christian luncheon, and we were talking about some of the ways that Jews and Christians express their faith. A smiling, well-dressed woman, whom we shall call Mrs. Ploni, asked my opinion of a particular rabbi who teaches on the interfaith circuit. Now this question put me in a double bind, because although Rabbi So-and-So bills himself as a kabbalist, he no longer practices the daily disciplines of Judaism. He eats pork, works on the Sabbath, and has a bad reputation for telling sexist jokes. Therefore, I felt that I could not honestly endorse his work. But at the same time, I did not want to get into mud-slinging. So I tried to be diplomatic, stating simply that I believed a good teacher should live the teachings, and just as I would not choose to learn body-building from a flabby gym instructor, so I would not go to any spiritual teacher who does not practice the path he professes.

Scarcely had I said this, than Mrs. Ploni flew into a rage and began loudly castigating me in front of the entire group. "It is because of narrow-minded people like you that Jews leave Judaism!" she yelled indignantly, demanding that I now leave the group because I was "certainly no teacher." This verbal attack took me so completely by surprise that all I could do was stammer. None of the other people present came to my defense, although a few seemed embarrassed.

Any possibility of communication was over, so I did leave for a while, hoping that Mrs. Ploni would calm down and we could make peace. But she would have none of it. When I returned to the table a few minutes later, she started in on me again. Needless to say, that was the end of the roundtable discussion.

I spent the rest of that afternoon wondering what could possibly have provoked such a violent emotional reaction. Only later did I learn from a third party that Mrs. Ploni was in fact Jewish, and she had idolized Rabbi So-and-So precisely because he gave the outward appearance of being authentic without actually making any demands on his followers. Now I had come along and reminded her that practicing any spiritual path meant genuine commitment—words that she simply did not want to hear in the context of Judaism.

The story does have a happy ending, however. Although Mrs. Ploni avoided me for two days, she apparently did some soul-searching, and we eventually talked privately. She believed that she had died as a Jew in the Holocaust and was now reincarnated as a Jew once more. But although Mrs. Ploni felt comfortable in her current life as a secular Jew, she had nothing but negative associations with what she disparagingly called "the religion." Apparently the horrible experiences of the Holocaust incarnation had so imprinted themselves on her soul that the very suggestion of doing *mitzvot* evoked nothing but shame, rage, and pain. Much of this negative feeling had now subsided, and, although Mrs. Ploni was a long way from ever becoming Orthodox, at least she was no longer hostile toward other Jews who affirmed the traditional practices.

Rabbi Shlomo Carlebach, who was cited earlier, was once asked why so many Jews had joined Eastern religions. He replied that during the formative years of the "baby-boom" generation, the Jewish community was in such terrible mourning because of the Holocaust that there was no joy left in our spiritual house. The people went through the motions of Jewish worship, but their hearts were heavy and the prayers were filled with unspeakable pain.

The children born into this "house of mourning"

did not understand what this sadness was about and thought that pain and guilt were all there is to Judaism. Therefore, many Jews left their religion of birth to look for a faith where joy still flourished. Some found that joy in the Eastern religions. Now they were returning to Judaism, bringing the joy back with them.

It is not an easy task for Jews to come back to the "heaviness" of post-Holocaust Judaism after having experienced transcendental bliss on some other path. How much simpler it would be to remain a Hindu or a Buddhist, adopting a culture that never had a Holocaust! Yet many Jewish seekers are not really comfortable praying to Shiva or Krishna and long for something authentically Jewish that will still resonate with their inner being.

Such teachings do exist, but, before we can embrace them with true joy, we must confront and heal the pain from so many centuries of exile, including the Holocaust. I have no simple answers for how to do this, but the following true story may provide us with a clue:

A few years ago I was leading a small group retreat on the festival of Shavuot, also called the Feast of Weeks. Shavuot commemorates the giving of the Torah at Mt. Sinai and is traditionally observed with an all-night study session, followed by a dawn worship service and a feast. Usually this is done in the synagogue, but on this occasion we were using my home in northern Minnesota, with plans to walk to the river at dawn.

The theme of our retreat was "What are the stumbling blocks which keep us from accepting the Torah?" Throughout the night we studied Jewish texts, sang traditional songs, and shared personal stories. The atmosphere was very open, and many people were quite candid about what had turned them off to Judaism. There were tales of insensitive Hebrew school teachers, materialistic parents, sexist congregations, and hypocritical rabbis. One woman felt that modern Jews were worshiping the state of Israel instead of God. Another young man told how he had learned to spontaneously pray from the heart while working a twelve-step recovery program, only to be (erroneously) told by his rabbi that "Jews can't pray like that."

By the end of the night, we had come to grips with dozens of personal issues about Judaism and Torah, and were ready for the next stage of our quest. About forty-five minutes before dawn, we left the house and headed for the river. It was already light enough to see without a flashlight, and the birds were just beginning to sing. I had instructed the group to maintain silence throughout the walk, focusing on the natural beauty around them and the questions we had explored together that night.

Walking at the head of this silent procession, I could just make out some large rocks lying in the middle of the trail ahead, not far from where we would pass under the old train trestle. The rocks hadn't been there when I had planned the walk yesterday, and I assumed that they must have rolled down the hill from the vibrations of a passing train. I decided to break the silence momentarily, warning the group to watch out for other possible falling rocks.

Imagine our horror as we came up to that place in the path and discovered that the "fallen" rocks were actually arranged in a huge *swastika!* This was clearly no accident—somebody had purposely come here and put a giant swastika right in the middle of our path! Talk about stumbling blocks! It was as if the one subject that we had avoided all night was now staring us in the face: the Holocaust was, indeed, our biggest fear! Needless to say, this cruel prank upset the equilibrium of our peaceful retreat.

What to do with the stone swastika? Some people did not even want to touch it. Others suggested scattering the stones in the bushes, as a way of "wiping out Amalek." What we finally did was rearrange the stones into a circle. Chanting *shalom* (peace) as we worked, we quickly transformed a symbol of hate into a circle of wholeness. In this way we took back our own power once again and were able to proceed down the path to our destination.

I never did find out who put the swastika there. But unknown to themselves, the swastika-makers had given us the very answer we were seeking. What kept us all from wholeheartedly embracing the Torah was not just our negative Hebrew school experiences, although these certainly played a part. But what really blocked our spirituality was the deep-seated terror we all carried in our hearts because of the Holocaust. This had kept us from going within, for fear that instead of inner peace we would find unbearable pain. Facing that fear and conquering it became our focus for the rest of the retreat and was a big step toward spiritual healing.

Chapter 7:

Healing the Karma of the Holocaust

By now you are probably wondering, "What about forgiveness? Aren't we supposed to forgive and forget?" I most certainly do believe that forgiveness plays a big role in healing negative karma. But forgiveness is not the same thing as amnesty. Nor is it social amnesia. In fact, by linking "forgive" with "forget," we are often working against the very healing process that we want to facilitate.

All too often, when people say "forgive and forget," they somehow expect the victim to put his or her brain on "erase" and just go back to the way things were, as if the offensive behavior had never happened. But this simply is not possible. Even if both parties work through their issues with each other and agree to "bury the hatchet," the relationship will never be the same as before. Forgiveness can provide the basis for building a new—perhaps even better—relationship, but it cannot restore the old one.

I once publicly asked Dr. Usharbud Aryah, noted Sanskrit scholar and disciple of Swami

Rama, the following question: "Mahatma Gandhi forgave his assassin; what is the karma in that?"

Aryah's answer was that Gandhi would not be karmically tied to the assassin because he had forgiven him, but that the assassin, unless he himself repented, would still be responsible for his own karma concerning the murder. In other words, I might forgive Hitler, but unless Hitler himself also has a change of heart, he must face the consequences of his own bad karma in one way or another. Hindu thought and Jewish thought are the same on this issue: forgiveness is not amnesty, nor does God practice moral amnesia.

Judaism teaches that for sins between a person and God alone, simply asking God for forgiveness is enough. So, for example, if I fail to say my daily prayers, that is between me and God to work out. But if I have harmed another human being, then I must ask forgiveness directly from that person. Plus I must make restitution directly to the victim of my crime. If I have stolen, I must repay what I stole. If I injured someone, I must pay for the healing. And if I murdered someone, I may, through the courts, be required to pay with my life, either literally or through life imprisonment. Only when I have made things right between myself and society can I be forgiven by God.

This concept of making amends directly to the person harmed, known in secular law as "victim's rights," was also the original intent of *ayin tachas ayin*, "an eye for an eye" in the Bible.[1] Contrary to popular conception, "an eye for an eye" does *not* mean taking revenge. In Jewish law the "eye for an eye" has always been applied as *monetary compensation for loss of the eye* (similar to a modern

insurance policy that pays a fixed sum for the loss
of a body part) and was meant to say that one
person's eye was not worth more than another's.
In other words, the king's eye was worth the same
as a peasant's eye. The original reason for this law
was to limit the claim of the injured party. In
addition, the type of compensation to be paid was
determined by a court of law, not by the individuals themselves taking personal revenge.

How does this Jewish interpretation of "eye for
an eye" apply to reincarnation? I believe that the
principles are exactly the same. While karma is
indeed a process of cause and effect, it does not
necessarily have to be tit-for-tat. Therefore, rather
than take the karmic law into our own hands, we
should leave the responsibility of judgment to the
Heavenly Court and trust that God will, in His own
time, call all people to account for their deeds.

This does not mean that God is angry and vengeful, but rather that God is indeed the Judge of the
universe, who judges justly. The idea that God
carries out justice can actually free up the victim
to be able to forgive. One of the reasons that so
many Jews are reluctant to forgive the Nazis is
that they feel the world will then release the Nazis
from responsibility. Which may be true; the world
is notorious for rewriting history to omit the sufferings of minority peoples. But even if a Nazi war
criminal is put to death for his crimes, can that
one death really be equal to the untold suffering he
caused to perhaps thousands of others? Justice on
the earth plane is necessary for an ordered society,
but it is often unequal to the severity of the crime.

However, once we realize that God is indeed a
God of justice, then it becomes possible to turn the

anger over to God and not carry it around in our own hearts. Forgiving our enemies does not let the enemies off the hook, but it does prevent our own anger and hate from poisoning our souls. This is why we must eventually "let go and let God," knowing that even those Nazis who seemed to get away with it on earth will be called to account in another lifetime.

Occasionally I have heard Jews say that it is impossible to forgive the Nazis, because only the victims themselves can grant forgiveness to their persecutors, and the victims are dead. If one does not believe in a life after death, then this is certainly true. But I personally do not believe that God would create a universe in which it is impossible for a soul ever to repent. After all, Jews do not believe in eternal damnation—even for Nazis.

It is a misunderstanding to think that Jews cannot unilaterally forgive. Although it is best for a person to ask forgiveness from the one harmed, the victim can, if he or she wishes, decide to forgive without being asked. This idea of "grace" is a very Jewish one and existed long before Jesus, who was himself a Jew and merely reiterating a principle that already existed in the Judaism of his day. The Hebrew word for "grace," *chesed*, appears many times in the Bible as well as throughout the Jewish prayerbook and is from the same root as *Hasid*, which means "pious." *Chesed* is even used to name one of the ten levels of consciousness on the Kabbalistic Tree of Life diagram. (See Chapter Eight.) ("Love your neighbor as yourself," by the way, is also originally a Jewish teaching, from the Book of Leviticus.)[2]

It is a standard axiom in Jewish teachings that

our Creator is a forgiving God, who desires repentance, not punishment. Although in English the word "repentance" often brings to mind the imagery of self-flogging and castigation, in the Hebrew language it has a totally different meaning. The Hebrew word for "repentance," *tshuvah*, literally means "returning" to the ways of God. The soul, according to Jewish theology, is pure and holy; there is no concept of original sin as in some sects of Christianity. However, because of our own actions and mistakes, we often turn away from the path of God and get lost in a jungle of confusion. But no matter how far we might have strayed, we need only turn away from error and back toward God to get on the right trail again. This is what a Jew means when he or she speaks of "doing *tshuvah.*" Although repentance may or may not involve outward signs like fasting, it always requires an inward returning to God.

Every year on Yom Kippur, the Day of Atonement, Jews everywhere read the entire Book of Jonah in the synagogue. This Biblical story tells of Nineveh, an evil city that was filled with robbery, violence, idolatry, and corruption. The prophet Jonah is sent by God to Nineveh to warn the people that if they do not change their ways, the city will be destroyed. The people heed the message, fast, and repent in sackcloth and ashes, and *therefore Nineveh is not destroyed.* While it is true that the prophet Jonah himself appears to be more interested in revenge than forgiveness, he is chastised by God for this in the Biblical text, and in Jewish oral tradition he is severely criticized for not showing compassion. Jonah is the classic example of what *not* to do as a Jew.

If there is indeed life after death, either on another plane of consciousness or as reincarnation, then it would be possible for Nazis to repent and seek forgiveness from those whom they formerly hated. In such a case, it is not necessary for the victim to kill the perpetrator in the next life, which would only perpetuate the cycle in future lives. It can also happen that the murderer in one life *gives birth* to the victim in the next incarnation, thus replacing the body that was destroyed.

I know of one case where past-life regression revealed that a woman had been a "witch" during the time of the Crusades. In that lifetime, she held such hatred against one particular knight, a Crusader who was slaughtering her people, that she killed him through black magic. In this life, the knight came back as her son, whom she loved and nurtured as a child, but there was always a certain uneasiness between them.

In later years, the mother and son went through a simultaneous past-life regression, in which they relived the moment of the knight's death. The emotions involved were so intense and seemed so real that, had there not been a third person present as a control, the regression might have ended in violence. But, with the guide reminding them that this was only a flashback, they were able to work through the fear and anger to forgive each other. The son eventually became a soldier in this life, too, but now submits to a moral code. The mother believes she has atoned for the murder of the knight by giving him birth in this life and is now free to progress spiritually.

This story is a perfect example of karma-stopping without tit-for-tat. But it does not mean that the people involved can simply forget that the incident ever happened. On the contrary, both are now consciously applying what they learned from the experience. Ten years after the regression, when the mother was confronted by the Persian Gulf War, she felt the same intense rage toward President Bush that she had felt toward the knight during the Crusades. But instead of casting spells, she directed her energy into the peace movement—a karmically positive way to express her anger. The soldier son, in turn, had to learn to practice tolerance for his mother and others who did not agree with his support of the war. Because both have learned and grown spiritually, it is not likely that they will ever make the same karmic mistakes again.

We can, therefore, see that "forgive and forget" is a fiction, because in order to really learn from our mistakes, we must be able to remember them! In fact, a great deal of past-life regression therapy centers around remembering specific incidents from previous lives which are causing problems in this life. When such a memory surfaces, we should bring it out into the open so we can examine it and understand what really happened. Rather than "forgive and forget," we need to *forgive and move forward.*

When people share these past-life memories with me, I always assure them that the Jews and others who died in the camps were not being "punished." This is an extremely important point. Self-blame is very common among abuse victims, especially if the abuse happened during childhood. Many of my subjects have asked, "What did I do to deserve this?" Time after time, when I have explained that the Jews who died in the Holocaust were martyrs for a beautiful and noble religion, the clients breathed a visible sigh of relief. In several cases it was apparent that the idea of Judaism as a "religion worth dying for" had never occurred to them before.

Why not? Because, unfortunately, among members of certain Christian churches there is a belief that all of the suffering of the Jews down through the centuries has been caused by their having supposedly killed Jesus. As a result, this false accusation often becomes a self-fulfilling prophecy used by bigots of all varieties to justify more persecution of Jews. During the years when most of the people mentioned in this book were growing up, it was very common for Jewish children to be harassed on the playground as "Christ killers." Although this attitude is far less prevalent today, it is by no means dead. While I do applaud the Roman Catholic church for removing this accusation from its doctrine at Vatican II, and I commend those Protestant denominations which have done the same, there are still many people, even in this seemingly enlightened age, who need to re-examine their attitudes toward Jews.[3]

It is certainly possible that some Jewish individuals of Jesus' time were involved in his death. Palestine was under the thumb of the Romans, and as in any occupied country there were traitors who collaborated with their conquerors. The Romans were very worried about rebellion in Palestine, and anyone who could gather a crowd of 5,000 was seen as a political threat. At the same time, it is not hard to imagine a disillusioned Judas Iscariot betraying his former teacher to the powers-that-be. Such things happen all the time. But an individual's betrayal to a particular political structure could never justify blaming "the Jews" for Jesus' death.

Whatever the circumstances that brought about his death, I cannot imagine that Jesus, a teacher of love and nonviolence, would have wanted revenge by slaughtering innocent people in a Holocaust, including over a million children. Nor can I believe that God would decree such a thing. To level this accusation against our Heavenly Parent is downright blasphemous. After all, Jesus himself prayed for the very Romans who nailed him to the cross: "Father, forgive them, for they know not what they do."[4]

Jewish oral tradition (midrash) teaches that the Creator wept at the Red Sea over the drowning of the Egyptian charioteers because they, too, were God's creations. If God could weep over the loss of Egyptian slave drivers, then surely God must deeply grieve over innocent men, women, and children who had committed no "crime" except to be Jewish. Contrary to popular misconception, Jews do not worship an angry, vengeful deity. The "bloodthirsty" Jehovah (not His real name) as preached by the Puritans has never been a part of Judaism.

Since the Holocaust could not possibly have been a punishment, then how does karma apply here? Didn't these people choose their own incarnations? Yes, on some level they did. But that does not mean that they chose to be tortured and brutally murdered. Between incarnations we decide the *general circumstances* of our next life, such as who our parents will be. But the details are not always mapped out in advance, because that would negate our free will and the free will of others. We are not puppets acting out a predetermined script, but free agents who have a role in creation from moment to moment. As such, each of us can choose what we wish to learn in the next life, but we do not always have control over the obstacles others may create for us while working out their own destinies.

Consider, for example, a soul who has spent many lives as a learned scholar. Between incarnations, the soul decides that it has mastered the intellectual plane and now wants to learn more about relating to people through the heart. In order to accomplish this as quickly as possible, it might choose a body that is mentally retarded. Without the ability to use the intellect, the soul will have no choice but to learn to communicate through feelings and emotions. If all goes well, the soul will be born into a loving, heart-filled environment where it will be nurtured and cared for as a fellow human being. After a full, rich life as a retarded citizen, the soul will return to the spiritual world, having succeeded in what it wanted to learn.

But suppose the environment becomes hostile toward retarded people and, instead of being nurtured, our hypothetical soul is rounded up and gassed to death as an inferior "subhuman." Can we really say that such a death was consciously chosen by the soul while on the spiritual plane? No, we cannot, because that would deny the moral responsibility of those who did the gassing. They, too, have free will and must answer for the karma of choosing to murder others.

We can say that the people who died in the Holocaust chose to incarnate in Europe at that time, but that does not mean that they predetermined for themselves a horrible death in a concentration camp. It is very dangerous to fall into a "blame the victim" mentality when dealing with karma. Nobody "deserves" to be abused and tortured, no matter what the crime in this life or another. Even the Biblical death penalties were carried out in a merciful way, and nowhere does Jewish law ever condone torture. The excesses of the Nazis were of their own doing and not something predetermined by either God or the victims themselves.

As we can see, there are many factors which go into the circumstances of our next incarnation. Perhaps it would help if we remember that the word "karma" literally means "action" in Sanskrit. The Talmud says that "all your *deeds* (actions) are written in a book."[5] There is really no difference between the Eastern concept of "karma" and the Jewish concept of "Divine Judgment." Both call us to account for our actions. While we can and do choose the general circumstances of our lives on earth, the sum total of our previous actions must also be taken into account. These "karmas" seem to fall into the following four categories:

1. The karmic group to which we belong. Most souls incarnate with other souls that they already know from previous lives, because emotional attachment among human beings is a very powerful force. This can be either positive or negative, depending on the nature of the relationship between the two souls. A religious teacher and disciples may come back as a group, but so can a band of thieves return again as thieves! Simply

knowing somebody from a previous life does not
guarantee that the relationship is a healthy one.
However, we are not trapped into any particular
group behavior. Souls can both progress and
regress spiritually, often changing karmic groups
as they do so.

2. *The past history of the group into which we are
born.* We are greatly influenced by the values
around us, as well as the history and culture of the
family, race, religion, or nation into which we are
born. If a soul incarnates into a military family, it
will probably accept war as a natural part of life,
although it may reject this later. A soul that is born
black or Indian will be influenced by attitudes of
the general society toward minorities, while a soul
born into poverty will face different tests than one
born into great wealth. Again, these "problems"
can be viewed as opportunities for growth and
change. Inner peace can be found everywhere,
under all circumstances, and sometimes those
who are tested the hardest will progress the most.

3. *Our own karma from previous incarnations.* It
has been said that an astrological natal chart is a
summary of our karma at the moment of birth.[6]
This does not, however, mean that we are locked
into predestined behavior for the rest of this earth
life. Although we cannot alter the circumstances
of our birth, we can all take control of our own lives
and overcome negative karma. Each of us has
been born into this world for a purpose, and we
each have specific things to do that nobody else
can accomplish. At the same time, we all have
problems to overcome and tests to meet. These

personal challenges are unique to each soul, and, although we can seek advice from teachers or other guides along the spiritual path, we must do the actual walking by ourselves.

4. *The choices we make through our free will.* We must also bear in mind that each soul has its own unique journey, and there is a wide variation in personality types within each karmic group. Mere membership in a group does not guarantee a certain life pattern. The group karma provides a frame of reference in which to grow, but how the individual uses this opportunity is still a matter of free will.

There have always been individuals in every society who decided to go against the current of group karma. Thus, there were seekers among the pagan "sons of Belial" who sat in the tent of Abraham and Sarah to learn about the one God. Conversely, individual Jews have sometimes backslid into hedonism and idolatry, as the Bible itself testifies. During the Holocaust there were Germans who helped hide their Jewish neighbors, and Jews who collaborated with the Nazis—both examples of free will overruling group karma.

Therefore, we cannot say that membership in any historical group automatically means such-and-such. No matter what situation we find ourselves in, we can always renounce evil and do good. Jewish tradition teaches that even Amalek, the very personification of evil, could repent if he chose to do so and that God would accept his change of heart the same as that of any other sinner.

We can see, therefore, that in each individual

life these four factors are delicately intertwined. Those of us who are in the pastoral and counseling professions must be very careful not to give pat answers, because what is true for one person may not be true for another, even if the outward circumstances are similar. This is why I generally do not "prescribe" for my clients, but simply listen to the stories and allow people to work out the karmic implications for themselves. Rather than serve as their "guru," I prefer to be a sympathetic sounding board.

As I am not a hypnotist, I have not done actual past-life regression work with any of my clients. Usually at the point when people contact me, they have already gotten in touch with their past-life memories through self-hypnosis, dreams, visions, or déjà vu. Occasionally someone does ask my advice on whether or not to go through hypnotic regression. In most cases it is not necessary to know every detail about a horrible death in order to get beyond it. However, there may be cases where detailed recall will help as, for example, with a phobia that seems to have no logical reason for its existence. Hypnosis can be useful, but be sure that the hypnotist is both competent in the technique and aware of the issues surrounding the Holocaust.

The same goes for choosing a psychic reader. While I believe that there are indeed genuine psychics out there, there are also a lot of people claiming to do clairvoyant or channeling work who have very stereotyped ideas about Jews and Judaism. Being psychic does not guarantee freedom from prejudice, nor even profound insight. Before having a reading on Holocaust issues, it is very important to be sure that the reader respects Judaism as a valid spiritual path and that he or she is not going to interpret your experience as some kind of punishment against "the Jews." Without gentle, loving guidance and support through the process, recalling a life in the Holocaust can be extremely traumatic and is not something to be taken lightly. One of the reasons I wrote this book was to provide both counselors and seekers with a broad framework for dealing with some of these issues and healing the karma involved.

Sometimes it has been enough for me to simply affirm that reincarnation is possible. Many of these people had never told anyone about their dreams and visions for fear of being labeled "crazy." After all, it does sound pretty bizarre to claim to have reincarnated from the Holocaust! But after they read case histories of others with similar past-life memories, the fear of "going crazy" usually subsided and inner healing began.

It is my belief that the healing process from one incarnation to another is not really much different from healing within the same lifetime. Therefore, many of the techniques for dealing with grief and abuse issues can also be used for healing the trauma of an incarnation during the Holocaust or any other past-life tragedy. One psychological model which has proven very useful to me is the five-step grief process originally developed by Dr. Elisabeth Kübler-Ross in her work with terminally ill patients. The Kübler-Ross model has since been shown to be applicable to any serious personal loss, and I believe it can help us with inter-incarnational healing as well.

Grief has been defined as the process of restructuring one's life after a deep tragedy. Kübler-Ross has identified five stages to the grieving process, steps which everyone must go through in order to recover. These five stages are: (1) denial, (2) bargaining, (3) anger, (4) depression, and (5) acceptance. The steps do not always occur in this order, and two or more of them can happen at the same time.[7] Both the terminally ill patient and the family go through these stages; the patient, because he or she is leaving this world, and the family, because they are losing a loved one.

I first came into contact with this five-step process while training as a hospice volunteer in 1986. Since then, as I have worked with terminally ill patients and residents in the nursing home where I serve as chaplain, I have come to realize that the grieving process is also a type of spiritual healing. In our society, we do not openly talk about death, and yet every one of us must one day face it. Patients who have worked through the first four steps and come to the "acceptance" stage usually meet their deaths with serenity and peace. On the other hand, those patients who are still in one of the other four stages have a much more difficult time at the moment of death. The same is true for family members. I cannot help but believe that the way in which we deal with death will ultimately affect our next incarnation.

In talking with people who remember their deaths from previous lives, I often see one or more of these stages still manifesting itself, especially if they died violently before their allotted time. Some are very angry at their abusers or at God, while others are depressed. Still others are in the "bargaining" stage, feeling that they were somehow "cheated" out of something in their previous lives and trying to make up for it in this one. Being aware that these feelings can come from unresolved issues surrounding death in another life can be helpful in solving problems in this life.

The story of Mrs. Ploni in the previous chapter is a good example. The level of rage which she unleashed on me was obviously coming from something far deeper than a mere reaction to my comments at a religious discussion. I have met many others like her, who find themselves in fits of rage or the depths of depression for no apparent reason. Some have been to numerous doctors and therapists who repeatedly find nothing medically wrong with them. Very often, getting in touch with past-life memories has produced a healing where all else has failed.

I am certainly not suggesting that past-life regression is some kind of miraculous cure-all. But if you find yourself overwhelmed with unexplainable emotions and standard therapy has not helped, it might be worth a try. You can also begin by journaling these experiences. Are there particular people, places, or situations which seem to trigger your emotions? Are there words or phrases which you associate with these feelings? Do they fit a pattern? If so, try meditating on them, and record any images which come to mind.

You may also attempt to do this by finding a quiet, peaceful place where you will not be disturbed. Next, ask God to protect you, surrounding you with a gentle white light that will shield you from any negativity. Then, close your eyes and take a few relaxed, even breaths. When you feel centered, suggest to yourself that you will remember the incident from your past life which is triggering these reactions. If you are afraid that the memory will be traumatic, try imagining that you are watching it on a movie screen. That way, you will "see" what happened without reliving the actual pain and suffering.

Don't be disappointed if you are not successful on the first try. Although I believe that everyone has some psychic ability, developing it is just like any other skill—it takes practice. When you do get past-life images or impressions, write them down or draw pictures. Include everything you remember, even if it seems irrelevant. There are sometimes details that may not make sense to you now but can later be verified as historically accurate.

Once you have remembered an incident from another life, try to understand it from a karmic point of view. Is this event still affecting your life now? What lesson can you learn from it? Do you need to change attitudes or behavior patterns that were set in motion by this event? Is there something you must do to make amends to others, or do you yourself need to forgive those who harmed you?

After you have come to understand the incident and your role in it, begin to work on letting go of negative emotions. Remember, by forgiving your oppressors, you are not granting amnesty but simply turning the responsibility for judgment over to the Heavenly Court. Ask the Creator, in whatever way you conceive of Him or Her, to remove this karmic burden from your shoulders. Even if you do not believe in God, ask anyhow, and trust that, in some way you may not understand right now, this prayer will be effective. Then, after you have released the negative emotions, ask for a blessing to heal any scars that may remain. Visualize yourself surrounded with holy light and enveloped in unconditional love. Sit in silence for a few minutes, until you have returned to normal consciousness. Then take a stretch and do something nice for yourself.

In addition to healing karma on the individual level, I believe we must also work on raising group consciousness. While many Christians focus primarily on individual salvation, the Jewish understanding of karma is much more communal. "All Jews are relatives" and "All Jews are responsible for one another" are strong sayings in our tradition. This is why our liturgical prayers are always expressed in the plural, such as "We have sinned" or "Bless us with peace." This reminds us that no person's actions are isolated from the whole. As a community, we are interconnected.

Other cultures also have this communal perspective. The Lakota Indians say *mitakuyasin,* which means "all my relatives." Many Buddhists take the *boddhisatva* vow, promising that once they themselves have become enlightened, they will continue to reincarnate until "all sentient beings" are also free from the wheel of karma. In the Biblical tradition, we are indeed our brothers' and sisters' keepers. Therefore, I believe that if we really want to heal negative karma, we must all work together, Jews and non-Jews, to confront the issues in our communities as well as on the individual level.

In many ways, the Jewish community today is still in the midst of grieving over the Holocaust, and this deeply affects the way we Jews see the world. The destruction of European Jewry has had as profound an impact on the Jewish people as the destruction of the Second Temple in the year 70. In some circles, the Holocaust is even being referred to as *Kurban Shlishi*—"the Third Destruction." The Old World is gone forever to us. There is no turning back, no way to reverse the finality of the murder of a civilization.

But how do we Jews share this grief with global neighbors who know so little about our culture? Everyone has heard of "the Jews," but what do they really know about us as people? In the popular mind, the 1,900 years of Jewish history between the death of Jesus and the Nazi Holocaust is one big blank. Yet this is precisely the period which has had the greatest influence on Judaism today. Kabbalah developed during this period, and, as we saw in Chapter Three, it was during the European Middle Ages that Jewish teachings on reincarnation were finally written down. To Jews, this "1,900-year blank" is filled with teachers, philosophers, saints and sinners, rabbis, soldiers, beggars, poets, and martyrs.

But who outside our community has ever heard of them? Even in this age of renewed spiritual enlightenment, Jews are still frequently referred to as people who worship "the angry Jehovah," a negative stereotype carried over from Christian Sunday school. This adds to the feeling of alienation which many Jews experience and contributes greatly to perpetuating the anger and depression created by the Holocaust. We Jews often feel as if we are mourning the loss of a family whom our neighbors never even knew existed.

Non-Jews can help heal this alienation by educating themselves about Jewish history and culture and by including authentic Jewish rituals, stories, and traditions in multicultural programs. When non-Jews publicly affirm that Judaism is a spiritual path, as beautiful and valid as any other, then the Jews themselves will begin to feel welcome in the global family.

In May of 1992 I was invited to speak on "Beyond the Ashes" at a conference sponsored by the International Institute for Integral Human Sciences (I.I.I.H.S.) in Montreal. When I looked at the schedule, I saw that, although there would be a number of ceremonies from different religions throughout the weekend, the only thing Jewish on the program was my speech about the Holocaust. I pointed this out to the conference planners, requesting that we add something joyful from Jewish tradition, so that the participants would not think Judaism was only pain and suffering. They agreed.

The opening speaker for the conference was Matthew Fox, well-known Catholic theologian and teacher of "Creation Spirituality." I suggested that since his speech would be on Friday night, it might be appropriate to do something related to the Jewish Sabbath, which also focuses on the theme of Creation. We decided to light Sabbath candles on stage. Because this is usually done by the woman of the house, I asked Dr. Marilyn Rossner, internationally known Jewish children's therapist and psychic who is co-founder of the I.I.I.H.S., to do the honors.

The idea worked perfectly. Matthew Fox's talk centered on bringing back the feminine imagery of

God for the healing of Planet Earth. When he had finished, Marilyn and I took the stage and shared Jewish teachings about how the Sabbath is like a return to the Garden of Eden, when everything is in harmony. Marilyn told how her grandmother would say that "if all the Jews would light Sabbath candles, we would have peace on earth." Then I taught the chorus to *Lecha Dodi*, a mystical hymn sung in all synagogues around the world on Friday evening. In this song, the Sabbath is personified as a beautiful bride or queen. Everyone on stage and in the audience then linked arms, swaying and singing *Lecha Dodi* to welcome the Sabbath in ecstatic joy. When the program ended, a man came up to me and said, "Tonight you made me proud to be a Jew."

Ritual can be a powerful force for karmic healing. This is one of the reasons why the Holocaust has been incorporated into the modern Jewish liturgy. In this way, the story is being preserved for future generations. Most synagogues have also set up a Holocaust memorial, often an eternal light burning somewhere in the building. And, of course, there is *Yom Ha-Shoah*, Holocaust Remembrance Day. At first there was an attempt to combine the memory of the Holocaust with *Tisha B'Av*, a day of mourning already on the Jewish calendar. But the general feeling was that even in Jewish history, a history so sadly punctuated with savage persecutions, the Holocaust was somehow unique and deserved a day of its own.

Many people in the non-Jewish world do not always understand this need to memorialize the Holocaust. But if you stop to think about it, this is not much different than setting up a gravestone for a deceased family member. Every one of those six million Jews — and the millions of others who also died in the war — was a unique human being with a family and friends, hopes and dreams. We Jews cannot simply forget the Holocaust, because that would mean wiping out the names and deeds of our ancestors and relatives. What group of people anywhere on earth would be willing to do that? The Sioux Indians, over 100 years after the Wounded Knee Massacre, still honor those who died there. Why should it be any different for Jews?

Rabbi Zalman Schachter-Shalomi once suggested that the world needs an international week of mourning for the Holocaust, a time when all people of all nations and faiths would grieve this tragedy *together* and really accept what happened. When the world comes to the point of accepting how the Holocaust has changed human consciousness forever, then real healing for both Jews and non-Jews can begin to take place. Otherwise, we will all continue to bounce back and forth among denial, bargaining, anger, and depression.

It is to be hoped that humanity has also learned something from the terrible lesson of the Holocaust and will not, heaven forbid, have to repeat it. The events of World War II changed the course of history, not only for Jews, but for all of us. I believe that the Holocaust was experienced simultaneously by enough people to have caused a "hundredth monkey" effect, entering the collective human consciousness as an archetype. Just as the Exodus from Egypt became a symbol of all liberation movements, so does the Holocaust stand as an eternal warning about the misuse of our technol-

ogy. We can and should individually forgive but
can never collectively forget. The horrors of
Auschwitz and Treblinka are forever engraved in
the depths of our memory.

What we do with this collective memory is the
important thing. It is no accident that World War
II was followed by the civil rights movement, the
peace movement, women's liberation, and other
struggles for equal rights. Nowadays, whenever
there is oppression of one people by another, the
symbolism of the Holocaust is invoked. If it can be
said that there is healing benefit from the concentration camps, it is this: never again will it seem
acceptable for one group of humans to consider
themselves superior to another. The Holocaust
has permanently transformed human consciousness. Although there is still war and persecution
in the world, it no longer seems "normal" to us, and
along with the tragedies there is now also protest.
Seen in this light, the "victims" of the Holocaust
were in reality martyrs who laid down their lives
for truth and religious freedom.

Chapter 8:

Journeys of the Soul

Throughout this book I have been using the word "soul" to refer to a reincarnated individual, because I feel it is more personalized than the usual metaphysical term "entity." As we continue our exploration of reincarnation in connection with the Holocaust, the question now arises, just what is this "soul"? What part of a person survives death? How are the past-life memories preserved? Which person are we in the next world? These are some of the questions which we will explore in this chapter.

The Hebrew language has several different words for "soul," and these have specific technical meanings. However, scholars down through the centuries have sometimes interpreted these levels of the soul in different ways, based upon their own experiences and the general knowledge available at the time they lived. As we have seen in previous chapters, Judaism was never a static religion but has continued to evolve and expand. Whenever new scientific discoveries were made, Jewish philosophers sought to incorporate them into their views of the universe. This explains why the ideas in later Jewish texts often seem so different from those of the "originals" on which they are based. The Torah itself remains the same, but the ways in which Jews understand it are continuing to evolve.

Because human knowledge in general is constantly growing, a new generation can sometimes perceive the world very differently from the previous generation. The story is told of a student who once asked a philosopher, "How could anyone have ever been so stupid as to believe that the sun was circling the earth? Surely common sense would have said that it must be the other way around."

"True," replied the philosopher. "But I wonder, what would it look like if the sun *were* circling the earth?"

The obvious answer is that on the physical level it would look exactly the same. Yet more than 400 years after Copernicus, we still speak of "sunrise" and "sunset," even though we know perfectly well that the sun neither rises nor sets. Rather than invent new language, we have continued to use the old terms *with new meanings*. Almost everyone nowadays has learned to read "sunrise" as referring to "that moment when, as the earth revolves on its axis, the side on which we are standing has just begun to turn toward the sun, which therefore becomes visible to us." What has changed is not the level of human intelligence, but rather our understanding of how the solar system works.

This same kind of reinterpretation in the light of new discoveries has frequently occurred within kabbalistic circles. I believe that mystics are often on the "cutting edge" of religious understanding, because they are directly experiencing the spiritual dimensions of consciousness. Describing these "alternate realities" to non-mystics is very difficult, however, because there is frequently no suitable vocabulary. In some cases, new words are invented, but more often the older terminology is redefined with another "layer" of meaning.

Space does not permit a full explanation of how I evolved my current understanding of the "journeys of the soul"—that would take another book! Let it suffice to say that I, too, have been deeply influenced by recent scientific discoveries and am now trying to integrate them into the Jewish world view. Readers who are already familiar with kabbalah will still benefit by reading the following. For those to whom the study of kabbalah is new, it is important to know that this chapter is based on a combination of Jewish mysticism, modern psychology, and my own personal observations.

Kabbalah teaches that there are five levels to the soul. As was stated above, not all sources agree on the exact interpretation of these five levels. In the light of modern psychology and metaphysics, I believe we can define them as follows:

(1) *nefesh,* the biological life force of the body
(2) *ruach,* the lower emotional spirit or "ego"
(3) *neshamah,* the individual higher consciousness
(4) *chayah,* the collective unconscious of the group
(5) *yechidah,* the level of unity with creation and God

Some medieval Jewish mystics were of the opinion that we are not necessarily born with all five levels, but that some of them must be consciously developed. One of the interpretations of the 613 *mitzvot* (commandments) in the Torah is that they serve to develop the "limbs of the soul." Of these 613 *mitzvot*, 365 are negative ("thou shalt nots"), corresponding to the days of the year and symbolizing that we must "reject evil and choose good" every day of our lives. The other 248 *mitzvot* correspond to the parts of the body as it was understood in medieval anatomy. These 248 *mitzvot* are the positive commandments ("thou shalts") and, according to this teaching, a Jew who fulfills them is not only carrying out the laws of the Torah on the earth plane, but also building a "spiritual body" for the next world.

But there is an obvious problem with this model. Because some of the *mitzvot* are specifically designated by the Torah as applying only to certain classes of people, how is it possible for any single person to fulfill all of them? A male cannot, for example, fulfill the Torah laws regarding menstruation, nor can a female be circumcised. Other *mitzvot* apply only to kings, judges, prophets, farmers, merchants, etc. Therefore, even the most devout Jew is bound to be lacking in some of the *mitzvot*, which in turn would mean not developing one or more "limbs of the soul."

The kabbalists solved this dilemma through the doctrine of reincarnation. According to Gershom Scholem, world-renowned academic authority on kabbalah, "the idea of transmigration (sic) was radically expanded from that of a punishment restricted to certain sins to that of a general law encompassing all the souls of (the people) Israel and, in a later stage, the souls of all human beings and even, in its most radical form, of all creation from the angels to insentient beings."[1] By being reborn many times into the Covenant at Sinai under different circumstances, a Jew could eventually fulfill all of the 613 *mitzvot* over many lifetimes.

But what about the non-Jews? If one must fulfill the 613 laws of the Torah in order to build a spiritual body and these laws are given to Jews only, then what happens to the rest of humanity? Some of the medieval Jewish commentators were of the opinion that Gentiles do not have the higher levels of the soul—an opinion that I emphatically reject.[2] As Scholem stated in the quote above, the doctrine of reincarnation within Judaism has long since evolved from being an ethnocentric interpretation into a more universal one. I personally believe that all souls have the same five levels but that they may be developed in different ways according to the karmic group to which the individual soul belongs.

Of these five levels, the *nefesh* (NEH-fesh) and *ruach* (ROO-akh) levels do not survive beyond death, because they are dependent upon the physical body. When death occurs, *nefesh,* the basic life force, dissipates back into the universe, and the body begins to decompose. The brain also decomposes, losing *ruach,* the sensory, emotional, and conditioned knowledge encoded within its nerve structure. The physical body, with its particular brain and personality, is gone forever.

The level of *neshamah* (neh-SHAH-mah), however, does survive. Since Talmudic times, this level has also been associated with the intellect and personal disposition. *Neshamah* is one of the levels that, according to some kabbalists, must be consciously developed. This is an amazingly modern insight when viewed in the light of recent discoveries about child psychology. The following outline of normal child development can be found in any introductory book on child psychology, although, of course, such a textbook will not make reference to reincarnation! What I have tried to do is integrate two systems of thought, kabbalah and psychology, in order to gain a better understanding of what the mystics were trying to say.

We now know that a child's awareness develops in very definite stages, based in part on the maturation of the brain. Newborn infants function primarily on the physiological level, spending their time eating, sleeping, and crying when their needs are not met. A newborn baby does not appear to recognize any boundaries between herself and her physical surroundings. From a kabbalistic standpoint, she is living primarily on the level of *nefesh*, the basic life force of the body. We could also say that the soul is not yet "well-grounded" into the physical world.

Gradually the infant explores her fingers, toes, and other body parts, discovering where she "leaves off" and the world begins. The next step is establishing an individual identity that is separate from her parents. Now the level of *ruach* begins to emerge, as the child forms emotional bonds with significant people, pets, and even objects, such as a teddy bear or other toy. She also begins to acquire language skills, which further "shape" her ways of defining the world around her. This stage is usually complete by the age of three-and-a-half years, at which time she can clearly express herself as an individual with her own likes and dislikes.

Between the ages of three-and-a-half and six years, the child explores more and more of the world around her. At this stage her world view is "magical," in that she does not necessarily understand the difference between "make believe" and physical reality. When a child in this age group "pretends" to be a soldier or a nurse, she feels as if she *really is* that character. Abstract reasoning, as we know it in adulthood, has not yet emerged.

By the age of six, the child has learned to differentiate between "make believe" and the objective, physical world. She now begins to explore social roles. At first, these will be imitations of the adults and other role models that she knows best, who provide her with some basic values and teach her which behaviors are acceptable and which are not. At this stage, the child may tend to think of "right and wrong" in very concrete, black-and-white terms, because she has not yet developed the skills necessary for more subtle, abstract reasoning.

Eventually these accumulated values fuse into an "inner voice," which stays with her throughout life and becomes her basis for making decisions.[3] The child has now begun to learn how to rationally weigh one idea against another, and to understand that there can be both positive and negative consequences for her behavior. From this point on, her mind continues to develop until, with the onset of puberty, she has become a young woman who now demands the right to "think for herself."

Neshamah, the intellectual level of the soul, has now begun to manifest itself and will continue to evolve throughout her life.

It is not clear to me whether the levels of the soul are literally "developing" during this process or already exist on the spiritual plane but must wait for the child's brain to mature enough to work through it. If the latter is the case, then we might view the brain as a very sophisticated computer that is "unprogrammed" at birth but which utilizes its childhood experiences to develop the "software" which eventually enables the higher levels of the soul to manifest themselves on the earth plane.

According to my understanding of kabbalah, the *neshamah* level is not limited to intellectual development alone, but is also the level of the "eternal soul" which survives death. In addition, the *neshamah* maintains a constant connection to *chayah* (KHAI-yah) and *yechidah* (yeh-KHEE-dah), the higher transcendental levels. Between earth lives, all the soul's incarnations are remembered on the *neshamah* level, although not necessarily in specific detail. What is retained are those lessons and truths that were significant to the spiritual growth of the individual soul. The rest is meant to be shed like an old garment, which explains why the majority of people cannot recall specific information, such as names, dates, and street addresses, which they knew in previous lifetimes.

This is not so difficult to understand if we remember that the same pattern occurs in our daily lives on the earth plane. We have both a long-term and a short-term memory. For example, you might call directory assistance for a phone number, then repeat it to yourself long enough to make the call. But unless you write that number down, you will not remember it tomorrow, because it was only stored temporarily in your short-term memory. On the other hand, you have probably memorized your own phone number, putting it into long-term memory, where it will be instantly available.

We might say that the entire physical brain is the "short-term memory" of the soul for one lifetime, while the *neshamah* and higher levels serve as the long-term memory from one life to another. Unnecessary details are usually forgotten. However, if there is "unfinished business" left over from one or more incarnations, then the soul may preserve some specific details about that life. This type of carry-over is frequently connected with a tragedy that would generate very strong emotions, such as being tortured during the Holocaust. As was explained above, emotions normally dissipate with the *ruach* level of the soul at death. But in the case of a murder or other injustice that is not resolved, the event may impress itself on the long-term memory of the *neshamah*, to be carried from incarnation to incarnation until it is finally dealt with. Once the "unfinished business" is somehow resolved, it, too, recedes from individual consciousness.

On the levels of *chayah* and *yechidah*, however, all the details are preserved forever, because these are the higher levels where the soul touches the light of the All-Knowing God. The level of *chayah*, which literally means "living being," is probably the least understood of the five levels, which is why there are so many disagreements among the classical commentators. Here is one of the areas where, I believe, modern psychology can shed some light. I would like to suggest that *chayah* represents the "collective unconscious" of one's particular karmic group. In other words, it is the level of Carl Jung's "archetypes."[4]

Unlike many Jungians, however, I do not believe that the symbolism of the archetypes is necessarily universal. As a member of a minority culture, I am constantly confronted with symbols that mean one thing in the "dominant" society and something quite different in the Jewish world view. For example, "Torah" to me is the dynamic, vibrant, living "blueprint" of God's universe, whereas to many non-Jews it means a harsh, rigid, unbending set of archaic laws. On the other hand, the color "red" is often used in Jewish writings to represent war, bloodshed, and harlotry, while to Native Americans it has the life-affirming symbolism of the "good red road." For this reason, I suspect that the interpretation of archetypal symbols is often conditioned by the culture in which we are raised.

Can the symbolism of the collective unconscious be changed? I believe that it can. As I have briefly suggested in previous chapters, a large-scale event like the Holocaust might have a "hundredth monkey" effect, which means that enough people experienced it simultaneously for it to become a new archetype. This, in turn, could make the symbolism of that event accessible to all those souls who are somehow "plugged in" to the karmic group which originally experienced it. I also believe souls can become connected to an existing archetype through learning about it after the fact. For example, the Exodus from Egypt, which was a specific event in the history of the Jewish people, has become a well-known archetype for non-Jews as well through their study of the Bible.

Education might also be a means for eliminating negative archetypes, such as those with sexist or racist connotations. Now that the world is linked together by mass communications, it is possible for large numbers of people to experience the same new interpretations simultaneously. The archetype itself would probably remain, but its *meaning* could be altered from a negative to a positive one. This has already happened with "the big bad wolf," who is no longer seen as a vicious beast attacking Little Red Riding Hood but as an endangered species to be protected.

On the level of *yechidah*, the soul is united with all creation and touches its origin in the mind of the Creator. In some religions this level is described as a total merging of the soul into the actual consciousness of God, but Jewish mystics by and large have been reluctant to go that far. According to Jewish theology, we do not "become God," because God is a completely unique and independent Being. One can, however, "touch" God and in so doing become "godly." By this it is meant that one's own will becomes so merged into the will of God that the two are essentially the same. In the words of the Talmudic sage, Rabban Gamaliel ben Judah Ha-Nassi: "Make your will His Will, that He may make His Will your will."[5]

A good way to understand this relationship to God is to think of an electrical system, with God as the "generator" and the individual human being as the "light bulb." Although the light is clearly visible within the bulb, we know that the electricity does not originate there but is produced in a power station many miles away. In the same way, the individual human heart manifests the Divine Light, but the ultimate Source of that Light is the Creator. From a Jewish standpoint, God is *both* immanent ("within") and transcendent ("out there"). The Creator did not just create the universe and then "walk away" but is consciously sustaining the universe from moment to moment. This is the meaning of the line in the Jewish morning prayers, "And in goodness, God renews *every day continuously* the work of creation." (Italics mine)

Carrying the "light bulb" analogy one step further, as long as we remain "plugged in" to God, we have access to an infinite supply of this Divine Light. But if we decide to "unplug" ourselves from God and run on our own "ego-batteries," we will eventually "run down," because without the connection to the Source of Light our own supply of "energy" remains limited. Fortunately, all it takes to re-connect ourselves to God is a humble heart and a sincere desire to do so, followed through with appropriate action.

Returning to the subject of "levels of the soul," many psychics speak of an "Akashic Record" which they can access while in trance. Other people can apparently do the same under hypnosis, either self-induced or guided by a hypnotist. I believe that a person in a genuine psychic trance is probably bypassing his or her own *nefesh, ruach,* and *neshamah* levels to get in touch with the level of *chayah.* From there, the psychic can sometimes see into the *yechidah* level and access the "Hall of Records," where God preserves everything that has ever happened.

Edgar Cayce described the Akashic Record as being like a huge library, where he would find the "life reading" for each soul. This is similar to statements found in both the Talmud and the Muslim Koran:

TALMUD: "Reflect upon three things, and you will not come within the power of sin. Know what is Above you: a Seeing Eye, a Hearing Ear, and all your deeds are written in a Book."[6]

KORAN: "Verily We shall give life to the dead, and We record that which they send before, and that which they leave behind, and all things have we taken account in a clear Book."[7]

Of course, these references to "books" and "libraries" are only metaphors. Preliterate cultures use other imagery, as, for example, the widespread belief that ancient records are encoded in stones and crystals. On the other hand, psychics born into the electronic age have sometimes compared the experience to watching a videotape! But whatever the symbolism, the basic idea is that knowledge about a person's incarnations is preserved beyond the grave. It appears that some things are remembered by the individual soul itself, while others can be accessed from the "Book of Life."

Once this information is accessed, however, it must pass back through the level of *chayah* and into the psychic's conscious mind. In the process of doing so, the information is "colored" by whatever symbolism the psychic has internalized. This would explain why even the most "universalist" mystics still tend to clothe their visions and dreams in symbolism that is consistent with their own cultures. If the brain can be compared to a computer, then the symbolism in the collective unconscious is the "software" which enables the information to take on a recognizable form.

Now that we have examined the five levels of the soul, I would like to explore how they apply to another basic kabbalistic concept, the Tree of Life diagram. (See Figure A.) Rather than burden the reader with yet another set of Hebrew words, I have chosen to dispense with the traditional terminology of the Tree and use what we have already learned. But first, a word about the Tree diagram itself.

The Kabbalistic Tree is so well known in Western mysticism that many people think of it as being synonymous with kabbalah. This has both advantages and disadvantages. On the one hand, there will be many readers of this book who are already familiar with it. But on the other hand, what they have learned may or may not bear any resemblance to what I am about to explain. This is because the Tree of Life has been adapted to many different philosophies, some of which are theologically different from Judaism. At the present time there appear to be three basic "schools" of kabbalah taught in metaphysical circles, which even use variant spellings of the word: (1) the original Jewish kabbalah, which is completely monotheistic; (2) the Christian Cabala, which presents a trinitarian view of the universe; and (3) the neopagan Quabalah, which incorporates the gods and goddesses of many ancient mythologies. Needless to say, my understanding of the Tree of Life is based on the Jewish version.

If you look at Figure A, you will see that it is composed of several circles, which are called *sephirot* (sfee-ROTE), connected by numerous lines or "paths." This particular version of the diagram represents the human consciousness or "microcosm." Other versions of the Tree also exist, which represent the universe or "macrocosm" and the divine attributes of God. As explained above, I have replaced the traditional Hebrew names of the *sephirot* with the five levels we have already defined, as well as some modern terminology.

At the bottom of the diagram are the "lower kingdoms" of animal, vegetable, and mineral. These, according to kabbalah, are also regarded as having a "holy spark" or "spirit of life," but they are not as highly developed as the human level. Each higher kingdom includes the attributes of the kingdoms below it. Thus, the mineral kingdom manifests the attribute of *cohesion*, that is, of atoms and molecules holding together; the vegetable kingdom has cohesion and, in addition, manifests the power of *growth;* the animal kingdom has both cohesion and growth, with the added attribute of *sense perception.* (I am aware that crystals "grow" and plants "sense" light. There is a great deal of overlap among the lower kingdoms, but space does not permit further explanation here.)

In this system, human beings are regarded as a separate level, which includes the mineral, vegetable, and animal kingdoms, but which also has

the added ability *to consciously know its Creator.*
Humans are, therefore, the only beings on the
earth plane who have true free will. Although
animals may feel emotions like love, anger, or fear
and in some cases can demonstrate intelligence,
they do not, according to this model, have moral
knowledge of "right and wrong." Our bodies may or
may not have evolved from apes, but our souls are
endowed by God with an extra measure of awareness that animals do not possess. With this
awareness goes a level of greater responsibility for
our behavior.

The Tree diagram itself represents an "enlarged
for detail" version of the human kingdom and can
be viewed in a number of different patterns, depending on which "paths" are emphasized. For our
purposes, we will analyze it as three Pillars: the
right-hand Pillar of Force (or energy), the left-hand
Pillar of Form, and the central Pillar of Balance. In
viewing the Tree, regard it as a mirror image: your
own right is the Right Pillar on the Tree, and your
own left is the Left Pillar on the Tree.

On the Right Pillar are those attributes which
relate to spiritual force or "energy" manifested on
higher and higher levels of consciousness. As we
master each level and "climb" the Right Pillar, we
find that "holistic creativity" on the everyday level
leads to "mercy" and "tolerance of grace" on the
religious level, which in turn leads to "spiritual
wisdom" on the transcendental level. All three of
these levels have the same thing in common: they
are ways of expressing good intentions (*kavannah*
in Hebrew) of the spirit.

On the Left Pillar are those attributes which
relate to preserving spiritual form. When we climb

this Pillar, we move from "objective logic" on the everyday level to "justice and strictness of cosmic law" on the religious level to "spiritual understanding" on the transcendental level. Again, these three levels have something in common: they all provide structure for expressing the spirit.

On the Central Pillar we find the five levels which were discussed above. The level of *chayah* is represented with a dotted circle because, although it is not technically one of the ten *sephirot,* many kabbalists have sensed that there should be another level there. The Central Pillar represents "balance," and on each soul level it is our task to find the equilibrium between the attributes of Form and Force. Theory must be balanced with Practice, Justice balanced with Mercy, and Understanding balanced with Wisdom.

One way of visualizing this is to think of Form as the "cup" and Force as the "wine." Ritual without the spirit is like an empty chalice, very beautiful but useless for quenching your thirst. On the other hand, the finest wine without a cup to hold it will run through your fingers before you have a chance to drink. In order to "make *kiddush,*" that is, bring holiness into the world, you need *both* the wine of Spirit and the cup of Ritual. The same analogy applies to all aspects of Form and Force.

This "cup and wine" example also helps explain why Jewish kabbalists associate the Left Pillar with Female and the Right Pillar with Male, which appears "backwards" to Western students of metaphysics. This is because modern gender stereotypes often portray men as "logical" and women as "intuitive." But the kabbalistic imagery is based on a different, much older set of symbols, where

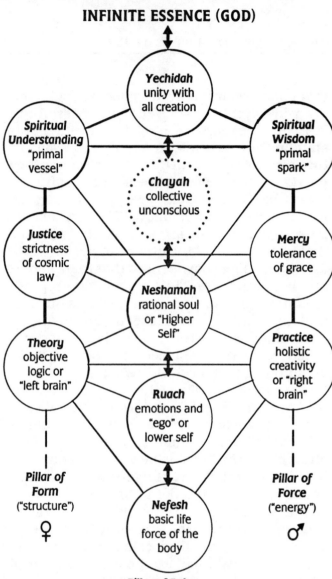

INFINITE ESSENCE (GOD)

Yechidah
unity with all creation

Spiritual Understanding
"primal vessel"

Spiritual Wisdom
"primal spark"

Chayah
collective unconscious

Justice
strictness of cosmic law

Mercy
tolerance of grace

Neshamah
rational soul or "Higher Self"

Theory
objective logic or "left brain"

Practice
holistic creativity or "right brain"

Ruach
emotions and "ego" or lower self

Pillar of Form
("structure")
♀

Pillar of Force
("energy")
♂

Nefesh
basic life force of the body

Pillar of Balance

Animal Kingdom (Senses)
Vegetable Kingdom (Growth)
Mineral Kingdom (Cohesion)

Figure A: *Kabbalistic Tree of Life:*
The Five Levels of the Human Soul

Arrows represent movement of consciousness up and
down the central Pillar of Balance.

© 1992 by Yonassan Gershom

"female" is the womb and "male" is the semen. The female Left Pillar, therefore, represents things which *provide structure* (the Cup of Ritual), while the male Right Pillar represents things which *infuse energy* (the Wine of Spirit). Once again, these two aspects, "male and female," must be balanced, regardless of the sex of the physical body.

According to most theories of reincarnation, we do, in fact, change sex from life to life. This is supported by modern research and, as we have already seen, many of the people whose stories are told in this book believe that they were the opposite sex in a previous incarnation. The *Zohar* indicates in many places that the soul is hermaphroditic while in the spiritual world and "splits" into two halves, one male and the other female, when it enters the physical realm. This is the textual basis for the idea of "soul mates," as well as the expression "my other half" for a spouse.

In light of modern research, I am more inclined to believe that the soul does not actually split in two but simply takes on the sexual role of the body it currently inhabits. "Soul mates," in my opinion, are not literally our "other halves" but those individual souls with whom we choose to share our lives. The feeling of "instant recognition" that many lovers experience is probably due to having known each other in previous lives. I believe that this model leads to healthier relationships, because it recognizes the autonomy of the two individuals, who are not "halves" of each other but independent souls choosing to make a home together.

How does all of this relate to personal spiritual growth? I believe that balancing all of these levels

on one's inner Tree can take many lifetimes and
that each level presents new tests and challenges.
In my kabbalah workshops I often ask participants to meditate on the Tree diagram, focusing
on which attributes are most appealing and which
are not. In the discussion which follows, we usually discover that the *sephirot* which we like the
least are the very ones we should be working on!
For example, if you tend toward rigid fundamen-
talism, then you probably need to exercise the
more tolerant attribute of Mercy. On the other
hand, if you tend to be too permissive, then it may
be time to focus on learning the laws of Justice.

This explanation of the Tree has barely scratched
the surface, and there are many, many more ways
in which you can grow and evolve toward the Light.
Each incarnation of the soul is unique, and,
although we may return many times, the precise
circumstances are never exactly the same. We
should, therefore, treasure every moment of life as
a priceless opportunity for spiritual growth.

How many times does a soul return? The Jewish
sources disagree on this. In the *Bahir* it is stated
that reincarnation may continue for a "thousand
generations" and, as we saw in Chapter Three,
both the *Bahir* and the *Zohar* frequently read
"generations" as "incarnations." For example, Exodus 20:5-6 says that God visits the sins of the
wicked unto the children for four generations, but
rewards the descendants of the righteous for a
thousand generations. Can this mean that God
literally punishes children for their parents' sins?
No, says the *Zohar;* it means that our own sins are
visited upon us in a future lifetime.[8] From this
verse it would seem that it can take up to four

rebirths for a soul to burn off negative karma—
assuming that the soul does not sin again!

Among the medieval Spanish kabbalists, it was
commonly believed that every soul returns three
times following the lifetime of the original body, for
a total of only four incarnations. This was based on
Job 33:29: "Behold, God does all these things
once, twice, three times, with a man [or woman]."
Rabbi Isaac Luria, the great sixteenth-century
kabbalist upon whose teachings most of modern
Jewish mysticism is based, took this one step
further. He taught that a soul which showed no
improvement after four incarnations not only did
not return, it completely ceased to exist.[9]

In reality, however, Luria's harsh scenario rarely,
if ever, actually happens, a fact which he himself
recognized. It is said that Luria could read all of a
person's past incarnations, and no doubt he realized that there is rarely a soul so wicked as to show
absolutely no improvement. Even the worst of
criminals has done some good somewhere. Therefore, Luria also taught, if even the slightest progress
is made toward good in only one of the incarnations, then the soul will be granted as many more
lifetimes as it needs to repent completely.[10] The
average soul, therefore, has already returned many
more than four times.

In later centuries, the Hasidic Jews of Eastern
Europe based many of their teaching tales on this
theme of how one small *mitzvah* can save a soul
from oblivion. This "spiritual optimism" remains a
basic tenet of Hasidic Judaism today. While some
segments of Orthodoxy tend to write off all non-
Orthodox Jews as hopelessly wicked, the Hasidim
do not. Instead, many Hasidim (especially the

Lubovitch sect) devote a great deal of energy toward getting less observant Jews to adopt even one new *mitzvah* in their lifetime. This tiny improvement in this life, they believe, will start the person on the path toward repentance in future incarnations.

Many kabbalists also taught that the righteous souls *voluntarily* return, for thousands of incarnations if need be, in order to help the rest of humankind—exactly like the Buddhist concept of *Boddhisattva*. These souls are known in Hebrew as *Zaddikim* or "righteous holy ones." Some of the *Zaddikim* reveal themselves publicly, like the miracle-working Hasidic Rebbes of Eastern Europe. Others remain anonymous, disguised as ordinary people. It is said that, at any given time, there are always at least thirty-six hidden Jewish saints on earth. These hidden saints, called *Lamedvavniks* from the Hebrew for "thirty-six," spend quiet but exemplary lives as living incarnations of the Torah. It is for the sake of these thirty-six that the world continues to exist.[11]

The question arises, if we do indeed live many lives, which person are we in the next world? I believe we are a combination of all of our lives. Although the personality of each earth life is both real and unique, it is not the true Higher Self, but merely a projection of that Self. On the higher levels of consciousness, all of our earth lives merge together.

Using a medical analogy, we could compare this to a case of Multiple Personality Disorder (MPD), in which several distinct "people" inhabit the same body. According to modern psychology, MPD is caused by extreme trauma in early childhood, at a time when the brain is still developing and its individuality is not yet clearly defined. In order to cope with the pain of the trauma, a separate personality splits off, so that one "person" is aware of the pain and the other is not. Once this mechanism is set up, any number of independent personalities may develop. Sometimes the personalities are "frozen in time," remaining at whatever age they were at the time of the split. Some of the personalities may be aware of each other, while others operate completely independently. However, there is usually a core personality who is constantly aware of all the others, and through its help the psychiatrist can learn what triggered the various splits in the patient and how to reintegrate them.

In the same way, our many incarnations on earth might be regarded as "multiple personalities" split off from the main core, which is the Higher Self. Just as the medical case of MPD is initially triggered by trauma, so is a case of multiple incarnations the result of the soul attempting to cope with previous experiences (karmas) on earth. And just as the MPD patient does not remember the traumas while in the waking state, so does the average person not remember what particular incidents caused the current incarnation.

Carrying this analogy one step further, we can say that the cure for MPD is similar to the process of stopping negative karma. In order to reintegrate multiple personalities, it is necessary for the personalities to get to know each other and consciously share memories and information. In this process, the initial traumas are remembered and con-

fronted. If the treatment is successful, the separate personalities eventually merge into one person
again. MPD patients have sometimes described
this process as the "death" of the personalities,
but their memories and experiences are not lost.
Instead, what was formerly known only to one
personality is now shared by the entire integrated
self.

In the same way, as the soul progresses, it
gradually incorporates all of its experiences on
earth into one consciousness. People who are not
spiritually advanced will remain fragmented and
rarely have any conscious awareness of former
lives. But as spiritual progress is made, the person
begins to recall the incidents in previous lives
which are currently affecting this one. More often
than not, these determining karmas are of a
traumatic nature, and once they are dealt with,
the karmic pattern does not repeat. Eventually,
the positive lessons which the soul has learned in
previous lives are brought into waking consciousness and, it is hoped, are used for the good of
humanity.

But sometimes a soul is so traumatized that it
doesn't return to the higher spiritual planes at all.
Instead, it becomes enmeshed in the events of its
last life and remains "earthbound" on the lower or
astral plane. As of this writing, I have not yet
visited any of the concentration camp sites, but I
have been told by numerous psychics that many
earthbound spirits are still tied to these places.
This is consistent with other parapsychological
findings, where "ghosts" often "haunt" the sites of
their deaths. In many such "hauntings" the death
was a traumatic one, with some kind of "unfin-

ished business" which prevents such a soul from going into the Light. Helping these unhappy spirits to full transition into the next world is one of the best-known types of work that psychics do.

While each case is unique, there do appear to be some common factors which hold spirits earthbound in the lower levels of the astral plane. These factors fall into three main categories:

1. The spirit does not know that it is dead. While it may seem incredible that someone could die and not realize it, this does happen. Such a soul often has no belief in life after death, and therefore reasons that, because it still has consciousness, it cannot really be dead. In addition, if the death happens suddenly, the transition to the afterlife can be so fast that the soul does not realize it has taken place.

I once lived in an apartment which began to manifest a great deal of psychic activity almost as soon as I moved in. Lights went on and off, pictures fell from the walls, and feelings of anger, frustration, and sadness could sometimes be sensed in the bedroom. I immediately suspected a haunting and tried chanting Psalms and other prayers on behalf of the spirit. When that did not work and the phenomena continued, I called in a trance medium who "channeled" the "entity" for me.

The story which emerged was that of two young lovers who were killed instantly in an automobile accident a number of years ago. The young woman had apparently gone on to the next world immediately, but the young man did not know he was dead. He was searching for his girlfriend in my apartment, where she had lived at the time of their deaths, and naturally the "ghost" was angry that another man—me!—was sleeping in "her" bedroom! All it took to free this earthbound spirit was to tell him that he could follow the Light to find his beloved in the next world.

2. The soul has stereotyped expectations of the next world. There are many people who do not realize that religious descriptions of the afterlife are only metaphors and expect them to be fulfilled literally. The absence of a Heaven with angels sitting on clouds playing harps may cause some Christian souls to remain earthbound because they will not accept the help of the spirits who have come to meet them, perhaps even fearing that they are demons in disguise. At the other extreme, the fear of being sent to a literal fiery Hell can also keep a soul from completing the transition.

I cannot help but wonder if there are Jewish spirits who remain earthbound because they believe that they must wait in their graves until they tunnel to Jerusalem on Judgment Day. As was explained in Chapter Three, the Jewish version of the physical resurrection includes the expectation that one's bones will someday be miraculously fleshed out again. It is possible that some spirits may feel trapped at the sites of concentration camps because that is where the ashes of their bones are. If so, it would seem that such souls could also be released by explaining that these symbols are not meant to be taken literally and that they should follow the astral "tunnel to Heaven" which has been described by so many people who have had near-death experiences.

3. The soul has "unfinished business" with events and people on the earth plane. This is the most difficult type of earthbound spirit to work with, because in order for a soul to be released into the Light, it must want to go. As long as it feels that it has not completed its work here on earth, the soul will continue to be attached to persons, places, or things in the material world.

Concerning victims of the Holocaust, there is no doubt in my mind that many of them vowed with their last dying breath never to forgive or forget. Others vowed to survive at all costs as an act of defiance and may still be "surviving" on the astral plane, perhaps unaware that they no longer have physical bodies. If such souls are earthbound at Auschwitz or Dachau, it will be very difficult to release them unless they can be reassured that history is now bearing witness to the Holocaust, and their deaths were not in vain.

It is important to tell these souls that the Jewish people not only survived the Holocaust but have gone on to experience a renaissance of religion, culture, and traditions, as well as a physical return to the land of Israel. Only upon being convinced that they have fulfilled their vows of Jewish survival will such souls be able to leave without feeling as if they have failed.

As was explained in Chapter Three, one of the reasons for saying *kaddish* (Jewish prayer for the dead) is to help the soul progress in the next world. *Kaddish* may be said anywhere in the world where there is a *minyan* (Jewish quorum) holding a service. Many Jews in this generation have taken on the custom of saying *kaddish* every day throughout the year on behalf of those who die in the Holocaust. This is a very praiseworthy practice, which I believe will help such souls to progress.

But there is also a negative side to this teaching about *kaddish*. Because it is usually the children (in very traditional circles, only the sons) who say *kaddish*, many Jews mistakenly believe that without living offspring, they are somehow doomed to wander after death. This belief was so prevalent in Eastern Europe that parents often referred to the eldest son as "our *kaddish*" and were greatly relieved when he was born.

Besides partially explaining the Jewish focus on having male children, this belief could also account for certain earthbound souls not progressing through the benefit of "communal" *kaddish* prayers on their behalf. Such souls may need to be educated to the fact that Jewish religious law does provide for appointing a proxy in the event that a Jew dies childless and that this is karmically the same as having a biological child say *kaddish*. Even though an entire extended family may have been wiped out in the Holocaust, leaving not one single survivor, the souls involved are still connected to the Jewish people and, therefore, are included in their prayers.

Rabbi Zalman Schachter-Shalomi, himself a Holocaust survivor, has expressed his support for people of all faiths to pray on behalf of the earthbound souls at the concentration camp sites. In a 1987 videotaped lecture, *Personal and Planetary Transformation*, Reb Zalman explained that "this blood is still crying out for revenge" and that as long as it continues to do so, there will be unrest in the world. Helping these unhappy souls to find peace is an important part of the process of planetary healing.

I agree that the work of healing Holocaust karma is very important for the general welfare of the planet and that this includes helping to release earthbound souls of victims. However, groups and individuals doing this type of work should be aware of the sensitive issues surrounding the Holocaust and approach it with a deep, abiding respect for the Judaism that these people died for. Whenever one is working with souls who died for a good cause, it is very, very important to affirm the validity of that cause and to assure them that their deaths were not in vain. Merely desiring to clear up "bad vibrations" and "get it over with" is not enough and may actually compound the problem. Doing psychic work is like any other kind of counseling. Sometimes we must do "therapy" with the soul, gradually helping it to grow toward the Light at its own pace and within its own belief system.

This chapter certainly does not exhaust all of the possible "journeys" that a soul might take. Thus far, we have focused primarily on the reincarnation of Holocaust victims. In the next chapter, we will examine a few cases of Nazis who have also returned and explore some of the karmic cycles which may have influenced events surrounding the Holocaust.

Chapter 9:

Cycles of Return

In 1984, when I was teaching at the Spiritual Frontiers Fellowship retreat in Northfield, Minnesota, a middle-aged Christian woman, whom we shall call Mrs. Brown, sat down next to me in the cafeteria and asked to talk. "You are the first Jew I have ever met who believes in reincarnation," Mrs. Brown said. "Perhaps you can help me."

Mrs. Brown was concerned, not for herself, but for her teen-age daughter Jenny, who had recently developed an obsession with Nazi paraphernalia. Jenny spent many hours in her room, listening to German military music, and liked to dress in uniforms with knee-high boots. She had also begun collecting books, photographs, and other memorabilia from the Third Reich, and there were many swastikas among the doodles in her school notebooks.

Understandably, Mrs. Brown was upset about all this. Nobody else in the family had any interest in Nazism—both parents were political liberals who had been actively involved in the peace movement. They had tried to teach all of their children to be loving and tolerant of others. At first, Mrs. Brown had thought that this "Nazi business" was just a "phase" that her daughter was going through, perhaps a way of rebelling against her parents' liberal values. But the obsession had long since gone beyond teen-age rebellion, and Mrs. Brown was now very worried.

"Could this be connected to reincarnation?" she asked, looking into my eyes from across the lunch-room table.

While Mrs. Brown was talking, I kept getting a psychic impression of a sixteen- or seventeen-year-old boy sitting in the cockpit of an airplane. The boy was smiling ecstatically, and in the background I could hear the roar of the plane's engines. The word "hero" kept coming into my mind, and I got the impression that this boy had been no hard-core Nazi, but an idealistic youth who was caught up in the excitement of being a fighter pilot. Was this his first flight? Did he die in combat? I did not know. But I was certain that I was tuning in to the reason for Jenny's obsession with military marches and uniforms.

When I described this psychic impression to Mrs. Brown, she responded by saying that the description fit her daughter very well. Jenny had always loved motorcycles and fast cars, and often said that she enjoyed hearing the roar of the engines. On the other hand, she had never really shown signs of anti-Semitism or racism. Apparently it was not the ideology of Nazism which had attracted Jenny, but the outward trappings that she "remembered" from a previous life. This insight gave Mrs. Brown and me a clue as to how Jenny's energy might be diverted into a more positive direction.

I suggested that Mrs. Brown talk about reincarnation with Jenny, to see if her daughter had any feelings about a previous life in Germany. In addition, Mrs. Brown might encourage Jenny to join a marching band, where she could legitimately wear a fancy uniform and play military music in public parades. Jenny should also look for an occupation or hobby where she could operate a fast, roaring machine, perhaps a motorcycle or racing car. In this way she could be a "hero" without the negative trappings of fascism.

I never heard from Mrs. Brown again, so I do not know what happened to Jenny. Perhaps she is even now winning trophies on the racetrack. But her story does bring up an interesting question. If the Jews and other victims from the Holocaust have returned, then what about the Nazis? Are they once again among us?

Yes, I certainly do believe that the Nazis are returning—it would be ridiculous to think that only innocent souls reincarnate! For obvious reasons, I doubt that any "hard-core" Nazis, reincarnated or otherwise, would want to consult with a rabbi. Therefore, I have not had any opportunity to personally meet with reincarnated individuals who still believe in Nazism. But if we consider the recent resurgence of right-wing organizations in America and around the world, then it is not too difficult to believe that the souls who were Nazis in a previous life are once again among us. Some such souls have, no doubt, learned from their mistakes and progressed beyond fascism. But I believe there are many other souls who are repeating the same mistakes this time around.

Of course, we could also offer sound sociological

reasons for the recent rise in hate crimes. The United States' economy is now in recession, and many youth today do not see much hope for the future. Demagogues of all varieties thrive on this feeling of hopelessness, attracting followers by providing simplistic answers to complex problems and by promising prospective recruits that they can "be somebody" by putting others down. Nor is this tactic limited to "white supremacists." The late Rabbi Meir Kahane, former member of the Israeli Parliament and founder of the Jewish Defense League in the United States, advocated deporting all Arabs from Israel. Kahane also used the same kind of demagogery as Hitler, so much so that "Kahanism" has become a synonym among Jews for this repugnant political platform. Unfortunately, hate comes clothed in all colors, religions, and ethnic groups.

But why do some individuals succumb to racist propaganda and others do not? From a kabbalistic perspective, what I believe happens in hate groups is that the members set aside (or never develop) the higher *neshamah* or rational aspects of the soul. Instead, they function primarily on the lower emotional levels of *ruach*. While intense emotions can sometimes make us "feel good," they are often mindless. Demagogues know this and purposely play on feelings of jealousy, anger, frustration, and hate in order to stir up the crowd. Without the "inner voice" of conscience to evaluate what the demagogue is actually saying, it is all too easy to get caught up in the mindless emotions of the mob.

This is why Torah gives a specific commandent that "you shall not follow a crowd to do evil."[1] This commandment affirms our free will to think for ourselves, rejecting hate and exercising love. But such a seemingly simple teaching is among the most difficult to put into practice, because it often means standing alone against the powerful forces of peer pressure. The rewards for doing this are not always obvious on the physical level, but learning to "do the right thing" under adversity is one of the most challenging tests a soul can meet. Consider the following story, told by a past-life reader at one of my workshops on "Reincarnation and the Holocaust," on August 4, 1986, in Minneapolis.

The client was a young woman who had come to the psychic reader with questions about a current love relationship. The reading revealed that, in a previous lifetime during World War II, the client had been a Jewish woman, whom we shall call "Malkah," and the boyfriend had been a German soldier, whom we shall call "Hans."

In physical appearance, Hans was the epitome of the Aryan ideal, tall and muscular, with straw-blond hair and deep blue eyes. But although he looked the part of Hitler's "master race," in his heart he was no fascist. Like so many Germans toward the end of the war, Hans had been drafted into the army quite young, so that now, at the age of seventeen, he found himself stationed at one of the concentration camps.

Hans hated being a soldier. In fact, he hated the whole nationalistic Nazi scene. But nothing had prepared him for the horrors which he was expected to oversee at the camp. Hans knew that if he openly disobeyed orders he would be executed on the spot, so he outwardly hid his feelings. But his heart went out to the suffering prisoners, and he wished there were some way that he could save them. Although Hans realized that he could do very little single-handedly, he tried to "soften" his orders whenever possible and "looked the other way" when necessities were smuggled in.

One day Hans met Malkah, a dark-eyed Jewish girl of about sixteen and was instantly attracted to her. Hans and Malkah fell in love, and he somehow managed to smuggle her out of the camp. For about a year Hans successfully hid Malkah, and she became his personal symbol of resistance against the whole barbaric system. If he could not save all the prisoners, then at least he could save this one woman. Eventually, however, they were both found out and shot.

For the client, having this man come back into her life again in this incarnation was very difficult. I asked the past-life reader what she had counseled her client to do. Although the reader could not give details for confidential reasons, she did say that "we've gone back to another lifetime before the Holocaust, when they also had a relationship, and are working on that." The relationship between "Hans and Malkah" in the camp was apparently based on yet another incarnation together, when their experiences had been much happier. This explained why they had been so attracted to each other during the Holocaust lifetime.

Another woman whose Holocaust incarnation had its roots in a previous lifetime is Esther, who lives in St. Paul, Minnesota. In this life, Esther is a gentle, self-assured Jewish woman who is interested in crystals, aura healing, and metaphysical studies. In the course of her aura healing work,

Esther, too, has met clients who remember dying in the Holocaust and who often carry "scars" from that lifetime in their astral bodies. Her "aura-cleansing" technique includes helping these clients to release the pain from past-life experiences, so that they can move forward in their personal growth.

Esther first heard of my work with reincarnation in 1988, when part of my article "Are Holocaust Victims Returning?" was reprinted in serial form by a local publication, the *Holistic Health Review*.[2] After reading the first installment, she immediately wrote me a letter, explaining that she had met similar cases and would like to talk with me. I phoned Esther and we agreed to meet, with the intention of comparing notes on our healing work.

What began as a meeting between two professionals soon moved into a more personal kind of sharing. When Esther and I came face to face, we both had an immediate sense of recognition. She then told me that after our first phone conversation, she had "remembered" knowing me from another life. Esther believed that I had once been her teacher, not during the Holocaust but in Eastern Europe during the nineteenth century. In that life, Esther told me, I was a rabbi who taught at an Orthodox *yeshiva* (religious school), and she was a male student in his mid-teens, whom we shall call Nathan. In order to understand what comes next in this story, I need to give some historical background.

During the 1800s in Europe, there was a strong conflict between the traditional Jews and the *Haskalah* or secularist "Enlightenment" movement, which had begun in the late 1700s. Because of political and social changes in Western Europe, especially in France and Germany, Jews were now able to move out of the ghettos and into the mainstream of society. But the price of this acceptance was assimilation into the dominant culture. The *Maskilim* or Jewish followers of the Enlightenment philosophy stressed adopting Western styles of dress and speaking cultured German, rather than Yiddish, which they labeled a "backward" language. (Yiddish is linguistically related to German.) Modern Reform Judaism also began in Germany during this period, purposely shedding the age-old Middle Eastern style of worship and patterning Jewish religious services on the German Christian churches. Both the Reform and Enlightenment movements were vigorously opposed by the Hasidim and other traditional Jews, who saw assimilation into European culture as selling one's birthright for a bowl of porridge.[3]

The "enlightened" Jews, on the other hand, wanted their freedom and were willing to pay the price of cultural assimilation. Many went even further, openly mocking the old ways and flaunting their new-found "freedom" by publicly desecrating the Sabbath and Jewish holidays. Others were attracted to the writings of Karl Marx, himself an assimilated German Jew, who coined the expression, "Religion is the opiate of the people." Still other Jews emigrated to the United States, where by and large they quickly shed their religious and cultural heritage to blend into the "melting pot."

Returning to Esther's story, she believed that I had been her rabbi during this period and that I had stood firmly on the side of the traditionalists.

Esther described how, as Nathan, she had once argued with me in favor of the Enlightenment, but I had maintained that it was nothing but foolishness that would eventually lead the Jews to disaster. Young Nathan, however, was disgusted with his teacher's "backwardness" and, therefore, left the *yeshiva* to follow his own heart into the secular world.

Because of this attraction to German philosophy and culture, the soul next returned as a German, whom we shall call Wolfgang. He was probably born sometime during the 1920s, because, like Hans above, he was drafted into Hitler's army as a teen-ager. Wolfgang did not mind serving his country as a legitimate soldier, but he was horrified to be assigned to duty in the death camps. The shock of what he saw there was too much for Wolfgang to bear, and he committed suicide.

This same soul now returned as Esther, who, like so many of the people in this book, was born during the "baby-boom" generation. In this incarnation she is Jewish, with dark hair and olive skin. Although Esther is not religiously observant, she does strongly identify with her people in the ethnic sense. This is apparently a balance between the extreme positions of her two previous lives, when as "Nathan" she had been a rebel who rejected Judaism altogether, and as "Wolfgang" she had been a Gentile assigned to kill Jews, even those who were "Germanized."

Today Esther does not practice in the Orthodox way, but neither does she deny her heritage. The road to freedom, she has learned, does not lie in suppressing one's own culture in order to assimilate, but rather in affirming one's own roots while respecting the roots of others. In addition, Esther believes that her current aura-healing work is a karmic atonement for the wrongs she had committed during her life as Wolfgang.

Let us now consider the subject of "roots" in general, to see how the Nazis might fit into the concept of karmic groups. Please keep in mind that we are not talking about "racial guilt" here, but about individual souls with free wills who choose to come back together life after life. As we have already learned, being born into a particular group or historical situation does not, in and of itself, predetermine one's behavior. Both Hans and Wolfgang above lived as Germans under Hitler, but consciously chose to reject Nazism and were reborn into a more spiritual environment.

Among Hasidic Jews (and many others as well), there is a belief that Hitler was a reincarnation of Amalek, the grandson of the wicked Esau through his son Eliphaz.[4] A later generation of Amalekites "came and fought with Israel at Rephidim"[5] but were defeated by Joshua. Jewish tradition teaches that since the Bible says they "came" and fought, the attack was without provocation. Not only that, the Amalekites did not honorably engage Joshua's troops at the front of the Exodus but attacked from the rear, where the women, children, and elderly were straggling behind.

Amalek thus became the Biblical archetype for those who prey upon the weak and defenseless. While he is a relatively little-known character in Christian theology, Amalek plays an important role in the Jewish world view. He is, in many ways, the closest thing that Judaism has to the concept of Satan. The very word *satan* means "the opposer" in Hebrew and, as we shall see, Amalek and his karmic group have opposed the Jews many times in history.

King Saul, too, fought the Amalekites, wiping out their entire army except for King Agag (also believed to be Amalek returned), who was put to death by the prophet Samuel.[6] Agag apparently had descendants, however, for we are later told in the Book of Esther that the wicked Haman was an "Agagite." (He, too, is regarded as an incarnation of Amalek.) Haman tried to deceive King Ahasuerus into wiping out the Jews, but ended up being hung on the very gallows he had erected for executing the saintly Mordechai.

We see, then, that the Biblical line of Amalek has attacked and attempted to exterminate the Jews in many generations and/or incarnations. Exodus 17:16 tells us that "YHVH will be at war with Amalek throughout the ages." I interpret this to mean that our Creator is on the side of the oppressed, not the oppressor, and we should always champion the cause of "the widow, the orphan, and the stranger," i.e., those who are most helpless and downtrodden.

Nowadays it is no longer possible to prove who is or is not a literal descendant of Amalek, which is probably just as well, because the Bible says that God will "utterly blot out the memory of Amalek from under Heaven."[7] Were it possible to identify Amalekites as a particular ethnic group, this might lead to genocide. Rather than being a genetically related group of people, Amalek and his followers could be a karmically connected group of souls, who have appeared in various guises throughout history. Today it is generally accepted in Jewish circles that "Amalek" refers to a particular type of behavior. In other words, it is now a matter of ideology, not geneology. Therefore, to "blot out" Amalek can mean to eliminate fascist behavior rather than actually killing anyone.

Whether or not Hitler was a literal reincarnation of Amalek, we do not know. But he did act in the same treacherous way, attempting to wipe the Jewish people off the face of the earth. Yes, there were others besides Jews who were massacred, but we must not play down the Nazi hatred of Jews as such. Other groups, like the Gypsies, gays, socialists, and Jehovah's Witnesses, were included in the "final solution" because Hitler perceived them as being somehow connected with the Jews. They died precisely because they were "Jew-like."

In Hitler's twisted world view, the Jews were the source of everything that he wished to destroy: intelligence, tolerance, forgiveness, religion, morality, and peace. Hitler especially despised the Jews for having produced Jesus, with his message of compassion, which Hitler considered a sign of weakness.[8] He also saw the Jews as a "subhuman" race who encouraged "racial impurity" through intermarriage. He therefore considered all other "inferior" races (such as the Gypsies and the blacks) to be in league with the Jews in a plot to destroy the "pure Aryan" race.[9]

Even a cursory reading of *Mein Kampf* ("My Struggle"), written by Adolf Hitler himself, makes it obvious that he considered the Jews to be the root source of every moral, social, and political problem which ever beset the German people. He therefore believed that the extermination of Jews was "necessary" in order to restore Germans to their "superior" role as a "master race." Hitler also saw Judaism and Marxism as synonymous; by linking these two groups, he was able to utilize the widespread fear of Communist revolution in Europe (on the heels of the Russian revolution in 1917) to win followers to his own cause. The complete, unexpurgated text of *Mein Kampf* was not available in English until 1939, which meant that many Americans did not realize the full racist intent of Hitler's program until six years after he had come to power.

But why were the Jews singled out by Hitler in the first place? Perhaps because we were witnesses to the laws of the one God and, therefore, hated by Hitler and all who opposed those laws. In many times and places throughout history, the Jews have been the scapegoats of dictatorships. In the case of Hitler, he did not invent German anti-Semitism, but simply built upon a longstanding and shameful tradition of Jew-baiting which had existed in Europe for many centuries, often encouraged by both the Roman Catholic and Lutheran churches, the two major denominations in Germany.[10]

What the German people under Hitler did not realize is that when one group is scapegoated, the persecution eventually spreads to everyone. Consider the following analogy. Natural gas, which is odorless, is frequently found in coal mines. Before the invention of modern technology, the miners used to take a caged canary down with them, in order to know whether or not the air was good. As long as the bird was alive, the air was safe. But if the bird died, the miners knew to get out before they suffocated or before there would be an explosion.

Were the Jews the "canaries" of pre-World War II by virtue of the fact that they had been vulnerable "strangers" in so many lands? If so, then the rise of anti-Semitism in pre-war Germany should have been a warning signal to everyone that human rights were in danger. It should also serve as a warning to the world in the future. Unfortunately, the world did not heed the signal during the Holocaust until it was too late. By that time, the gas was killing not only Jews, but everyone else as well.

Martin Niemoeller was a German nationalist and anti-communist Christian who had thought, at first, that Hitler would be good for Germany. But Niemoeller was soon disillusioned as the Nazis began imposing their doctrines on the churches as well. Niemoeller's own evangelical denomination, the Confessional Church, publicly opposed the Nazis and their anti-Semitism. In 1937, Niemoeller was arrested and sentenced to Dachau, where he remained until he was liberated by the Allies in 1945. After the war, Niemoeller wrote:

> "First they came for the Jews, and I did not speak out because I was not a Jew; then they came for the Communists, and I did not speak out because I was not a Communist; then they came for the unionists, and I did not speak out because I was not a union man. Then they came for me — and there was no one left to speak out for me."[11]

There is an enduring truth in the words spoken by God to Abraham, "I will bless those who bless you, and curse the one who curses you."[12] History shows that countries which treat Jews and other minorities with love and respect will prosper, while those which do not eventually fall. For example, medieval Spain experienced a "golden age" of science, literature, and the arts under the tolerant rule of the Moorish Muslims, who allowed the Jews and Christians to live in peace. But when King Ferdinand and Queen Isabella had completed their conquest of Spain in 1492, the first thing they did, under the advice of the Queen's Catholic confessor, Torquemada, was to expell all the Muslims and Jews. The expulsion so disrupted Spanish society that the economy collapsed, and, as a result, Spain was never again a major power in Europe.

On the other hand, the Ottoman Empire welcomed the exiled Spanish Jews and thereby began to prosper from their many skills. When Ferdinand and Isabella issued the Edict of Expulsion, the Sultan of Turkey, Bayazid II, immediately issued a counter-proclamation inviting the exiles into his domain. The Sultan is reported to have said about Ferdinand, "Can you call such a king wise? He is impoverishing his country and enriching mine!"[13]

Hitler, too, ultimately destroyed his own country and lost the war largely because of his insane hatred of the Jews. After all, Hitler reviled Jewish scientists like Albert Einstein, whose work ultimately benefited the Allies. Karma always comes full circle.

But beyond the historical reasons behind the Holocaust, there may have been deeper, more mysterious forces at work. I personally believe in the Amalek theory explained above, that there is indeed a karmic group of anti-Semitic souls which has returned in many different guises throughout the centuries. This conflict, I believe, goes all the way back to the days before the Great Flood described in the Bible. To explore this idea, I would like to compare some Jewish materials with the Edgar Cayce readings.

The particular psychic readings relevant to this discussion were given by Cayce between the years 1924-1944, during the very lifespans of both the Nazis and the Holocaust victims. (Hitler himself was born in 1898 and died in 1945.) I realize that Cayce spent his entire life in the United States and, to my knowledge, was never once consulted by any Nazis. Nevertheless, I wondered if the readings contained any information regarding souls incarnate in the first half of this century, which could be useful in understanding the Holocaust. In fact, I did find something very interesting, which seems to support the Amalek theory from Jewish tradition.

Although Cayce was often consulted on specific medical questions, he also gave "life readings," which examined a person's entire life and karmic patterns. In many of the life readings, Cayce told his subjects that they had also lived during the time of an ancient civilization which existed before the Great Flood. In this civilization there were conflicting factions in society just as there are today. The two main opposing groups were called "the Sons of Belial" and the "Sons of the Law of One." It is not clear to me whether these were the actual titles which the two parties used at the time or simply names that Cayce gave them for identification.[14]

The first term, "Sons of Belial," is found in the Bible, where it first occurs in the Book of Deuteronomy in connection with idol worshipers.[15] The Hebrew word for "sons," *b'nai,* can also mean "followers" or "disciples" and, when used in this sense, refers to both males and females collectively. "Belial" is not the proper name of a specific person or idol, but a Hebrew word meaning "worthless." Therefore, the literal meaning of the Biblical Hebrew phrase, *b'nai belial,* is "followers of worthlessness." In the two most commonly used Jewish translations, *b'nai belial* is translated as "base fellows"[16] and "scoundrels."[17] In the Cayce readings, the pre-Flood Sons of Belial were also scoundrels, as we shall see.

The second term, "Sons of the Law of One," does not occur as such in the Bible. However, it is consistent with the imagery and grammatical structure of the Hebrew language. If we were to translate "Sons of the Law of One" into Hebrew, we would have *b'nai torat echad.* As stated above, the first word, *b'nai,* means "followers." *Torat* is a grammatical variation of *Torah,* which, as we have already learned, literally means "teachings" but is often translated as "the Law." This word occurs 114 times in the Old Testament, so it was obviously well known in antiquity. In the Hebrew language today there is also a common phrase, *ben Torah,* which literally means a "son of the Law," that is applied to a Jew who studies Torah and carefully observes the Commandments. I do not know of any other people besides the Jews who specifically call themselves "Sons of the Law." Is it

possible that the Jewish *Torah* and the "Law"
mentioned in the Cayce readings are somehow
connected?

The third word in my Hebrew translation, *echad,*
is the last word of the most central prayer in
Judaism: "Hear, O [people] Israel, the Lord our
God, the Lord is One."[18] If there is any single word
which characterizes Judaism, it is *echad,* which
means "one." The Jewish people today still call
themselves *am echad,*[19] which can be translated
as "one people," "a unique people," or more poeti-
cally "people of the One [God]." Again, I do not
know of any other ancient people for whom the
word "one" is so intimately connected with their
group identity. The phrase *b'nai torat echad,* "Sons
of the Law of One," is very Jewish in both grammatical structure and meaning, and may indicate
that the beliefs of the Jews today have their origins
in the pre-Flood period described by Cayce.

Jews have always seen themselves as witnesses
to the unity of God. Even before the Covenant with
Abraham, which marked the official beginning of
the Jewish people as such, there were prophets
and other individuals who remained loyal to the
One God. The very fact that the Bible begins with
the Creation story and not just the birth of Abraham
(ancestor of the Jews) demonstrates that Jews see
their belief in monotheism as a continuation of a
much older tradition. Seth, Enoch, and Noah were
prophets of the One God, who passed the teachings down to Shem and his descendants.

In the fourteenth chapter of Genesis,
Melchezedek, King of Salem (an older name for
Jerusalem), blessed Abraham with bread and
wine,[20] which is the first mention of a ritual that

Jews of all denominations still do at home every Friday evening to usher in the Sabbath. The Jewish bread-and-wine blessing later became the basis for the Christian communion, complete with the white tablecloth and two candles that are traditionally lit on the Jewish Sabbath table. Melchezedek's bread-and-wine blessing, some mystics believe, was actually an initiation. According to Rabbi Schachter-Shalomi, this same Melchezedek was head of a school of prophets and "the last High Priest of monotheism in the Age of Taurus, passing the torch to Abraham, the first High Priest of monotheism in the Age of Aries."[21]

Through Abraham, the teachings were passed down to the Jews (as well as some other monotheists), who have continued to carry and preserve this belief in the oneness of God throughout the ages. Franz Rosenzweig, a turn-of-the-century Jewish philosopher, suggested in *The Star of Redemption* that it was the role of the Jews to keep the eternal light of monotheism burning, so that others could kindle their own flame of oneness. Christianity, according to Rosenzweig, was never intended to replace Judaism, but rather to supplement it by helping to carry the light of God into the non-Jewish world.[22] At times the Jewish "eternal light" has been only one small candle sputtering in the darkness, but it *was* kept burning, so that today many people around the world believe in the oneness of God.

If there is indeed an ancient connection between the teachings about the one God preserved by the Jews and the information about the Sons of the Law of One as described in the Cayce readings, then there may also be a karmic connection among the Sons of Belial, Amalek, and the Nazis. Although, to my knowledge, Cayce never openly made this claim, he did indicate that many souls from both of these pre-Flood groups were once again incarnating in the beginning of this century.[23] In describing the two groups, the Cayce readings say:

"[The Sons of Belial focused on] the gratifying, the satisfying, the use of material things for self, *without* thought or consideration as to the sources of such nor the hardships in the experiences of others. Or, in other words, as we would term it today, they were those without a standard of morality . . . The Sons of Belial had no standard, save of self, self-aggrandizement."[24]

"[The Sons of the Law of One believed] that the soul was given by the Creator or entered from outside sources *into* the projection of the *mental* and spiritual self at the given periods. *That* was the standard of the Law of One, but was *rejected* by the Sons of Belial."[25]

In other words, while the Sons of the Law of One affirmed the spiritual origins of all humanity, the Sons of Belial had sunk into selfishness and materialism. In the Dead Sea Scrolls, discovered in this century in a cave at Qumran, two opposing groups are also mentioned, called the "Sons of Light" and the "Sons of Darkness," who were engaged in a perpetual battle that would be settled in the Last Days. Many scholars believe that the Qumran sect was a branch of the Essenes, a

Jewish monastic movement mentioned in the writings of Josephus and Philo. Other scholars have
pointed out similarities among the beliefs and
rituals of the Qumran sect and those of the
Pharisees, Sadducees, Zealots, Ebionites, and other
groups of the same period. But all agree that the
sect at Qumran who wrote about the "Sons of
Light" and the "Sons of Darkness" was Jewish,
and that its origins pre-dated Christianity by at
least 150 years.[26] Could these teachings about the
"Sons of Light" battling the "Sons of Darkness"
have been passed down to the Essenes from an
even more ancient source?

From the Cayce readings, there appear to have
been two major issues disputed in pre-Flood days.
One dispute centered on the development of technology, which the Sons of the Law of One used for
healing and helping others. In Biblical times, the
Jewish priests (kohanim) were also responsible for
diagnosing certain diseases, a fact which accounts
for the chapters about leprosy in the Book of
Leviticus. In addition, the name "Essene" is believed to come from the Aramaic essyah, which
means "healer" in both the physical and spiritual
sense.[27]

The Sons of Belial, on the other hand, misused
technology for amassing political power and ultimately brought about the destruction of the
civilization. If the Nazis were indeed the Sons of
Belial returned, then the perversion of advanced
technology for cruel, selfish ends needs no more
comment.

The other issue over which the two ancient
groups argued was the status of certain living
beings whom the Cayce readings referred to as

"things." It is not clear exactly what these "things" were, but they may have been some kind of mutations produced through experiments carried out by the Sons of Belial. At times Cayce seems to be saying that there was a period in prehistory when human souls were not yet fully incarnated into the physical world, but were able to project themselves into animals and other living things on the earth plane.[28] A parallel to this teaching can be found in the kabbalistic idea that the "garments of skin" which God gave Adam and Eve after they left the Garden of Eden were not animal pelts but physical bodies.[29] Be that as it may, the Sons of the Law of One considered these "things" to be fully human because they had souls and, therefore, wanted to grant them equality and education to better themselves. The Sons of Belial, however, thought otherwise and wanted to keep the "things" permanently enslaved:

> "[In pre-Flood times] when there were those periods of disturbances owing to those confusions arising between those in authority that would make for the universality of knowledge of all natures and those that held for castes and for positions."[30]

One of the best-known doctrines of Nazism is that the Aryans were supposedly a "superior race." What is not so well-known is that Hitler was highly influenced by a German pseudoscientist named Hans Horbiger, a self-proclaimed "prophet" who taught that the universe was a constant battlefield for the occult forces of fire and ice. The planet Earth, according to Horbiger, had experienced a number of cataclysmic events in the distant past, when civilizations had risen and had been destroyed and monstrous mutations had occurred. One of these periods of mutation had supposedly produced the Jews, whom Horbiger blamed for the "degeneration" of Nordic supremacy. With the rise of Hitler to power, Horbiger's racist theories became official Nazi "science."[31]

Another important influence on Hitler's beliefs was Alfred Rosenberg, whose book *Myth of the Twentieth Century* became a fundamental part of Nazi thinking.[32] If Hitler's *Mein Kampf* was the "bible" of Nazism, then Rosenberg's *Myth* was its catechism. Rosenberg and Hitler were both initiated into an occult lodge called the Thule Society. Hitler appointed Rosenberg the official "theologian" of the Third Reich, with the task of rewriting history and creating a neopagan religion. Rosenberg's *Myth* attempted to "purge" Western civilization of all Jewish influences and resurrect the ancient gods of Nordic mythology.[33] (Jesus, to Rosenberg, was a blond-haired, blue-eyed Aryan child kidnapped into slavery.) Although people in metaphysical circles often think of "paganism" as a gentle, life-affirming Earth religion, the type of neopaganism preached by Rosenberg and his cronies was heartless and barbaric.

In reading the writings of these Nazi thinkers, I could not help but notice the similarities between their attitudes about non-Aryan peoples and the self-serving way that the Sons of Belial treated the "things" described in the Cayce readings. Were the Nazis reincarnations of souls from the generation of the Great Flood? Or is there an archetypal Amalek/Belial "mob psychology" which emerges among the followers of all demagogues who oppose the principles of freedom, justice, and equalty? Either way, the parallel is striking.

Whether or not Hitler's soul was literally from among the Sons of Belial, it is well known that he was interested in the occult, and many believe that he was a student of black magic. Hitler wanted nothing less than the complete reversal of the laws of God, as symbolized by his version of the swastika. (See Figure B.) This design, which appears in the art and rituals of tribal peoples around the world, is known as the "whirling logs" to the Navajos and Hopis. It was used in mosaic borders by the Romans and appears in Tibetan Buddhism. It is also used in India, which is apparently what led Hitler to see it as an "Aryan" symbol. Drawn in the ancient way, with the logs whirling clockwise, the swastika symbolizes the Four Directions and the harmony of the universe. But, in true satanic fashion, Hitler purposely *reversed* the swastika, turning it into a symbol of utter chaos.

While Hitler was working to usher in an age of chaos, there were other, more positive spiritual forces among both Jews and Gentiles, which were actively opposing him. According to the great sixteenth-century kabbalist Rabbi Isaac Luria, whom we have already mentioned in previous chapters, one of the main reasons for the Jewish rituals is the collective process of *tikkun olam* (tee-KUN o-LAHM) or "repairing the universe." Luria taught that during the primal creation process, the "Holy Vessels" *(sephirot)* which were intended to contain the Holy Light were shattered and "sparks" *(netzotzot)* of holiness fell into lower levels of consciousness. In other words, the universe

Meaning of the Swastika

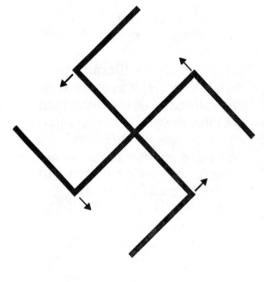

Traditional or "whirling logs" swastika, which turns clockwise, symbolizing harmony in the universe. This is the form used by Native Americans and others.

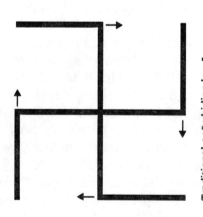

Nazi swastika is tilted and turns counterclockwise, symbolizing chaos. (Note: Versions of this swastika in an untilted form were also used by the Nazis.)

Figure B

Comparison of Swastika from "Earth Religions" with the Nazi Swastika
(To understand the way the swastikas "turn," picture them as four whirling flags streaming out behind the flagpoles.)

"slipped down" a notch, so that what was intended to be purely spiritual became emeshed in the material world.

According to Luria, the 613 *mitzvot* in the Torah are not only for the benefit of the individual Jew who observes them, but are also a theurgic vehicle for "elevating" these exiled "sparks" back to their proper place in the universe. This is why most of the *mitzvot* require the use of physical materials or objects. When the *mitzvot* are done with properly focused intention *(kavannah)*, the psychic energy contained within the physical objects is freed and sent back to the Creator, thus affecting the entire creation. This kabbalistic process is cumulative; when *tikkun olam* is completed, the universe will be ready for the Messianic Age of planetary unity and peace.

Obviously, in order for *tikkun olam* to take place, there need to be Jews performing the *mitzvot*, fulfilling their function as a "kingdom of priests"[34] by helping to keep the planetary energy in balance. Although it is recognized that individual Jews may choose to neglect this responsibility, as long as there are still some—a devoted remnant— who observe the Commandments, the process of *tikkun olam* will continue. (Gentiles, too, can participate in *tikkun olam* by observing the Seven Laws of Noah explained in Chapter Four.)

If Hitler was indeed a black magician, then he would have greatly feared the "white magic" of the thirty-six *Lamedvavniks*, the hidden Jewish saints for whom the world is preserved, as well as the spiritual power of the kabbalists and Hasidic Rebbes whose lives were so totally devoted to God. Somehow Hitler must have sensed that as long as a single Jew remained alive to uphold the Law (Torah) of a just and loving God, then the world as we know it would continue to exist. Only by eliminating every last witness to the Covenant at Sinai could Hitler have established his "Thousand Year Reich." Fortunately he did not succeed.

In 1986 during an informal group discussion in my home, my teacher Reb Zalman, in answer to a question about the meaning of the Holocaust, compared the cosmic role of the Jewish people to the white corpuscles of the human body. These, he pointed out, fight disease by absorbing the invading bacteria into themselves. Individual white corpuscles may die in the process, but the body itself is saved. In the same way, Reb Zalman explained, the Jews have sometimes served as "white corpuscles" in the spiritual body of humanity. When something evil arises in the world, the Jews are often the first to feel the negative energy and absorb its impact. Down through the centuries this has cost us a lot of Jews, but the "body of humanity" was saved.

This is not a popular stand among Jews today. After the Holocaust, many Jews deliberately rejected the age-old idea of "raising holy sparks" and purifying the world through our suffering. God, they said, either did not exist or had forsaken them. So they chose instead to glorify the resistance fighters who grabbed their guns and fought the Nazis with violence. It was as if 2,000 years of persecution suddenly burst forth into an uncontrollable rage. Warriors, not spiritual masters, became the modern Jewish heroes.

I do not fault my fellow Jews for this. I understand their anger, and I empathize. But I also feel that we have lost a great deal by completely denying the validity of martyrdom. Many Jews now ridicule nonviolence in general, saying that a live soldier is better than a dead saint and that Jewish survival takes precedence over all else. Perhaps. But until we can once again have faith in the existence of a life beyond this one, we will continue to find it difficult to regain our spirituality or find inner peace.

During the course of writing this book, I, too, have struggled with my rage at the Nazis. In 1989 I had a very vivid dream, in which I was standing in the lobby of a theater. I was dressed in the Sabbath garb of a Hasidic Rebbe, complete with long black coat, fur hat, and side curls. The name of the play I had come to see was "The Life and Times of Adolf Hitler." All of the people in the audience had already gone inside, and I was alone.

Just as the house lights were dimmed and the play was about to begin, Hitler himself walked in off the street. I expected to be frightened, but somehow I was not. Hitler looked very small, tired, and sad, as if he no longer had any will to live. He picked up a copy of the theater program and walked over to me.

"Look what they are saying about me!" Hitler lamented, pointing to the list of acts from the play about his life. I looked at the piece of paper and saw that all the things Hitler had ever done were listed there, in chonological order, scene by scene.

"Yes," I replied. "That is how you are remembered on earth."

A terrible look of pain came over Hitler's face. Then he broke down and began to sob like a heartbroken child. At first I thought to myself, "It serves him right," but then, before I even knew what I was doing, I had put my arms around the sobbing Hitler and was comforting him. I explained that if he was truly repentant, then the door to forgiveness was open to him the same as to any other sinner, but the road would be very, very difficult. Hitler nodded in agreement, expressing his willingness to try.

At that moment a van arrived outside the theater, and a dark-skinned man, a retarded boy, and an old woman in a wheelchair came out and entered the lobby. They said, "We have come to take him to the next level." Hitler left with the three people, and they all drove away in the van. Then I awoke.

Could I have hugged Hitler in real life? Probably not. But the world of dreams is a strange place, where logic is sometimes suspended in order to deliver a message. This dream was not really about Hitler repenting. It was about me letting go of my own anger. The battle between good and evil is enacted not only in the world at large but also within ourselves. Every one of us is a potential Hitler and a potential Rebbe. In my dream, these two opposing sides of me had finally met face to face and were reconciled. The angry side could then begin to heal. I have no idea whether the real Hitler ever repented in the next world, but because of this dream I now feel more at peace and much closer to God.

Chapter 10:

Phoenix from the Ashes

Judaism has always been a religion of hope. Even in the darkest periods of our history, Jews have looked forward to the "light at the end of the tunnel," when the world would live in peace. This theme of moving from the darkness into the light is deeply ingrained in the Jewish psyche and encoded in our liturgy. Jewish days begin at sundown, following the pattern of creation in Genesis: "There was evening, and there was morning." The months on the Jewish calendar begin at the dark of the moon, progessing toward the light. The Passover seder, too, affirms this promise of better days in the opening lines: "This year we are slaves, next year we will be free!"

Perhaps nowhere is this Jewish focus on hope more clearly expressed than in the observance of Tisha B'Av, which marks the destruction of the First and Second Temples in Jerusalem, as well as many other tragic events in the long centuries of our exile. On one level, Tisha B'Av is the saddest day on the Jewish calendar, observed by fasting and chanting the Book of Lamentations in a mournful dirge. But at the same time, it is also a day filled with infinite hope, because a longstanding tradition says that the Messiah will be born on this date. Therefore, although the observance of Tisha B'Av begins at sundown with a heavy focus on tragedy, by the following afternoon, even in the midst of our fast, we are already looking toward the future, when the Messianic Age will rise like a phoenix from the ashes. Tisha B'Av is thus a day which begins in darkness but moves toward ever-lasting light.

In 1969 I was in South Dakota on Tisha B'Av, far from any Jewish congregation where I might join in the communal observances. I therefore decided to observe the fast as a personal vision quest. Toward sundown I climbed to the top of a hill in the middle of the South Dakota prairie, taking only a blanket, a candle, and a Bible. The night was chilly but perfectly clear, with the Milky Way and stars so bright that they seemed only inches away. I was both awed and humbled. After completing the required prayers and Bible reading by candlelight, I curled up in my blanket and fell asleep.

Toward dawn I had an out-of-body experience, in which I was shown a panorama of all my incarnations in the various periods of Jewish history. Then, still in the vision, I was flying over the prairie, looking down on a huge circle of people from all races, religions, and nationalities, who were dancing around the Tree of Life. They were clad in their national costumes and wearing rain-bow-colored prayer shawls, singing a line from Psalm 97 in Hebrew: "Light is given to the right-eous, and joy to the upright in heart."

The meaning of the vision was obvious, but one

thing baffled me. Why were all these different peoples wearing *Jewish prayer shawls* and singing in *Hebrew?* I rejected outright the idea that the world would become Jewish—not only did that contradict the rest of the vision, but it was chauvinistic as well. Nevertheless, I puzzled over this for eighteen years.

Only recently have I come to understand the full meaning of the vision. The people in the circle were not converting to my religion but affirming together that "Jewish is beautiful." By clothing themselves in Jewish prayer shawls, they demonstrated their belief that Judaism is a valid spiritual tradition in its own right, as deep and strong as any other.

Back in the sixties, even the Jews themselves were not so sure about that. The trauma of the Holocaust had driven us from our own house of mourning to other spiritual paths, in search of joy and love. I believe that many of the Jews born after World War II had indeed reincarnated from the Holocaust, but we (and I specifically include myself here) came into the world filled with unspeakable pain and with internalized victimization. We therefore tended to conceal our Jewishness under cloaks of fear or hide in the "closet" of the dominant culture. Although there were many, many Jews involved in the peace movement, the civil rights movement, and other activities for social change, rarely did we do it *as Jews.*

In the non-Jewish world, too, there was seldom any real acknowledgment of the spiritual side of Judaism in those days. I remember how, when Biblical verses about beating "swords into plowshares" were read at peace rallies, they were generally thought of as "Christian." Even in more recent decades, people in metaphysical circles still tended to believe that the role of the Jews in planetary evolution had ended with the coming of Jesus. This inaccurate theology has, in my opinion, contributed to a "blind spot" when it comes to understanding the religious life of Jews today.

In April 1987, a Midwestern Catholic college sponsored a major symposium on "The Development of the Human Person in Eastern and Western Spirituality." The roster included representatives from a wide cross-section of religious and philosophical backgrounds; there were Buddhist and Catholic monks, Hindu yogis, Native American shamans, and a Chinese T'ai Chi master, as well as secular psychologists, philosophers, and feminist thinkers. It was, the planners thought, a well-balanced and inclusive program.

But when the publicity hit the streets, the college began receiving irate phone calls from members of the Jewish community. Why, the callers asked, were there *no Jews* included in this rainbow of religious speakers?

The planning committee was genuinely embarrassed. When I was called in at the last minute, their representative explained apologetically, "After it was pointed out to us, we asked ourselves how such an oversight could have happened. In the course of our discussion we realized that although the assumption was unspoken, it was there: none of us thought that Jews had any spirituality."

I agreed to go to the conference and had many wonderful conversations with spiritual teachers from all over the country. As a direct result of my

participation in this symposium, I was invited to
be the Jewish speaker for another multicultural
gathering, this time in Denver, Colorado, for the
observance of the Harmonic Convergence on August 16-17, 1987. The Convergence was billed as
a cosmic event based on the Mayan calendar,
when, according to their prophecies, an age of
peace would begin. As it turned out, it was in
Denver that year where I would finally see my 1969
vision fulfilled.

But first, I had to overcome the same "blind
spot" about Jewish spirituality in these "new age"
circles that I had encountered in the Christian
world. During all of the national publicity about
the Harmonic Convergence celebrations, there
was virtually nothing said about Jewish prophecies, in spite of the fact that the Jewish calendar
and the Mayan calendar are only twenty-three
years apart. For Mayans it was 5725, while for
Jews it was 5747. Not only that, but the two
calendars actually meshed during the Convergence!

The Mayan calendar is quite complicated and is
said to be more accurate than the Gregorian
calendar commonly in use. In addition to days,
months, and years, the Mayan calendar also marks
larger cycles of time. The cycle which ended in
1987 began in the early sixteenth century in the
year 1519. Note that this was not too long after
Columbus "discovered" America in 1492. We have
all heard how the Aztec Indians mistook the Spaniards for gods. This was apparently based on the
fact that they arrived near the end of a major
calendar cycle, when messianic changes were
expected.

The Spaniards, however, turned out to be false messiahs, ushering in "Nine Hells" of horror and conquest. The Harmonic Convergence marked the end of the "Nine Hells" and the beginning of the Mayan Messianic Age. The focus of the Mayan prophecies was not on any particular individual as the peacemaker but rather on an outpouring of blessings from the Cosmic Tree of Life to the entire planet. (This concept of a "collective messiah" parallels some Jewish beliefs, as we shall see later.)

The Convergence itself was preceeded by twelve days of purification, beginning on August 4, during which individuals and nations were supposed to prepare themselves for entry into the coming new age. Strangely enough, the first day of this purification period coincided with another day on the Jewish calendar—Tisha B'Av, the date when, as explained above, the Messiah would one day be born. (The Jewish calendar is lunar, not solar, and the last time Tisha B'Av had fallen on August 4 was in 1949; it will not do so again until the year 2033.) Even stranger, the day before Columbus set sail in August of 1492 was also the deadline set by Ferdinand and Isabella (who financed his voyage) for the Jews to leave Spain—and it, too, fell on Tisha B'Av!

In addition to Columbus' voyage, the Spanish Inquisition, which would eventually burn thousands of Jews, Muslims, and pagans at the stake in both Europe and the Americas, was also set into motion that same year. For both Jews and Native Americans, the year 1492 marked the beginning of centuries of persecution and exile. And both cultures, it now seems, are still struggling with the impact of those events 500 years later.

Arthur Waskow, who teaches at the Reconstructionist Rabbinical College in Philadelphia, has also noted the parallel between Native American and Jewish histories. The years from 1492 to 1945, Waskow says, were two sides of the same coin, which he terms the "Modern Age." It began with the shattering of traditional communities—the Jews of Spain and the Incas in South America—and ended in the gas chambers of Auschwitz:

> "These dates, these milestones in the biography of the human race and of the Jewish people—from 1492 to 1945, from the 'discovery' of America to the invention of the atom bomb; from the expulsion from Spain to the 'invention' of the Holocaust—are profoundly intertwined . . . We stand in the ruins of the old world-systems, barely covered by the ruins of the more recent ones. We have not yet drawn the blueprints for some new living spaces where we can live out a human span."[1]

At the Convergence gathering in Denver, I had many opportunities to meet with tribal peoples from all over North and South America. I also learned about another parallel in our histories: Hitler had patterned his treatment of the Jews on the way in which the ruling powers in the Americas had treated the Native peoples, a point which he had discussed in *Mein Kampf*. The Indian reservations of the nineteenth century were, according to several speakers, primitive forerunners of the concentration camps, differing in their levels of technology but with basically the same intent. Whereas the Nazis had used sophisticated means for exterminating the Jews, the American military had relied on imprisonment, starvation, and smallpox-infected blankets to wipe out entire tribes who had no resistance to this disease. But in both cases, the oppressors had rounded up the people, confiscated their land and possessions, then force-marched them to isolated locations where they could be demoralized and destroyed.[2] Many Native Americans, therefore, believe that they, like the Jews of Europe, were victims of a systematic attempt at genocide. Fortunately, both the Jewish and Native peoples have survived, although both are still deeply wounded by the experience.

I have frequently been asked how long it will take to "get over" the Holocaust. When I reply that it will probably be many generations before this karma is completely healed, the listener is invariably disappointed. Yet if we look at how the negative impact of the "Columbus encounter" is still being felt by Native peoples five centuries later, then it is not unreasonable to assume that the Jews, too, will be affected by the Holocaust for many years to come. However, I do believe that we can speed up this healing process for both Jews and Native Americans by actively confronting our prejudices and by working toward a more humane and loving world. In addition, we can each continue to work on our own individual karma.

At the Denver gathering I learned that many Native Americans believe in reincarnation and attribute their recent cultural revival to the return of the souls of "medicine people" who died a

hundred years ago. These people, it seems, are
"remembering" the ceremonies that had been lost
so long ago. This parallels my own feeling that
many Jews from previous centuries are once again
incarnating—a subject we shall return to later.

On the morning of the Convergence itself, we
gathered in a huge circle on the rotunda of the
Colorado State Capitol for a sunrise ceremony
conducted by descendants of the Mayans and
Aztecs who had come from Mexico. Hundreds of
people from every possible tribe and nationality
were there, dressed in a colorful array of traditional costumes. I was the only person actually
wearing a Jewish prayer shawl (rainbow-striped,
of course), and we danced to drum beats rather
than Hebrew chants, but in all other ways it was
a fulfillment of my vision. Although there was no
visible Tree of Life in the center of the circle,
symbolically it was there, because the Convergence itself focused on that theme. I felt as if
the Cosmic Tree was indeed standing among us,
even though it was invisible.

Seven weeks after the 1987 Tisha B'Av that
ushered in preparations for the Harmonic Convergence, a new year began on the Jewish calendar
which also had special significance. Because the
Hebrew alphabet originally had no numerals, dates
are traditionally written by using Hebrew letters
according to their numerological values. These
letters often spell words or acrostics and are
regarded as an omen for the coming year. The
Jewish year, 5748, which began on September 24,
1987, is represented by the letters TAV-SIN-MEM-
CHET. What does that spell in Hebrew?
Tismach—"You shall rejoice!" In the Jewish com-

munity, *totally independent of the Harmonic Convergence*, many people saw this as the most hopeful sign in decades, because some of the letters for previous years had spelled out rather ominous messages. So hopeful was the omen, "You shall rejoice," that some Hasidic Jews even expected 5748 to be the year of the Messiah.

Why the writers and planners who publicized the Convergence did not pick up on this incredible merging of two ancient calendars I do not know, except that it was obvious many people were simply ignorant of our calendar and our teachings. I am inclined to believe that, at the time most of the Convergence participants were still thinking in terms of "Judeo-Christian tradition" and simply did not realize that Judaism and Christianity are independent religions with two separate sets of prophecies.

Sharing prophecies was one of the most interesting parts of the Convergence gathering for me. I admit that I am not entirely sure how to relate to this phenomenon of prophecy. Are these foretellings merely the archetypal dreams and visions of oppressed peoples, yearning for a new and better day? Or do prophets really see into the future? If so, what about free will? I have no easy answers to these questions. What I currently believe is that, although we have free will, there are major patterns in history which prophets sometimes glimpse from afar. From a Jewish perspective, these glimpses are not necessarily written in stone; the prophet states *what could happen if* the people continue on their present path. However, there is always room for repentance, and a sincere change of heart can "avert the evil decree," as we saw in the story of Jonah. (See Chapter Seven.)

I find it fascinating that so many of the prophecies from peoples around the world seem to converge on this century. If that is so, then World War II may have been far more than a political confrontation among secular superpowers. In fact, even before the war broke out, interpreters of prophecy in many traditions were predicting that the "End of the Age" would occur in this century.

In 1868 the chief rabbi of Rumania, Meir Loeb ben Y'hiel Mikhael Malbim, expected the Redemption to begin in 1913 and the Temple to be rebuilt in Jerusalem by 1928.[3] Although this obviously did not happen, it is interesting that 1914 marked the beginning of World War I, which, in turn, set the stage for the rise of Hitler. If World War II plays a role in Jewish prophecy, then perhaps Rabbi Meir Loeb was correct in his calculations. But instead of ushering in the Redemption itself, 1913-'14 was the beginning of a conflict that might have been the "birth pangs of the Messiah," i.e., the "Great Tribulation," after which the Messianic Age is expected to rise like a phoenix from the ashes.

As Hitler rose to power, students of the writings of Nostradamus saw in the Third Reich a fulfillment of some of his prophecies. Nostradamus, they claimed, had accurately foretold the American Revolution, the French Revolution, and the rise and fall of Napoleon. After Napoleon, there were to be two more tyrants: a German who "rules from the most horrible throne ever known" and an Arab or Persian in a blue turban. "The Germans and their neighbors will be in a war for the control of the regions of the clouds," wrote Nostradamus in the 1500s, four centuries before the invention of the airplane. He even named the German tyrant and was off by only one letter; Nostradamus had called him "Hister."[4]

Also during World War II, many Jehovah's Witnesses saw in Hitler the fulfillment of the anti-Christ prophecy depicted in the Book of the Revelation and were preaching that the end of the world was at hand. To this day Jehovah's Witnesses everywhere refuse to belong to political parties or serve in any army, and because of this stand they were systematically persecuted by the Nazis as soon as Hitler came to power in 1933. By refusing to wear the swastika, which they regarded as the "mark of the beast," on their arms or salute the Nazi flag, many of these Witnesses went to their deaths in the concentration camps.[5]

Other Christians, too, saw Hitler's "crooked cross" as a sign of Satan and the Time of the End. They pointed to the fighter planes overhead as being the "locusts" prophesied in the ninth chapter of the Revelation, with their "iron breastplates" and "faces of men" looking out of the cockpits. The planes did indeed roar "like many chariots" and their "sting was in their tail," in the form of strafing bullets and bombs which exploded into "fire from the sky."

Meanwhile, in the southwestern United States, the Hopi Indians were also seeing the fulfillment of their own ancient prophecies. It was foretold that when the "black road" crossed the land and the "white road" (jet trails) crossed the sky, then two powerful populations would appear, one with the sign of the sun (Japan) and the other with the sign of the reversed swastika (Germany). These two powers would "shake the earth twice" (World Wars

I and II?) before the Great Purification Day. After this "shaking the earth" happened, the Hopis were to journey to a large meeting house by the Big Waters, where "the sun shines through the walls" and the "chiefs of all nations meet."

In 1957, six spiritual leaders of the Hopi and their interpreter, Thomas Banyaca, journeyed eastward to the glass-walled United Nations building with the intention of addressing the General Assembly. They were unable to get through the bureaucracy, however, and were told that it would take four months to get on the agenda.

The Hopi leaders left the U.N. building and journeyed to the Pentagon in Washington, D.C. But once again, they were confronted with red tape. Fortunately the local news media picked up on the story, and the Hopis were then able to deliver their ancient warning: we must all live together in peace or a "gourd of ashes" will fall on the earth, poisoning the water and atmosphere.[6]

Can all of this be mere coincidence? I doubt it. In fact, I personally believe that World War II does fulfill the "last days" prophecies from many different cultures and that the Holocaust was indeed the "birth pangs of the Messiah" foretold in Jewish prophecies. I wish to make it clear that I am *not* saying that God ordained the Holocaust. What I do believe is that psychic warnings were given about this century which, had they been heeded, might have prevented a great deal of suffering. In Jewish prayers we ask for the "rebuilding of Jerusalem" and the Messiah to come "speedily in our time." One traditional way of reading this says that, sooner or later, the Messiah *will* eventually arrive; "speedily" in God's time, if we all consciously work toward it, but otherwise "in our [earthly] time," with all the trials and tribulations in between.

But before I can take you further into this theme, I must first clarify what Jews mean by "Messiah," because this word means many things to many people. To begin with, the word "messiah" comes from the Hebrew *mashiach* (pronounced "mah-SHEE-akh") and simply means "anointed." *Mashiach* can be used either as a noun or an adjective, and there are also verbal forms. The term first appears in Genesis 31:13 in connection with a stone pillar where Jacob poured out holy oil and made a vow. The word *mashiach* does not appear again in the Bible until the twenty-eighth chapter of Exodus, where it is used many times as part of the instructions for consecrating the Tabernacle and the Israelite priesthood. These instructions were first carried out by Moses, as described in the eighth chapter of Leviticus:

> "Then Moses took the anointing oil and anointed the Tabernacle and all that was in it, thus consecrating them. He sprinkled some of it on the altar seven times, anointing the altar, all its utensils, and the laver with its stand, its base, to consecrate them. He poured some of the anointing oil on Aaron's head, and anointed him, to consecrate him."[7]

Aaron the High Priest was thus the first "anointed one" or "messiah" in the literal sense. This practice of anointing individuals with consecrating oil continued throughout Biblical times, both for ordaining priests and for installing kings in office. King Saul and King David, for example, were both "messiahs." The prophet Isaiah, who was neither a priest [God] nor a king, declared that "YHVH has *anointed* me to preach,"[8] indicating that *mashiach* can imply a mission as well as an office.

In all of these examples, the people or objects which were anointed became holy (*kadosh*) and were specifically designated or "set apart" for the service of God. Holiness in the Jewish sense does not mean superiority or flawless perfection, nor does it mean that the person becomes a god. Holy people serve God, but they remain human and can still make mistakes. Only God is perfect; all else is constantly evolving toward ever-increasing perfection.

In addition to referring to specific individuals as anointed, the Bible also uses the word *mashiach* in a more collective sense. In the nineteenth chapter of Exodus, God sends Moses with a message to the Jews gathered at the foot of Mt. Sinai: "If you will obey me faithfully and keep my Covenant, you shall be My treasured possession among all the peoples. Indeed, all the earth is Mine, but you shall be to Me a kingdom of priests and a holy nation."[9]

While this verse does not specifically use the word *mashiach*, it does refer to the Jews as "a kingdom of priests" and, as was mentioned above, priests were always anointed when they assumed their office. Therefore, whenever the phrase "God's anointed" appears in a collective sense in the Bible, Jews today understand it as referring to the entire people, the anointed kingdom of priests; in other words, a collective messiah.

This is not to say that there are no Jewish traditions about a personified human messiah.

Throughout the centuries, many individuals have claimed to be messiahs, and many sects of Jews (and sometimes non-Jews, too) have followed them. But in addition to the usual understanding of *mashiach* as a specific person who delivers the people from oppression, there is also a strong argument within Judaism for a collective messiah.

As we have already learned in Chapter Nine, the kabbalists of the Lurianic school saw the process of *tikkun olam* ("repairing the world") as a necessary prerequisite for the coming of *mashiach.* According to Gershom Scholem, this teaching represented a very radical shift in focus, because it meant that instead of the Jewish people waiting for the Messiah to come to them, the people themselves now took an active role in the redemptive process. In a mystical sense, *mashiach* was no longer seen as a single person with miraculous powers to transform the planet but rather the collective soul of the Jewish people.[10] Many post-Holocaust Jews now speak of a "Messianic Age" rather than any one individual acting as the Messiah. Arthur Waskow, who was cited above, frequently refers to "bringing *mashiach*" in connection with social activism.

My purpose in citing all of these prophecies and traditions is to show that Jews continue to play a very important role in the spiritual evolution of the planet and that we are not as "separate" from the rest of the world as some people imagine. The "modern" metaphysical concept of collective shifts in consciousness is not really so new but is a restating of the Jewish concept of a group messiah. Jews have always maintained that *mashiach,* in whatever form it finally comes, will

bring concrete, physical "peace on earth" right
here on the planet. If, as I believe, we have already
passed through the "great tribulation" foretold in
so many traditions, then we are now at a very
crucial moment in history. And if there is indeed
a "collective Messiah," then we are all part of that
process.

What this means on the individual level is that
each and every one of us, Jew or Gentile, can
participate in the redemption of planet Earth.
Every spiritual act, every prayer, every "good work"
that we do is one more step toward the Messianic
Age. Seen in this light, the everyday activities of
our daily lives take on a significance of cosmic
proportions. "Run to do a minor *mitzvah* as you
would to do a major one," says the Talmud.[11] But
do we really know which deeds are "major" and
which are "minor"? A seemingly insignificant act
of kindness can set up a chain of events that may
change the course of our lives—perhaps even the
course of history.

We began this chapter by focusing on the metaphor of moving from darkness into light. It is a
curious fact that every major destruction of a
Jewish community has been followed by a revival
of Jewish spirituality fifty to seventy-five years
later. And each time the phoenix has risen from
the ashes, bringing new insights into Jewish
thought.

The Babylonian Captivity, in which the First
Temple was destroyed and the people carried off
into slavery, must have seemed like the end of the
world to the Jews of that generation. With no
Temple, no sacrifices, and so far from home—how
could they "sing the Lord's song in a strange

land"?[12] Yet that very exile brought about the establishment of the first synagogues, where people realized that they did not need a central Temple in order to worship. God, they had learned, was not limited to any one place but could be found everywhere. Seventy years later, when the Jews returned to Jerusalem to build the Second Temple, they were stronger in their faith than before. God would once again have a house in Jerusalem, but was one and the same in all places.

The destruction of the Second Temple brought another exile, followed by another transformation of Jewish life. This time, the Temple was not rebuilt and remains destroyed to this day. So every Jewish home became a temple, and the Sabbath table was the altar. The everyday activity of eating food became a holy act of worship. Plus, the Jews now discovered what Abraham Joshua Heschel has termed "the architecture of time."[13] For many centuries to come, Jews would be denied any control over land or living space. Synagogues, houses, businesses—all these tangible aspects of life—could be confiscated at a moment's notice. But nobody could take away the Sabbath, which became a sanctuary from an increasingly hostile world.

The expulsion from Spain in 1492 was yet another shock to the Jewish community. But it, too, was followed by a phoenix from the ashes, namely, the flowering of kabbalah in the Safed community in Israel, which, in turn, infused a deeper level of spirituality into Jewish life everywhere. The *mitzvot* were no longer just commandments to be obeyed; now they had become a vital process for repairing the universe by "elevating holy sparks" to bring *mashiach.*

Then in the mid-1600s, the Cossack leader Bogdan Chemielnicki led a revolt against the Polish gentry and took the opportunity to slaughter the Jews in the process. For a while this tragedy appeared to have broken the spirit of the Jewish people, but a generation later they were once again lifted out of their despair, this time by the Baal Shem Tov, founder of Hasidism. He took kabbalah from the realm of the scholars and gave it to the common people, teaching the ordinary Jews how to worship with true joy under all circumstances. Now even the most commonplace acts of daily life became infused with holiness.

On Rosh Hashanah in 1746, the Baal Shem Tov "ascended to Heaven," where he met the Messiah and asked him, "When will you come?" The Messiah answered, "When your teaching will spread and be revealed in the world . . . then all the 'husks' [negativity] will perish, and that will be the time of grace and salvation."[14] When the Baal Shem Tov had this vision, Hasidism was an obscure Jewish sect in the "backwoods" of the Carpathian Mountains. Within a generation it would spread like wildfire throughout Eastern Europe. But it would take another disaster of enormous magnitude to spread Hasidism to Jews around the world.

That disaster was the Holocaust. Fifty years have now passed since this latest tragedy, and Hasidism is now "spread abroad" to Jewish communities everywhere, as well as to non-Jews who can now read the Hasidic teaching tales in many languages. Once again, the phoenix is rising, and we can see the beginnings of a Jewish revival.

What is the secret of this resiliency, this ability

which Jews have to not only survive disasters of such magnitude but to come out stronger than before? Sociologists, anthropologists, psychologists—all probably have their explanations for this phenomenon, and they are probably valid. But I also think that reincarnation plays a big role. I believe there is a core group of souls who are committed to returning as Jews and that this "holy remnant" always comes back within a generation or two after the tragedy, when the community has healed enough to move beyond the negative experiences and grow in a new direction.

In the course of collecting material for this book, I have often been asked, "Where are the souls of the Hasidic Rebbes who died?" It is a good question. From the eyewitness accounts, it would appear that many religious Jews faced martyrdom with unwavering faith, secure in the belief that their deaths were *kiddush hashem*—for the sanctification of God's name. Such martyrs probably did not feel the need to come back right away but spent a longer period of time in the Other World. Now that nearly fifty years have passed since the Holocaust, I believe these souls, too, are once again returning and that this partially accounts for the revival of interest in traditional Judaism among youth in the past decade.

In the early 1980s I once asked Rabbi Manis Friedman, a well-known teacher and writer among the Lubovitcher Hasidim, the following question: "If we are getting closer and closer to the time of *mashiach*, why are the Jews of today so much less observant of the Torah's teachings than our ancestors?"

His answer was very interesting. There were, he

said, many very holy souls who had purposely chosen to incarnate in secularized families in order to experience the joy of returning to the Torah. In other words, there was no challenge to being born into it. These particular souls wanted the special *mitzvah* of "doing *tshuvah,*" of soul-searching and finding it for themselves. Over the past decade since I asked this question, there has indeed been a phenomenal return to Judaism among secularized Jews from my generation. In addition, many Jewish children in the younger generations are now more observant than their parents. And the grandchildren often seem much more spiritual than we ever were at that age. Are they, indeed, the souls of saintly martyrs returned?

In addition to these questing souls, I believe that there are many other souls, both Jews and Gentiles, who, although initially traumatized upon reincarnating so soon, have now healed enough to be able to access the spiritual knowledge they carry from pre-Holocaust incarnations. No doubt this same process is also taking place in other karmic groups as well. Mention has already been made of Native Americans who believe that they are accessing spiritual knowledge from past lives before Columbus. In the black community, too, there is a resurgence of African religion and culture, although I do not know if this is ever attributed to reincarnation. But whatever the source of their insight, as all of these people now move into their mid-life years and assume roles of responsibility within their respective communities, they are bringing a new perspective. That perspective, I believe, is *global consciousness.*

In 1971 anthropologist Margaret Mead voiced
the opinion that the "generation gap" of the sixties
was not really about children rebelling against
their parents but about the vast differences among
people born before and after World War II. "What
we're talking about as the generation gap happened only once," explained Mead. "It isn't about
parents not getting along with children, or children rebelling, or changing styles of morality. It's
simply that at the time of World War II *the whole
world became one,* so that there is a complete
difference between all young people and all old
people [in the sixties generation]."[15] (Italics mine)

World War II did indeed unite the world, but it
was a unity based on fear of mutual destruction.
For the first time in recorded history, the entire
planet was involved in the same war. Even those
countries which remained neutral were, nevertheless, affected by it. The war shrank the world to a
global village, and our technology had reached the
point where we could literally destroy the planet.
While people born before this war were still able to
think in terms of "us" and "them," the generation
which followed had a totally different perspective.
With the explosion of the atomic bombs at
Hiroshima and Nagasaki, the entire world became
"us."

But if World War II produced the potential for
total destruction, then the Apollo space mission
gave us the symbol for peace. Once we saw that
magnificent photograph of the bright blue Earth
floating in outer space, it became possible to
visualize planetary unity, because we could "step
back" and see the Earth as it really is. These two
powerful symbols—the atomic bomb and the blue

planet—represent the choices which face us today. Never before have we seen such a literal fulfillment of the words in Deuteronomy 30:19: "I have put before you life and death, blessing and curse. Choose life, if you and your offspring would live."

In 1979 I was part of an intercultural program at the Hillel House (Jewish student center) on the University of Minnesota campus. Also on the program was Eddie Benton Banai, an Ojibwa holy man from Minnesota. As we shared stories and traditions, the discussion turned to the subject of prophecy. Eddie told the group about an Ojibwa prophecy concerning seven "fires" or periods of time, each about 1,000 years long. We are now at the end of the sixth fire and the seventh will either bring complete peace or, according to Ojibwa tradition, total destruction.

I was amazed at how closely this prophecy parallels a Talmudic teaching about Four Ages of Jewish history:

> Two thousand years of chaos;
> Two thousand years of receiving the Torah-teachings;
> Two thousand years for the birth pangs of Messiah;
> And one thousand years of the World to Come.[16]

As I write this, the year (1992) on the Jewish calendar is 5752. Almost 6,000 years. Could the "seventh fire" of the Ojibwa and the "World to Come" of the Jews be the same event? And if so, what kind of world is coming?

The Talmud also says that "the Son of David (i.e., the Messiah) will only come in a generation which is either wholly innocent or wholly guilty."[17] Now if there were ever a generation that was wholly innocent, then the light of love and peace should long since have spread around the world. So obviously the prophecy must go the other way— does this mean that we are all guilty?

I think the answer leans toward yes. Our planet is now so interconnected on the social and economic levels that there is probably not a single person alive who has not caused pollution, hatred, war, violence, or injustice, either directly or by using the products of these things. Don't we all share the guilt, every one of us, for the current mess on this planet, and are we not all partly responsible for one another's actions? If our generation does not come together and bring about the necessary shift in consciousness, there may not be much of a world left. Was there ever a generation that was more "wholly guilty" than ours?

Another Jewish tradition, which Marilyn Rossner cited in the name of her grandmother at the Montreal conference (see Chapter Seven) but which also has its source in the Talmud,[18] says that "the Messiah will come when the whole Jewish people keeps Shabbat twice in a row." Now the Jewish Shabbat is very different from the Puritan-style Sabbath, not only because Jews observe it on Saturday and Christians on Sunday, but also in the spirit of the observance itself. While both groups close their businesses and refrain from work and secular activities, that is where the resemblance ends. For the Puritans (from whom many Americans have inherited their religious concepts), the Sabbath is a heavy, gloomy day for dwelling on one's sins. The Jewish Shabbat, on the other hand, is a day of light and joy, when even thinking about sins is forbidden. Instead, Jews come together in celebration, with prayer, food, songs, and fellowship around a festive table. Shabbat, according to Jewish tradition, is a "taste of the World to Come," a bit of Heaven on earth.

According to this prophecy, if all the Jews around the world simultaneously observed Shabbat, that would create spiritual unity among them regardless of sects or denominations. If they could then maintain that unified consciousness throughout the following week and observe a second Shabbat together, this would presumably set up enough psychic vibrations to cause a "hundredth monkey effect," that is, a collective shift in human consciousness. (The same idea has also been expressed by other groups. For example, Maharishi Mahesh Yogi, the originator of Transcendental Meditation, believes that if only one percent of the world were practicing meditation, it would have a calming effect on the entire planet.)

Both traditions are true. The whole planet needs to work together as one humanity but, at the same time, Jews and other minority cultures need the freedom to work within their specific paths. "Unity in diversity" is what we should strive for, not the stifling conformity of Hitler's *ein Reich, ein Volk, ein Fuehrer* (one kingdom, one people, one leader).

Again, we have a life-and-death polarity. We can choose the fascist path of trying to convert, assimilate, or destroy everyone who is not exactly like us, or we can choose the pluralistic path of appreciating the magnificent diversity of individuals and cultures. As human beings who share the same planet, we are interconnected, yes; in that sense, we are "one people." But at the same time, each culture is special and each person is unique, with a specific "spark" that only he or she can elevate. Not only that, if we prevent others from raising up the "sparks" that they have incarnated to work with, then the entire process of *tikkun olam* is impaired, and the "repairing of the universe" is slowed down. We are, in a sense, a spiritual ecosystem, with each individual part contributing to the welfare of the whole.

The *Zohar*, considered by many to be the "bible" of kabbalistic thought, contains the following beautiful prophecy:

> "Do not expect the coming of the Messiah until the rainbow will appear, decked out in resplendent colors which will illuminate the earth. Only then expect the Messiah."[19]

I do not need to elaborate on the current use of the rainbow as a symbol of unity in diversity. We are rapidly evolving out of Piscean dualism of "us" and "them," and beginning to realize that the world is not "black and white with gray areas." Between the White Light of Emanation and the Black Light of Absorption there is a whole rainbow of possibilities. And each band in that rainbow—each culture, tribe, religion, or whatever—is a legitimate color in its own right. If any color is missing, the rainbow is not complete. And that includes the Jews.

At the present time, many Jews do not really feel

a part of the Global Rainbow, because the scars of the Holocaust are so very deep. Not only that, but many centuries—and incarnations!—of persecution preceded it, and the trauma of these events is still vivid in the Jewish psyche. For many Jews, the very idea of intercultural dialogue is threatening, because in the past the only "dialogue" was when the dominant culture tried to convince the Jews that they should give up their own religion and adopt another faith. Genuine dialogue built on mutual respect is a new experience for all of us, and the process of building trust will require much patience and understanding on all sides.

I deeply regret that it has taken four decades for the world to "break the silence" and begin talking openly about the Holocaust, but perhaps the world needed "forty years in the wilderness" to recover enough to deal with such heavy karma. Each of us, Jew or Gentile, carries some of the pain from that archetypal event. Until we can all freely discuss that pain, it will be very difficult to get beyond it. I wish that I could offer you instant healing, but I would be misleading you. Genuine *tikkun olam*—repairing the world—is a slow and difficult process, and unfortunately there are still many "holy sparks" languishing in exile.

Nevertheless, we must never become discouraged. "It is not for you to complete the work [by yourself]," said Rabbi Tarfon 2,000 years ago, "but neither are you free to quit."[20] Even if we cannot yet see the sun on the horizon, we must always remember that the birds begin to sing an hour before dawn, when it is still quite dark. We in the Aquarian Age are like those first singing birds, announcing that the long night is almost over and taking the first steps toward healing.

And the sun *will* rise. Already we can see the first rays of hope. Within Judaism a spiritual renewal is taking place, and there is also a greater appreciation of Jewish teachings in the world at large. For the first time in many centuries, Jews are being treated as equals. Many colleges now offer Jewish studies programs, while metaphysical publications have begun to feature articles on kabbalah and Hasidism. Some retreat centers, like the Lama Foundation in New Mexico, have actually incorporated Shabbat into their crosscultural programming. Rabbis regularly appear on the rosters of interfaith programs, churches hold Passover seders, and Pope John Paul II has sought reconciliation by officially visiting the synagogue of Rome. In recent years even the Dalai Lama has consulted with Jews of many denominations to discover our secrets for surviving in exile. Judaism, so long battered and rejected by Western civilization, is at long last beginning to be loved, embraced, and respected.

And that, perhaps, is the greatest way to heal the karma of the Holocaust, so that we can all get beyond the ashes. As we have seen in this book, many of the souls who died in that conflagration are once again incarnate among us. This time around, let us all work to heal their wounds by providing a genuinely loving, caring, supportive environment where they can be free to celebrate Jewishness and add their special light to the Global Rainbow. Only when Jews and Gentiles alike can sit "beneath their vine and fig tree, in peace and unafraid," will we finally be able to leave the horrors of the Holocaust behind us, so that the

Age of Peace can rise like a phoenix from its ashes. Now is the time for us all to take the first steps and begin walking toward the sunrise together.

"And on that day shall YHVH be One, and God's Name shall be: One."

"May the One who creates peace in the heavens above, give peace to us, to Israel, and to the whole world. Amen."

Appendix:

Varieties of Jewish Experience

What is a Jew? There is no simple answer. Jews are not a race, which implies a separate biological basis for their identity. There are Jews of all colors and racial types, from the black Jews of Ethiopia to the olive-skinned Jews of the Arab countries to the pale-skinned Jews of Europe. Obviously these people do not represent a separate race, but rather a cross-section of all races.

At the same time, being Jewish is more than a religion, because there is a distinct ethnic identity which has secular dimensions as well. I personally prefer to define Jews as a tribal culture in the anthropological sense. Jews have common ancestors (Abraham and Sarah), a common language (Hebrew), a common land base (Israel), a common religion (Judaism), and common customs revolving around traditional festivals and specific foods. Therefore, "religion" is only a part of being Jewish. There are many secular Jews who have no religious affiliation within Judaism—some are even atheists—but who, nevertheless, still identify themselves as Jewish and are considered as such by other Jews. In the current Israeli population, only about ten percent of the Jews are "religious."

I am sometimes asked how modern Jews could all be descended from Abraham and Sarah, when so many people have obviously converted to Judaism from other groups throughout the centuries. This is easily answered in two ways. First of all, individuals who convert to Judaism are "adopted into the tribe," so to speak, and considered *bona fide* children of Abraham and Sarah. A convert is actually called "son or daughter of Abraham and Sarah" for liturgical purposes. In addition, a child with a Jewish mother and a non-Jewish father will name Abraham as the father for liturgical purposes, because, although membership in the Jewish community itself is passed down by the mother, certain religious functions are inherited from the father. This is similar to many tribal cultures which have both matrilineal and patrilineal clan functions.

Secondly, once a person converts to Judaism, he or she usually marries into the Jewish community, so that their children are "grafted" onto the family tree. In the past, some rabbis were even of the opinion that a convert *must* marry a born Jew, and that marriages between two converts were not valid. (Nowadays this is not so, except perhaps in some very traditional sects.) However, even when two converts do marry each other, *their* children will probably not marry converts, so that at some point there will be a geneological joining of the converted family with the main community.

Theoretically, therefore, all Jews can trace their ancestry back to Abraham and Sarah. In reality there is rarely documentation beyond the Middle Ages because, in the course of so many persecutions and book burnings by anti-Semites, the records have been lost. During the Holocaust, especially, the Nazis attempted to destroy every vestige of Jewish identity, including the synagogue records. However, even if we cannot literally prove that all Jews are descended from Abraham and Sarah, in the mythological sense it is still true. Again, this is a very tribal perspective, where the common ancestors, real or imagined, are considered to be the origins of the people.

Another issue which should be addressed here is the idea of Jewish "separateness." To begin with, there are several different words in Hebrew which are translated "separate," and they do not all mean the same thing. To be "a separate people" does not necessarily imply aparteid but simply to remain a distinctive group within the surrounding society. Therefore, the phrase "a distinctive people" would probably be a better translation. The *Mechilta* (a classical Jewish commentary) says, in reference to the Jews enslaved in ancient Egypt, that they kept their Hebrew names, their language, and their mode of dress. In other words, they did not become assimilated into the dominant culture.

Within the Jewish community itself there is a great deal of diversity, so that speaking of "the Jews" is often meaningless without some further clarification. Although the Gentile world tends to think of Jews in terms of "Orthodox, Conservative, and Reform," these denominational divisions are only about a century old and do not really reflect the lines along which Jews have aligned themselves down through the centuries. Within each of these three groups there are differences of opinion, plus there are many smaller sects outside the "big three." To further complicate matters, many Jews belong to more than one group at the same time, often attending synagogue in one place but studying somewhere else. When it comes to mystical topics, things get even more diversified, because all of the Torah writings belong to all of the people, and Jews in all denominations can now study kabbalah in both the original and in translation.

To help make sense of all this for the non-Jewish reader, I have chosen to follow the usual outline of modern denominational and ethnic differences, putting the groups in alphabetical order for easy reference. Because space is extremely limited, I have not gone into depth about doctrines but have simply given a basic description of each group. The interested reader is encouraged to read further.

Ashkenazic Jews are descended from the Jews of medieval Germany and Eastern Europe. The Ashkenazic (ASH-ken-nazz-ik) culture expresses itself in characteristic foods, music, dances, and style of liturgy, which has a strong European flavor. Many Ashkenazic Jews speak the Yiddish language, which is related to medieval German. The majority of Jews in the U.S. are Ashkenazic, and they can be found in all Jewish denominations. See also "Hasidic Jews."

Conservative Jews are a "middle of the road" denomination between Orthodox and Reform. Although the word "conservative" in the non-Jewish world has political connotations, within Judaism it refers primarily to the style of liturgy. In Israel the Conservative movement is called *masorati,* which means "traditional." Conservative Judaism is the largest denomination in the United States and provides a meeting-ground for Jews who want to keep many of the old ways but also make accommodations to modern society. Most Conservative synagogues conduct services in Hebrew but have equal participation by women and men in all litugical functions. Conservative theology tends toward rationalism, with no official mention of reincarnation, although there are some individuals who believe in it.

Ethiopian Jews are black Jews from Ethiopia who trace their origin to the time of Solomon and Sheba. Because they were cut off from the rest of the Jewish world for many centuries, their rituals and customs do not reflect the teachings of the Talmud but are much closer to the Biblical tradition. Although the Ethiopian Jews have sometimes been called "Falashas," this is actually a name put on them by the non-Jews around them and is considered insulting. The majority of Ethiopian Jews now live in Israel.

Hasidic Jews are followers of the teachings of the eighteenth-century mystic, Rabbi Israel ben Eliezer, known as the Baal Shem Tov or "Master of the Good Name." The Hasidic movement originated in Eastern Europe, and this is still reflected in their style of dress, pronunciation of Hebrew, and customs. Hasidic communities are organized around a Rebbe or holy man who is considered to be an enlightened master. These communities are usually named after a town or city, either the place where the group originated or where their Rebbe now resides, as, for example, the Lubovitcher Hasidim who originally came from the town of Lubovitch, Russia. Because of the Holocaust, very few Hasidic Jews currently live in Europe; the majority now live in Israel, the United States, and Canada. Hasidim are very orthodox in their religious observance but give the rituals a more mystical interpretation. All sects of Hasidim believe in reincarnation.

Havurah does not really refer to a specific sect of Jews but rather to a type of small, informal community. The *havurah* movement began in the 1960s with Jews in the "counterculture" who were dissatisfied with mainstream Judaism. They began meeting informally in each others' homes for worship, study, and social activities. Eventually the movement evolved into a loose network of groups nationwide and began to have an impact on mainstream Judaism as well. Today some Conservative and Reform synagogues also sponsor *havurah-style* groups within their own congregations as a way of building a more intimate feeling of community. Many Jews in the *havurah* movement are open to new ideas and often invite metaphysical speakers to these living-room discussions. See also "Reconstructionist Jews" below.

Orthodox Jews are very traditional, keeping as many of the Torah laws and rituals as possible. Within Orthodoxy there are many different groups, ranging from the modern Orthodox who wear a skullcap but otherwise dress like everyone else to the *haredim* ("ultraorthodox") who dress in long black coats and white shirts, with full beards and dangling earlocks. Orthodox Jews do not usually use the term "orthodox" among themselves but say instead "observant." Although Hasidim are technically "orthodox," the term is not usually used to designate them but rather to refer to the non-Hasidic observant Jews. Regarding the study of kabbalah and belief in reincarnation, this is a matter of individual choice.

Reconstructionist Jews are followers of a philosophy which originated in the United States during the 1930s by Rabbi Mordechai Kaplan. Kaplan wished to remove the "supernatural" aspects of Judaism, such as revelation, miracles, and "choseness." In theory, therefore, Reconstructionism is the most nonmystical of the modern Jewish denominations. In practice, however, this is not so, because over the years the Reconstructionist Rabbinical College in Philadelphia has attracted many "radicals" who were not satisfied with mainstream Judaism and wanted the freedom to experiment. The seminary has been relatively tolerant of this trend, with the result that, somewhat ironically, the Reconstructionist movement has become a harbor for many of the more "new age" theologians and laypersons. Although there are few Reconstructionist congregations outside of major cities, many smaller communities may have an informal group. See "Havurah" above.

Reform Jews are the most "modernist" of the three main denominations, with services conducted mostly in the local language rather than Hebrew. In most Reform Temples the wearing of a prayer shawl or head covering is a matter of individual choice as is observance of the Sabbath, dietary laws, and other traditions. Reform Jews are very active in many movements for social change, regarding such actions as a continuation of the tradition of the prophets. Theologically, Reform tends toward rationalism, often rejecting the authority of texts besides the Bible. Kabbalah is rarely taught in Reform circles, although the individual is free to believe as he or she sees fit. In recent years I have met many Reform Jews who believe in reincarnation.

Secular Jews do not believe in "the religion" but, nevertheless, identify with the Jewish community in the ethnic sense and may be very active in Jewish politics, social services, charities, etc. Many secular Jews also observe some of the holidays, giving them a cultural rather than a religious interpretation. There is even a small seminary for "humanistic Judaism," founded by Rabbi Sherwin Wine in 1969, which trains rabbis who serve more as community social leaders than spiritual mentors.

Sephardic Jews are descendants of the Jews who were expelled from Spain and Portugal during the Middle Ages. Today Sephardic Jews can be found throughout the world. Their culture expresses itself through characteristic foods, music, dances, and styles of liturgy, which have a strong Spanish-Arabic flavor. Many Sephardic Jews speak the Ladino language, which is related to medieval Spanish. Kabbalah flourished among the Jews of Spain and is still studied today, with the result that many Sephardic Jews believe in reincarnation. Most Sephardic Jews in Arab countries have emigrated to Israel, so that Israeli society now has a Sephardic majority, who tend to be Orthodox but can be found in all denominations.

Traditional is a term I use for Jews who observe the old ways, regardless of denomination. I have adopted this word from the Native Americans, for whom "traditional" has the connotation of preserving the ways of the tribe. "Tradition," for Jews, does not necessarily have the negative connotations shown in the Broadway musical *Fiddler on the Roof* but can also mean preserving the religion and culture. The Israeli term for an "orthodox" Jew, *dahti,* literally means "keeper of the knowledge." We should also note that in Israel the Conservative movement is called *Masorati,* which means "traditional" in Hebrew. See "Conservative Jews" above.

Yemenite Jews come from the southern tip of the Arabian peninsula. Records exist of correspondence between the Yemenites and the Jewish philosopher Maimonides in the twelfth century. Today the majority of Yemenites live in Israel, where they continue to preserve their distinctive crafts, music, and traditions. Most Yemenites practice Orthodox Judaism. See "Orthodox Jews" above.

Zionists are Jewish nationalists who regard Israel as the political as well as spiritual homeland of the Jews. When Jews use the word, it simply denotes Israeli nationalism but does not indicate a specific political platform. Zionism comes in many forms, ranging from very militant right-wing groups to equally radical left-wing pacifists. Zionists also come in all denominations and flavors of Judaism. Many anti-Semites claim that Zionists comprise an "international banking conspiracy" but what they really are is a large conglomeration of organizations and individuals who support Israel, even though they frequently disagree about what form that support should take. In Israeli society there is dissent, the same as in any other country. (We should also note here that the infamous "Protocols of the Elders of Zion" is not a Jewish text, but an anti-Semitic forgery originating in nineteenth-century Russia.)

Notes

Chapter 1:
Strange Encounter on a Snowy Night

1. Miller, Rhonda, "The Dilemma of Christ-Oriented Readings," *Venture Inward,* Nov./Dec. 1986, Vol. 2, No. 6, pp. 13-18.

2. Langley, Noel, *Edgar Cayce on Reincarnation,* Warner Books, New York, 1988 edition, pp. 7-10.

3. Baker, Sherry, "Holocaust Revisited," *Omni,* September 1988, p. 82.

4. *National Examiner,* October 18, 1988, p. 15.

Chapter 2:
Flashbacks to Another Life

1. As, for example, in the town of Dubossary, Hungary, on September 3, 1941, when the Germans rounded up 600 elderly Jews, locked them in eight synagogues, and set the buildings on fire. All 600 people died. Cf. Gilbert, Martin, *Holocaust: A History of the Jews of Europe During the Second World War,* Henry Holt and Company, New York, 1985, p. 188.

2. Cf. Zuker, Simon, *The Unconquerable Spirit,*

Zachor Institute, New York, 1980, p. 48.

3. *Op. cit.*, Gilbert, chapters 7-9.

4. Lanzmann, Claude, *Shoah: An Oral History of the Holocaust* (complete text of the documentary film), Pantheon Books, 1985, pp. 72-78.

5. *Ibid.*, pp. 101-102.

6. Langley, Noel, *Edgar Cayce on Reincarnation*, Warner Books, New York, 1967, pp.79-80.

7. For example, Zvi Michaelowsky, who survived the mass execution of 4,000 Jews in Eisysky, Lithuania, on September 25, 1941 (Rosh Hashanah). Zvi was sixteen at the time, and after escaping the death pit was instrumental in forming the Jewish resistance in the Eisysky area. Cf. Eliach, Yaffa, *Hasidic Tales of the Holocaust*, Oxford University Press, New York, 1982, pp. 53-55. See also the incident described in note 8 below.

8. *Op. cit.*, Gilbert, p. 445.

9. Khan, Hazrat Inayat, *The Sufi Message of Hazrat Inayat Khan*, International Headquarters Sufi Movement, Geneva, 1979, Vol. I, p. 129.

10. Edgar Cayce reading 5753-1. [Edgar Cayce's psychic readings are identified by numbers, which were assigned to protect the identities of the subjects. The first set of numbers indicates the person for whom the reading was given, and the second set indicates which number of reading in a series that the subject received.]

11. For example, *Twenty Cases Suggestive of Reincarnation* by Ian Stevenson, *The Search for Bridey Murphy* by M. Bernstein, and *Life Between Life* by Joel Whitton, M.D.

12. *Science Year: The World Book Science Annual 1974*, Field Enterprises Educational Corporation, Chicago, 1974, p. 143.

13. Moody, Raymond, M.D., *Life After Life*, Mockingbird Books, Saint Simons Island, Ga., 1975.

14. *Op. cit.*, Langley, pp. 109-110.

Chapter 3:
The Afterlife in Jewish Teachings

1. Talmud, Sanhedrin 4b.

2. Whitton, Joel, M.D., Ph.D., *Life Between Life*, Doubleday & Company, New York, 1986, p. 71.

3. Daniel 12:2. The Hebrew word, usually translated "everlasting" *(olam)*, can also mean "world," implying physicality.

4. Cf. Psalm 88:10 and Ecclesiastes 9:5, 10.

5. The belief that there is no immortal soul is a basic tenet of the Jehovah's Witnesses' doctrine and appears frequently in their literature. They do, however, believe in a physical resurrection. See *You Can Live Forever in Paradise on Earth*, Watchtower Society, Wallkill, New York, 1989.

6. Ezekiel 37:11-14.

7. Cf. Ezekiel 26:20 and Talmud, Ketubot 111a. Prophetic references to "the Land" *(Ha-aretz)* are standardly seen as referring to THE land, i.e., Israel, in rabbinical exegesis. The Hebrew language has separate words for the idea of "land" in the more general sense: *ha-adamah*, "the earth," and *ha-tevel*, "the planet."

8. Talmud, Ketubot 35b.

9. Morse, Melvin, M.D., *Closer to the Light: Learning from the Near-Death Experiences of Children*, Ballantine Books, New York, 1990, p.88.

10. *Midrash Genesis Rabbah*, 82:6. For an English translation of the *Hekalot Rabbati*, a major work in this genre, see Kaplan, Aryeh, *Meditation and Kabbalah*, Samuel Weiser, Inc., New York,

1982, pp. 41-54.

11. Birnbaum, Phillip, *High Holyday Prayer Book*, Hebrew Publishing Company, New York, 1951, pp. 840-842. The story of the Ten Martyrs is, to my knowledge, included in all Orthodox versions of the prayerbook. In "modernized" Yom Kippur services, however, it is sometimes skipped over or replaced with stories from the Holocaust.

12. Kaplan, Aryeh, *The Bahir*, Samuel Weiser, New York, 1979, "Introduction," p. v.

13. Burke, James, *The Day the Universe Changed*, London Writers, Ltd. (Quality Paperback Book Club ed.), London, 1985, p. 98.

14. This idea has a precedent in the Talmud (cf. Berachot 18b), which tells of individuals who slept in the cemetery on Rosh Hashanah in order to overhear the dead speaking about the future. Rosh Hashanah, of course, is when God writes our fate for the coming year, and the dead were presumed to have better access to this information.

15. Maimonides, *Treatise on Resurrection*, ed. by J. Finkel, American Academy for Jewish Research, New York, 1939, p. 17.

16. Buber, Martin, *Tales of the Hasidim*, Vol. 1, Schocken Books, New York, 1947, p. 61. This is only one example of many, many stories of this type, both written and oral, which are still told about the Baal Shem Tov and other Hasidic masters.

17. *Op. cit.*, Whitton, pp. 10-11, 38-41.

18. *Ibid.*, pp. 38-40.

19. This explanation of the levels of *Olam Ha-Ba* is based on the *Maavar Yabok*, a Hasidic text which, to my knowledge, has never been translated into English. I am grateful to Rabbi Zalman

Schachter-Shalomi for explaining this model to me. A less-detailed reference to "levels" in the next world can be found in Moshe Chaim Luzzatto's classic eighteenth-century text, *Derech HaShem* (see section II, chapter 2), which is a summary of Jewish teachings from previous sources. *Derech HaShem* has been translated into English under the title of *The Way of God*, by Rabbi Aryeh Kaplan, Feldheim Publishers, Jerusalem, 1978.

20. *Bahir*, section 121.

21. *Ibid.*, section 195.

22. John 9:2-3.

23. Deuteronomy 5:2-3.

24. Potok, Chaim, *Wanderings: Chaim Potok's History of the Jews*, Alfred A. Knopf, New York, 1978, pp. 70-78.

25. Exodus 19:8.

26. Deuteronomy 29:13-15.

27. Plaut, Gunter, ed., *The Torah: A Modern Commentary*, Union of American Hebrew Congregations, New York, 1981, p. 1542.

28. Genesis 17:7.

29. Scholem, Gershom, *Kabbalah*, Keter Publishing House, Ltd., Jerusalem, 1974, pp. 344-350.

30. *Bahir*, section 197.

31. *Gates of Reincarnation*, 32. A classic sixteenth-century text by Chaim Vital, one of Isaac Luria's major disciples.

32. *Op. cit.*, Kaplan, p. vii. Also note that the modern word "cabal" for a secret conspiracy is derived from "cabala," an alternate spelling for "kabbalah." The fact that this association was made between kabbalah and secrecy indicates that the existence of kabbalah must have been well-known, if not its actual contents. The mys-

tics, of course, were not "plotting" anything.

33. *Tehillat Hashem* prayerbook, p. 118.

Chapter 4:
Jewish Souls in Gentile Bodies

1. Wiesenthal, Simon, *Every Day Remembrance Day: A Chronicle of Jewish Martyrdom,* Henry Holt & Company, New York, 1987, pp. 198-202.

2. *Ibid.,* p. 250.

3. Stevenson, Ian, *Twenty Cases Suggestive of Reincarnation,* rev. ed., University Press of Virginia, Charlottesville, 1974, p. 385.

4. Quoted in "Holocaust Revisited," *Omni,* September 1988, p. 82. This remark was made by phone interview to *Omni* in response to my work. However, I wonder if Hyman had actually read my article, "Are Holocaust Victims Returning?" because he does not seem to be aware that I had already raised the exact same possibility.

5. Gilbert, Martin, *Holocaust: A History of the Jews of Europe During the Second World War,* Henry Holt & Company, New York, 1985, p. 425.

6. Talmud, Berachot 55b.

7. Lanzmann, Claude, *Shoah: An Oral History of the Holocaust* (the complete text of the film), Pantheon Books, New York, 1985, pp. 101-102.

8. Scholem, Gershom, *Kabbalah,* Keter Publishing House, Jerusalem, 1974, pp. 170-172. See also *On the Kabbalah and Its Symbolism* by the same author.

9. It has occurred to me that the statement in the Gospel of John 1:1, "In the beginning was the Word and the Word was with God," might have originally referred to this Cosmic Torah, which is, in some ways, analogous to the Logos. A Jew

would not say "the Torah was God," but "the Torah became flesh" could, from a Jewish perspective, mean that Jesus' disciples regarded him as a living personification of the Teachings. Hasidim today still regard their Rebbe as a "living Torah."

10. Whitton, Joel, M.D., Ph.D., *Life Between Life,* Warner Books, Inc., New York, 1986, pp. 46-57.

11. Fleer, Gedaliah, *Rabbi Nachman's Foundation,* Sepher-Hermon Press, New York, 1976, p. 55. Conceiving a soul "in purity" refers not only to motive but to the physical observance of the Jewish menstrual taboos and immersion in the *mikveh* (ritual purification pool). These laws are called collectively *taharas ha-mispocha,* "family purity."

12. I have heard this personally from academics on several occasions. I have also heard of many cases where high school students who chose to write about the Holocaust during the 1950s were called "morbid" or suspected of being "disturbed" because they were interested in atrocities.

13. Friedman, Thomas, *From Beirut to Jerusalem,* Doubleday, New York, 1989, pp. 277-278.

14. Genesis 17:14.

15. Cf. Exodus 12:15, 19. The phrase is never used in reference to social crimes, like theft or murder, which, although they carry severe consequences, do not represent a renunciation of Judaism.

Chapter 5:
The Souls of a Million Children

1. Cranston, Sylvia, and Williams, Carey, *Reincarnation: A New Horizon in Science, Religion,*

and Society, Julian Press, New York, 1984, p. 280.

2. Whitton, Joel, M.D., Ph.D., *Life Between Life,* Doubleday & Company, New York, 1986, p. 52.

3. *Op. cit.,* Cranston and Williams, p. 280.

4. Burke, James, *The Day the Universe Changed,* London Writers, Ltd., London, 1985, p. 125.

5. Wiesenthal, Simon, *Every Day Remembrance Day: A Chronicle of Jewish Martyrdom,* Henry Holt & Company, New York, 1986, pp. 4-6.

6. *Op. cit.,* Whitton, pp. 43-51.

7. Langley, Noel, *Edgar Cayce on Reincarnation,* Warner Books, New York, 1967, pp. 109-111.

8. Talmud, Shabbat 89b.

9. Morse, Melvin, *Closer to the Light: Learning from the Near-Death Experiences of Children,* Ballantine Books, New York, pp. 161-164.

10. *Ibid.,* p. 164.

11. *Orach Chaim* 225:2. The "contradiction" between the Talmud's age of twenty for being judged "On High" and the age of bar/bat Mitzvah at age twelve or thirteen seems to allow for a "learning period" where the new adult adjusts to his or her duties. While the person is considered old enough at puberty to be responsible for keeping the ritual commandments, he or she is still living in the parent's home and is not yet fully responsible on the societal level. The age of twenty in Jewish law also marks the time one is legally able to enter into a contract and is the recommended age for marriage.

12. Midrash Ecclesiastes Rabbah 7:28.

13. Genesis 18:27.

Chapter 6:
Black Boots and Barbed Wire

1. Jeremiah 31:15, cited by Matthew 2:18. It was not clear if Mary was quoting the Old or New Testaments, or both.

2. *Venture Inward,* January/February 1988, p. 52.

3. Rudow, Rita, *Voices from the Holocaust,* self-published by Rudow, 6050 S.W. 27th St. #109, Miramar, FL 33023, 1985, pp. 29-30.

4. Gilbert, Martin, *Holocaust: A History of the Jews of Europe During the Second World War,* Henry Holt & Company, New York, 1985, p. 614.

5. Jacobs, Susan, "A New Age Jew Revisits Her Roots," *Yoga Journal,* March/April 1985, p. 34.

6. Netherton, Morris, Ph.D., and Shiffrin, Nancy, *Past Lives Therapy,* Ace Books, New York, 1978, pp. 24-25.

7. *Op. cit.,* Gilbert, p. 101.

8. *Ibid.,* pp. 101-102.

Chapter 7:
Healing the Karma of the Holocaust

1. Leviticus 24:20.

2. Leviticus 19:18.

3. This includes metaphysical circles. In recent years I have noticed an ominous metamorphosis of the "Christ killer" accusation into an accusation that the Jews also "killed" the Goddess! Many neo-pagans and feminists, coming out of (and rebelling against) Christian backgrounds, have, nevertheless, continued to scapegoat the Jews in their anger against what they call the "Judeo-Christian" tradition. The basic argument, which I have heard and read many times, is that there was once

a matriarchal utopia which worshiped a loving earth goddess, but this was ruined with the rise of the "patriarchy" supposedly introduced by the Jews. "The patriarchy" is then blamed for all the current problems of the world. Not only is this historically inaccurate, it also contributes to alienation among Jewish women who would like to be feminists but not at the expense of defaming their own culture. I myself have been verbally "attacked" numerous times by feminists using this simplistic argument. I wish to make it clear that I support women's rights, and I do recognize the harm which has been done by the misuse of the Bible by many groups, but it was hardly "the Jews" who caused this. Within Judaism there is also an active feminist movement which is confronting the issues of sexism both in Jewish liturgy and the world at large.

4. Luke 23:34.

5. Talmud, Pirkei Avot 2:1.

6. Yogananda, Paramahansa, *Autobiography of a Yogi*, Self-Realization Fellowship, Los Angeles, 1946, p. 169.

7. Kübler-Ross, Elisabeth, *On Death and Dying*, Macmillan, New York, 1969.

Chapter 8:
Journeys of the Soul

1. Scholem, Gershom, *Kabbalah*, Keter Publishing House, Ltd., Jerusalem, 1973, p.161.

2. A possible explanation for this attitude of some medieval rabbis might lie in the vast difference in educational levels between Jews and non-Jews at that time. In an age when Gentile kings were often illiterate, the average Jewish

male began learning to read the Bible in Hebrew at the age of five and was studying basic Talmudic texts by the age of ten—a course of study which had already become commonplace in Roman times. Medieval Jews were often used by the ruling classes as accountants, bankers, merchants, and tax collectors precisely because they were able to keep and decipher the records.

In addition, there was a long period during the Dark Ages when free interaction between Jews and non-Jews was forbidden by the ruling powers, and all too often the Jews experienced only the worst behavior of Gentile society. The rabbis did not have the benefits of modern psychology to explain these behavioral cycles of ignorance, scapegoating, and abuse. Therefore, they apparently concluded that Gentiles must have "animal souls" because they so often acted like vicious beasts without any apparent shred of "humanity."

I have heard Holocaust survivors express similar opinions about the Nazis, i.e., that they were "heartless beasts without souls." German psychologist Alice Miller, author of *For Your Own Good*, attributes this "heartlessness" to the abusive system of child-rearing prevalent in Germany at the turn of the century, which shaped the generation that followed Hitler. In addition, Miller traces patterns in Hitler's behavior to specific incidents in his childhood. I think Miller is on target. In my opinion, abusive behavior is a matter of learned behavior, either in this life or a previous one, and not a question of "animal" versus "human" souls.

3. This development of an "inner voice" could be a scientific explanation for a Jewish teaching

which has previously made no sense to me. It is commonly believed among Orthodox Jews that a child before the age of bar/bat mitzvah has the *yetzer hara* (evil inclination) but not the *yetzer tov* (good inclination). Then, at the age of twelve for girls and thirteen for boys, the "good inclination" is somehow "miraculously" bestowed upon the child. I have always thought that this teaching seems to contradict the idea that Judaism has no teaching of "original sin." However, if what we are really talking about here is *learned behavior,* then it makes sense. I believe that the rabbis noticed the emergence of the "inner voice" at this age, but, lacking the benefits of modern psychology, they interpreted it as a matter of theology rather than a stage in brain development.

4. See Jung, Carl, *Man and His Symbols,* Aldus Books, Limited, London, 1964, pp. 67-82.

5. Talmud, Pirkei Avot 2:4.

6. Talmud, Pirkei Avot 2:1.

7. Koran, Sura 26:12.

8. Zohar Chadash 33a.

9. *Gates of Reincarnation,* p. 32. In Talmudic times, some of the rabbis had taught that the "wicked" received their reward for any good deeds they might do while still in this world, so that, upon dying, they simply ceased to exist. This was based, in part, on the line from Psalm 92:7: "When the wicked spring forth like the grass, and the workers of iniquity do flourish, it is that they shall be destroyed forever." The good people who suffered, on the other hand, were being "purified" of their sins while still on earth, so that they could enter Paradise immediately. (Some rabbis were of the opinion that *everyone* ceased to exist at death, and

that only the righteous would be resurrected on Judgment Day—a view still taught by Jehovah's Witnesses.) By Luria's time, however, this somewhat simplistic attitude was no longer philosophically satisfying. While it answered the question of why "bad things happen to good people," it did not solve the problem of how the wicked were to be held accountable for their actions. Luria and his kabbalistic contemporaries, therefore, taught that karma is worked out over many lifetimes.

10. Berg, Phillip, *The Wheels of a Soul*, Research Centre for Kabbalah, New York, 1984, p. 48.

11. The number thirty-six in Hebrew numerology is twice eighteen, the numerical value for the Hebrew word *chai*, meaning "life." For an excellent scholarly treatment of the teaching on the thirty-six *Zaddikim*, see "The Tradition of the Thirty-six Hidden Just Men," included in Scholem, Gershom, *The Messianic Idea in Judaism*, Schocken Books, Inc., New York, 1971, pp. 251-256.

Chapter 9:
Cycles of Return

1. Exodus 23:2.

2. Gershom, Yonassan, "Are Holocaust Victims Returning?" *Holistic Health Review*, Overman Publishing, Minneapolis, Winter 1987 and Spring 1988 issues. Reprint of article which originally appeared in *Venture Inward*, Nov./Dec. issue, 1987.

3. Cf. Genesis 25:27-34, the story of Jacob and Esau. Jews do not interpret this story as Jacob "cheating" his brother, but rather as Esau's lack of spiritual responsibility. The "birthright" in those days included being the religious functionary for

the clan. As first-born son, Esau would have inherited this position. But that was far in the future, and Esau was hungry right now. So he "dispised his birthright" (verse 34) in order to fill his belly.

4. Genesis 36:10-16.

5. Exodus 17:8.

6. I Samuel, chapters 14 and 15.

7. Exodus 17:14.

8. Bamberger, Bernard, *The Story of Judaism,* Schocken Books, New York, 1970, pp. 393-394.

9. Jetzinger, Franz, *Hitler's Youth,* London, 1958, p. 273. (*Op. cit.,* Gilbert, p. 13.)

10. Cf. Luther, Martin, *Von den Juden und ihren Lugen* ("On the Jews and Their Lies"), Wittenburg, 1543. In this document, Luther advocates burning down synagogues, depriving Jews of their homes, and driving them from the country forever. Not until after the Holocaust did some branches of Lutherans re-examine and disavow the attitudes of their founder. Roman Catholics have also changed many of their teachings about Jews since the Holocaust.

11. Taylor, James, and Shaw, Warren, *The Third Reich Almanac,* World Almanac Books, New York, 1987, p. 238.

12. Genesis 12:3.

13. Raphael, Chaim, *Journey from Babylon,* Harper and Row, New York, 1985, p. 134.

14. Cf. Cayce, Edgar Evans, *Edgar Cayce on Atlantis,* Association for Research and Enlightenment, Inc., Virginia Beach, Va., 1968.

15. Deuteronomy 13:13. Judaism, in contrast to modern anthropology, teaches that humanity began with a monotheistic world view and only

later degenerated into polytheism and idolatry. According to tradition, the worship of idols is believed to have begun in the days of Enosh, the great-grandson of Adam, in the days before the Flood.

16. Hertz, Dr. J.H., *Pentateuch and Haftarahs*, Soncino Press, London, 1987, p. 807.

17. Plaut, W. Gunther, *The Torah: A Modern Commentary*, Union of American Hebrew Congregations, New York, 1981, p. 1431. (English translation from Jewish Publication Society, 1967.)

18. Deuteronomy 6:4.

19. Based on II Samuel 7:23: "And who is like Your people Israel, one nation (or "a unique nation") on the earth . . . ?"

20. Genesis 14:18.

21. From a lecture by Rabbi Zalman Schachter-Shalomi, 1982. Schachter-Shalomi, who currently teaches at the Reconstructionist Rabbinical College, has developed an in-depth presentation in which he uses the framework of the four astrological ages (Taurus, Aries, Pisces, and Aquarius) to trace the evolution of Jewish ritual. Included in this presentation is the above reference to Melchezedek as the "last High Priest of the Age of Taurus" passing monotheism on to Abraham. Although I heard this lecture several times while studying under Reb Zalman from 1980-'82, I do not know of any place where it can be found in print. His basis comes from kabbalistic sources and the longstanding Jewish tradition that there were academies of Torah study (in whatever form the Torah took at that time) that had existed since before the days of the Flood. A brief reference to Schachter-Shalomi's model using the astrological

Ages can be found in Waskow, Arthur, *These Holy Sparks*, Harper and Row, New York, 1983, pp. 172-173. On the idea of prophetic schools in Biblical times, see Kaplan, Aryeh, *Meditation and the Bible*, Samuel Weiser, New York, 1978.

22. Rosenzweig, Franz, *The Star of Redemption*, Holt, Reinhart, and Winston, New York, 1971. Rosenzweig went further than any other Jewish theologian before him in trying to find a place for Christianity in his philosophy. He was the first philosopher of either religion to suggest a "two-Covenant theology," in which two separate Covenants were made by God with both Judaism and Christianity. These two Covenants are equally valid but have different roles to fulfill. Therefore, according to Rosenzweig, Christianity does not "replace" Judaism but co-exists with it side-by-side. Based on Rosenzweig's work, the "two-Covenant" theology is now being further developed in liberal circles among both Jews and Christians.

23. *Op. cit.*, Cayce, Edgar Evans, pp. 161-164.

24. Cayce reading 877-26, May 23, 1938.

25. *Ibid.*

26. See "Essenes" in *Encyclopedia Judaica*.

27. *Ibid.*, p. 900.

28. *Op. cit.*, Cayce, Edgar Evans, pp. 53-60. This suggests to me the interesting idea that our bodies may have evolved from the animal kingdom before joining with our souls. If so, then "leaving the Garden of Eden" can represent descending from the spiritual plane to incarnate on the material plane.

29. Halevi, Zev ben Shimon, *Adam and the Kabbalistic Tree*, Samuel Weiser, New York, 1974,

p. 34. The verse in question is Genesis 3:21. One area where the Cayce readings and Jewish tradition differ, however, is in the number of such "projections" which took place. The readings maintain that there were five simultaneous projections, resulting in the "five races" of human beings. (See reading 364-13.) The Talmud, on the other hand, maintains that only one Adam was created, "that no one may say, my ancestors are greater than yours." (See Tractate Sanhedrin.)

30. Cayce reading 1302-2.

31. Pauwels, Louis, and Bergier, Jacques, *The Morning of the Magicians,* Avon Books, New York, 1968, pp. 223-232.

32. Taylor, James, and Warren, Shaw, *The Third Reich Almanac,* World Almanac Books, London, 1987, p. 282.

33. Rosenberg, Alfred, *Myth of the Twentieth Century (Mythos des Zwanzigstes Jahrhunderts),* published in 1930 in Germany.

34. Cf. Exodus 19:5-6.

Chapter 10:
Phoenix from the Ashes

1. Waskow, Arthur, *These Holy Sparks: The Rebirth of the Jewish People,* Harper and Row, San Francisco, 1983, "Foreword," p. xi.

2. According to Hitler's statements in *Mein Kampf,* he clearly was "impressed" with the way in which the United States had treated the Indians and saw the reservation system as a solution for the "Jewish problem" in Europe. For a well-documented history of the United States' policies of genocide against Native Americans in the nineteenth century, including the use of small-

pox-infected blankets, see Dee Brown's classic book, *Bury My Heart at Wounded Knee; An Indian History of the American West*, Holt, Rinehart, and Winston, New York, 1971.

3. Patai, Raphael, *The Messiah Texts*, Wayne State University Press, Detroit, 1979, p. 156.

4. Robb, Stewart, *Prophecies on World Events by Nostradamus*, Liveright Publishing Corporation, New York, 1961, pp. 42-46.

5. Cf. letter to the editors by Martin Poezinger, Jehovah's Witness Holocaust survivor, *New York Times*, May 14, 1985, reprinted in the April 8, 1989, issue of the Jehovah's Witness publication, *Awake!* Poezinger states: "As soon as Hitler came to power in 1933, he commenced a systematic persecution of Jehovah's Witnesses because of their stand of neutrality in politics and war. As a result, thousands of Witnesses became not only Holocaust victims, but also martyrs . . . " The Witnesses were known in German as *Ernste Bibelforschern* and were designated by a purple triangle.

6. Villasenor, David V., *Tapestries in Sand*, Naturegraph Company, Healdburg, Calif., 1966, pp. 106-108. See also in *The Book of the Hopi*, by Frank Waters, the chapter on "Hopi Prophecies."

7. Leviticus 8:10-12.

8. Isaiah 61:1.

9. Exodus 19:5-6.

10. Cf. Scholem, Gershom, *Shabbetai Sevi, the Mystical Messiah*, Princeton University Press, New Jersey, 1973, p. 52.

11. Talmud, Pirkei Avot 4:3.

12. Psalm 137:4.

13. Heschel, Abraham Joshua, *The Sabbath: Its*

Meaning for Modern Man, Farrar, Strauss, and Giroux, New York, 1951, pp. 8-9.

14. Patai, Raphael, *The Messiah Texts,* Wayne State University Press, Detroit, 1979, p. 271.

15. Cited by Skolnick, Arlene, *The Intimate Environment,* 1975.

16. Based on Talmud, Sanhedrin 97a-b.

17. *Ibid.,* Sanhedrin 98a.

18. *Ibid.,* Shabbat 118b.

19. Zohar I, 72b.

20. Talmud, Pirkei Avot 2:16.

Bibliography

Abramson, David M., "The Aquarian Jew," *New Age Journal*, pp. 30-36, 81-82, February 1984. Excellent article on "new age" Judaism.

Bamberger, Bernard, *The Story of Judaism*, Schocken Books, New York, 1970. Basic Jewish history text, from Biblical times to the present.

Berg, Phillip, *The Wheels of a Soul*, Research Centre of Kabbalah, New York, 1984. Jewish teachings on reincarnation by a disciple of the late Rabbi Yehudah Ashlag of Jerusalem.

Burke, James, *The Day the Universe Changed*, London Writers, Ltd., Quality Paperback Book Club edition, 1985. Book based on the BBC series about discoveries that changed the way we see the world.

Buber, Martin, *Tales of the Hasidim*, Vols. 1 & 2, Schocken Books, New York, 1947. Classical collection of stories about the lives of the pre-Holocaust Hasidic masters.

Cayce, Edgar Evans, *Edgar Cayce on Atlantis*, Association for Research and Enlightenment, Inc., Virginia Beach, Va., 1968.

Cranston, Sylvia, and Williams, Carey, *Reincar-*

nation: *A New Horizon in Science, Religion, and Society,* Julian Press, New York, 1984.

Dresner, Samuel, *The Zaddik,* Schocken Books, New York, 1974. Life and teachings of Rabbi Yaakov Yosef of Polnoye, one of the closest disciples of the Baal Shem Tov and author of the first book on Hasidic teachings and thought.

Eliach, Yaffa, *Hasidic Tales of the Holocaust,* Oxford University Press, New York, 1982. True stories of Hasidic Jews who kept their faith during the Holocaust. Very inspiring.

Epstein, Perle, *Pilgrimage: Adventures of a Wandering Jew,* Houghton Mifflin Co., Boston, 1979. Autobiographical account of a woman's personal search for Jewish spirituality in the 1960s. Although names have been changed, all the teachers described are real. See also *Kabbalah, the Way of the Jewish Mystic* by the same author.

Fleer, Gedaliah, *Rabbi Nachman's Foundation,* Breslov Research Institute, New York, 1976, pp. 55-59. Interesting material on the birth of a soul and its subsequent rebirths down through the ages.

Friedman, Thomas, *From Beirut to Jerusalem,* Doubleday, New York, 1989, pp. 277-278.

Gershom, Yonassan, *49 Gates of Light: Kabbalistic Meditations for Counting the Omer,* self-published, 1987. Available directly from the author, c/o Box 555, Sandstone, MN 55072. Experiential workbook for a seven-week process exploring Jewish mysticism and spirituality.

Gershom, Yonassan, "Shamanism in the Jewish Tradition." Article tracing shamanic and psychic practices through Jewish history. Included in the anthology *Shamanism: An Expanded View of Real-*

ity, edited by Shirley Nicholson, Quest Books, 1987.

Gilbert, Martin, *Holocaust: A History of the Jews of Europe During the Second World War,* Henry Holt and Company, New York, 1985.

Gnosis magazine #3 (Winter 1986-'87): Entire issue is devoted to kabbalah, both Jewish and non-Jewish forms.

Greenbaum, trans., *Restore My Soul,* Breslov Research Institute, 3100 Brighton 3rd Street, Brooklyn, NY 91053. Devotional excerpts from Nachman of Bratzlav. Very readable and uplifting.

Halevi, Zev Ben Shimon. Several titles including *The Way of Kabbalah, Adam and the Kabbalistic Tree, A Kabbalistic Universe, Kabbalah and Exodus.* Samuel Weiser, Inc., New York. Technical but accurate explanations.

Heschel, Abraham Joshua, *The Earth Is the Lord's,* Farrar, Strauss & Giroux, New York, 1977. Spiritual description of pre-Holocaust Jewish life in Eastern Europe. Reincarnation story, pp. 58-59.

Jacobs, Louis, *Jewish Mystical Testimonies,* Schocken Books, New York, 1977. Firsthand accounts of Jewish mystical and ecstatic experiences gleaned from a variety of classical texts.

Jacobs, Susan, "A New Age Jew Revisits Her Roots," *Yoga Journal,* March/April 1985, p. 34.

Jetzinger, Franz, *Hitler's Youth,* London, 1958.

Jung, Carl, *Man and His Symbols,* Aldus Books, Limited, London, 1964, pp. 67-82. Classic text on archetypal symbolism.

Kaplan, Aryeh, *The Bahir* (translation and commentary), Samuel Weiser, Inc., New York, 1979. Reincarnation references, pp. 46, 71, 77.

Kaplan, Aryeh, *Meditation and Kabbalah,* Samuel Weiser, Inc., New York, 1982. In-depth study of various schools of Jewish meditation, with clear translations of many source texts.

Kaplan, Aryeh, *Meditation and the Bible*, Samuel Weiser, Inc., New York, 1978. Traces Biblical references to meditation.

Khan, Hazrat Inayat, *The Sufi Message of Hazrat Inayat Khan*, Vol. I, International Headquarters Sufi Movement, Geneva, 1979. Excellent essay on Sufi understanding of reincarnation.

Klein, Aaron and Jenny, translators, *Tales in Praise of the Ari*, Jewish Publication Society, Philadelphia, 1970. Classical stories about Isaac Luria, sixteenth-century Jewish mystic. Explanations of the levels of purification in the afterlife, spirit possession, etc. Brief references to reincarnation, pp. 20, 26, and 40.

Kübler-Ross Elisabeth, *On Death and Dying*, Macmillan, New York, 1969.

Kushner, Lawrence, *Honey from the Rock: Visions of Jewish Mystical Renewal*, Harper and Row Publishers, New York, 1977. A modern Jewish mystic's thoughts and insights, told in short anecdotes. Chapter Six, "Gilgulim: Circles of Return," deals with reincarnation.

Langer, Jiri, *Nine Gates to the Hasidic Mysteries*, Behrman House, Inc., New York, 1976. Stories and experiences among pre-Holocaust Hasidim in Eastern Europe.

Langley, Noel, *Edgar Cayce on Reincarnation*, Warner Books, New York, 1988 edition.

Lanzmann, Claude, *Shoah: An Oral History of the Holocaust* (the complete text of the film), Pantheon Books, New York, 1985.

Levin, Meyer, *Classic Hasidic Tales*, Penguin Books, New York, 1975. Includes two Baal Shem

Tov stories, "Two Souls" and "Rabbi Israel and the Horse," which deal with reincarnation.

Maimonides, *Treatise on Resurrection*, ed. by J. Finkel, American Academy for Jewish Research, New York, 1939.

Miller, Rhonda, "The Dilemma of Christ-Oriented Readings," *Venture Inward*, Nov./Dec. 1986, Vol. 2, No. 6, pp. 13-18. Article on Jews studying the Edgar Cayce readings.

Mintz, Jerome, *Legends of the Hasidim*, University of Chicago Press, Chicago, 1968. Academic study of Hasidic folklore and culture. References to reincarnation, pp. 93, 127, 182, 190-191, 201.

Moody, Raymond, M.D., *Life After Life*, Mockingbird Books, Saint Simons Island, Ga., 1975.

Morse, Melvin, M.D., *Closer to the Light: Learning from the Near-Death Experiences of Children*, Ballantine Books, New York, 1990.

Netherton, Morris, Ph.D., and Shiffrin, Nancy, *Past Lives Therapy*, Ace Books, New York, 1978.

Patai, Raphael, *The Messiah Texts*, Wayne State University Press, Detroit, 1979. Excellent compilation of all classical references to the Messiah from Jewish sources, Biblical to Hasidic periods.

Pauwels, Louis, and Bergier, Jacques, *Morning of the Magicians*, Avon Books, New York, 1960, pp. 223-232.

Plaut, W. Gunther, *The Torah: A Modern Commentary*, Union of American Hebrew Congregations, New York, 1981.

Potok, Chaim, *Wanderings: Chaim Potok's History of the Jews*, Alfred A. Knopf, New York, 1978.

Raphael, Chaim, *Journey from Babylon*, Harper and Row, New York, 1985.

Robb, Stewart, *Prophecies on World Events by*

Nostradamus, Liveright Publishing Corporation, New York, 1961, pp. 42-46.

Rosenzweig, Franz, *The Star of Redemption*, Holt, Reinhart, and Winston, New York, 1971.

Rudow, Rita, *Voices from the Holocaust* (self-published). Available directly from the author, 6050 S.W. 27th Street #109, Miramar, FL 33023. A book of channeled poems, each telling the story of a Holocaust victim who is now on the "other side."

Sadeh, Pinchas, *Jewish Folktales*, Doubleday, New York, 1989. Contains five reincarnation legends: "Gehazi the Dog" (pp. 135-136), "Menashe, Alias Moshe" (pp. 162-163), "The Reincarnated Bride" (p. 243), "The Pony's IOU" (p. 354), and "The Father, the Dog, and the Fish" (pp. 361-362). Also many other Jewish tales of wandering earthbound souls and trials before the Heavenly Court.

Schachter, Zalman, *The First Step: A Guide to the New Jewish Spirit*, Bantam, New York, 1983. A useful introduction to Jewish spirituality.

Schachter, Zalman M., and Hoffman, Edward, *Sparks of Light: Counseling in the Hasidic Tradition*, Shambhala, Boston, 1983. Highly readable rewrite of Schachter's Ph.D. thesis on the role of the Hasidic Rebbe as a personal counselor and spiritual director.

Scholem, Gershom, *Kabbalah*, The New York Times Book Co., New York, 1974. Chapter on reincarnation ("Gilgul"), pp. 344-350.

Scholem, Gershom, *Shabbetai Sevi, the Mystical Messiah*, Princeton University Press, New Jersey, 1973. Chapter One includes a good overview of kabbalistic concepts and their impact on Judaism.

Schwartz, Howard, *The Dream Assembly: Tales of Rabbi Schachter-Shalomi*, Amity House, Inc., Warwick, New York, 1988. "The Tale of Malka Nehamah," pp. 87-89, deals with a soul reincarnated from the Chemielnicki massacres in Poland in 1648.

Schwartz, Howard, *Judaism and Vegetarianism*, Michah Publications, Marblehead, Mass., 1988. Not just a book on vegetarianism, this work covers many questions about Jewish teachings on ecology, holistic living, and world peace.

Siegel, Richard, and Strassfield, Michael and Sharon, compilers, *The Jewish Catalogue*, 3 Vols., Jewish Publication Society, Philadelphia, 1973. Jewish "do-it-yourself" manuals with very holistic approach to rituals, holidays, and life cycle events.

Stevenson, Ian, *Twenty Cases Suggestive of Reincarnation*, rev. ed., University Press of Virginia, Charlottesville, 1974.

Taylor, James, and Shaw, Warren, *The Third Reich Almanac*, World Almanac Books, New York, 1987.

Villasenor, David V., *Tapestries in Sand*, Naturegraph Company, Healdburg, Calif., 1966. Excellent compilation of Native American prophecies from many tribes. Hopi prophecies, pp. 106-108.

Waskow, Arthur, *These Holy Sparks: The Rebirth of the Jewish People*, Harper and Row, San Francisco. 1983. A holistic look at post-Holocaust Judaism by a well-known Jewish peace activist.

Weiner, Herbert, *9 1/2 Mystics: The Kabbala Today*, Collier Books, New Rabbi York, 1969. Personal encounters with a wide variety of Jewish mystics, individuals and groups, both traditional and radical.

Whitton, Joel, M.D., Ph.D., *Life Between Life*, Doubleday & Company, New York, 1986. Study by a hypnotherapist who regressed subjects to the *bardo* state between incarnations.

Wiesenthal, Simon, *Every Day Remembrance Day: A Chronicle of Jewish Martyrdom*, Henry Holt & Company, New York, 1987.

Winkler, Gershon, *The Soul of the Matter*, Judaica Press, New York, 1981. A Jewish Talmudic/kabbalistic perspective on the human soul before, during, and after life on the earth plane. Reincarnation discussed, pp. 17-22.

Yoga Journal, March/April 1985. Four articles on Jewish mysticism.

Yogananda, Paramahansa, *Autobiography of a Yogi*, Self-Realization Fellowship, Los Angeles, 1946.

Zuker, Simon, *The Unconquerable Spirit*, trans. by Hirschler, Gertrude, Zachor Institute, New York, 1980. True stories of faith and martyrdom of Orthodox Jews during the Holocaust.

Glossary

The following glossary contains vocabulary and technical terms used in this book. Hebrew pronunciations are a mixture of Ashkenazi and Sephardic, tending to follow the most common way in which American Jews pronounce these words. In some cases, both pronunciations are given. Although I am aware of the current system of Hebrew transliteration used by scholars, I have chosen to use spellings which will be easiest for the English-speaking reader.

Adonai (Ah-doe-NIGH): Literally "lord" or "ruler," it is used in place of the sacred four-letter name YHVH, which Jews never pronounce. See "YHVH."

aggadah (ah-GAH-dah or ah-gah-DAH): General category of non-legal Jewish writings, including parables, homilies, etc. Used especially of parts of the Talmud.

Amalek (ah-mah-LAKE): A Biblical character first mentioned in Genesis 36:10-16. Because the Amalekites attacked the Israelites from the rear (Exodus 17:8), they became the archetype of senseless brutality.

Ashkenazi Jew (ASH-keh-nazz-ee): A Jew from Eastern Europe or a descendant of such living in another part of the world.

Baal Shem Tov (bahl'-shem-TOVE): Rabbi Israel ben Eliezer, eighteenth-century founder of Hasidism. (Not related to the idol "Baal" in the Bible.)

Bahir: Jewish mystical text, attributed to Nehunia ben ha-Kana, first-century Jewish mystic. First published in the twelfth century.

Bardo (BAR-doe): A Tibetan word which Literally means "the space between islands," used to designate the plane of consciousness where the soul stays between earth lives. From *Bardo Thodol,* the *Tibetan Book of the Dead.*

bar mitzvah (BAR MITS-vah): Literally "son of the Commandments." A male Jew thirteen years or older. Also, the ceremony marking this religious coming of age. See "Bat Mitzvah."

bat mitzvah (BAHT MITS-vah): Literally "daughter of the Commandments." A female Jew twelve years or older. Also, the ceremony marking this religious coming of age. See "bar mitzvah."

B.C.E.: "Before Common Era." Used by archaeologists and others instead of "B.C." (before Christ) to avoid Christian connotations.

Belial (b'LEE-al): "sons of Belial," a Biblical term meaning "worthless" or "scoundrel." Used by Edgar Cayce to refer to an evil group of people who existed before the Flood.

Bet Din (bait DEEN): A rabbinical court, made up of three judges, one of which must be an ordained rabbi. Also the Heavenly Court.

B'nai Or (B'nay OAR): "Children (or Disciples) of Light." Originally a term from the Essene writings, where the "Children of Light" fight the "Children of

Darkness" in the Last Battle. Today, it is the name of a network of people dedicated to Jewish spiritual renewal. Founded by Rabbi Zalman Schachter-Shalomi in 1962. In 1985 they changed their name to "P'nai Or," the "Faces of Light."

Boddhisatva (Bode-hee-SAHT-vah): A vow taken by some sects of Buddhists, promising that, upon achieving personal enlightenment, they will voluntarily continue to reincarnate in order to serve as teachers to guide other souls.

Breslover (BRES-love-er): A follower of the eighteenth-century Hasidic Rebbe, Nachman of Breslov. After Reb Nachman's death, his followers did not appoint a successor but have continued to regard him as their leader in spirit to this day.

C.E.: "Common Era." Used by archaeologists and others instead of A.D. (Anno Domini, "in the year of our Lord," i.e., Jesus) to avoid Christian connotations.

chayah (KHAI-ah): Literally "living being." The fourth level of the soul, corresponding to the collective unconscious.

chesed (KHEH-sed): Hebrew word for "loving kindness" or "grace." Sephirah on the Tree of Life associated with the Right Hand of Mercy.

covenant: A binding agreement between two parties. There are three covenants in the Bible: (1) the Rainbow Covenant between God and Noah after the Flood, which applies to all people; (2) the Covenant between God and Abraham, which applies to all descendants of Abraham; (3) the Covenant at Sinai, between God and the Jews.

dybbuk: Soul of a dead person who possesses the living.

Gehenna (ge-HEN-ah): Purgatory.

Gentile (GEN-tile): A person who is not Jewish. The term "Gentile" is not usually used by Jews but is used in some places by the author because of its familiarity to the non-Jewish reader.

gilgul: Hebrew term for reincarnation.

halachah (hah-LAH-khah): Jewish law as revealed in the Torah and interpreted by oral tradition through rabbinical authority. Literally means "the way to walk." (adj. halachic)

Hasid (KHAH-sid): A follower of Hasidism (plural: Hasidim; adj. Hasidic).

Hasidism (KHAH-see-dism): A mystical, pietist movement within Judaism, founded by the Baal Shem Tov and characterized by fervent devotion to God and meticulous observance of the commandments.

ha'takah (ha-TAH-kah): "Transference." Older term for reincarnation; not commonly used today.

havdalah (hahv-DAH-lah): Ritual to end the Sabbath or a festival, using a braided candle, a cup of beverage, and sweet-smelling spices.

havurah (hah-voo-RAH): A group of Jews who meet informally for worship or study. See also entry in the Appendix.

hundredth monkey: A scientific theory which states that learned behavior, normally passed from individual to individual, can enter the group consciousness of a species once enough individuals have learned the behavior. (Cf. *The Hundredth Monkey* by Ken Keyes, Prometheus Books, Buffalo, New York, 1991.)

ibbur (EE-boor): Entry of another soul into a person for the purpose of a good deed or commandment; a type of "benign possession."

kabbalah (kah-BAH-lah *or* kah-bah-LAH): The collective body of Jewish mystical teachings. There is no one book called "the kabbalah." (adj. kabbalistic)

Kabbalistic Tree: Also called Tree of Life. A diagram of levels of consciousness, mapping energy flow in the universe and the human soul. Originally Jewish, it is used today by other groups as well.

kaddish: A Jewish prayer often said in memory of the dead. The text makes no mention of death but is an affirmation of God's majesty.

kallah (kah-LAH): A Jewish retreat gathering.

karet (kah-RATE): Literally "cut off." Banned or excommunicated from the Jewish people. In practice, this meant ostracism. Not generally practiced today, except among some Hasidic and Orthodox groups, where *karet* is similar to the Amish practice of "shunning" an offender.

karma (CAR-mah): Sanskrit word meaning "action," used in Eastern religions to refer to the Law of Cause and Effect. Jewish equivalent is "Divine Judgment."

karmic group: A group of souls that are connected together because of some experience in a previous incarnation.

kavannah (kah-VAH-nah or kah-vah-NAH): "Intention"; the inner focus of prayer; the "spirit" of the Torah. Also, a meditation before doing a mitzvah. (plural kavannot: kah-vah-NOTE)

kiddush (KIH-dish): Special blessing said over a cup of wine (or grape juice) to usher in the Sabbath or other holy day.

kiddush Hashem (KIH-dish ha-SHEM): Literally, "sanctification of the name of God." Jewish martyrdom.

kohen (ko-HAIN *or* KO-hain): A descendant of

the Jewish Temple priesthood from Biblical times. Although Jews no longer perform animal sacrifices, there are certain verbal liturgical functions still reserved to these descendants today. The status of *kohen* is passed through the father. Many families named Kohen, Cohen, Katz, Kaplan, and Kahane are *kohanim* (ko-hah-NEEM, the plural form).

Koran (ko-RAHN): The Muslim Holy Book, channeled through Mohammed in the seventh century.

Lamedvavnik (LAH-med-VAV-nik): One of the thirty-six hidden Jewish saints. The name is derived from the numerical value of the Hebrew letters *lamed* (30) and *vav* (6).

Lecha Dodi (leh-KHA-doe-DEE): "Come, My Beloved," a mystical Sabbath hymn written by Rabbi Solomon Alkabetz of the Safed community in the sixteenth century. It is sung today by Jews throughout the world on Friday evening and has been set to literally hundreds of tunes. This hymn contains beautiful feminine imagery, personifying the Sabbath as a bride or queen.

Lubovitcher (loo-BAH-vich-er): Of or pertaining to the Lubovitch sect of Hasidim. A member of this group. Lubovitchers follow the teachings of the eighteenth-century Hasidic master, Rabbi Schneur Zalman of Liady. The current Lubovitcher Rebbe (spiritual master) is Rabbi Menachem M. Schneerson, who resides in Brooklyn, New York.

Luria, Isaac: Sixteenth-century Jewish mystic in Safed, Israel. Regarded as one of the greatest kabbalists. (adj. Lurianic)

mashiach (mah-SHEE-akh): "Anointed one"; messiah.

Merkavah (mer-KAH-vah *or* mer-kah-VAH): Literally "chariot." A type of Jewish mysticism which flourished during the Talmudic period, involving meditations on the visions of Ezekiel and "palaces" of God.

midrash (me-DRASH): Torah commentaries of a non-halachic nature, often stories, legends, and exegesis from oral tradition. (plural: midrashim)

mikveh (MIK-vah): A special ritual immersion pool used by women after menstruation, by men after nocturnal emissions, and by all Jews for other purification purposes. A convert to Judaism is also immersed in the *mikveh*. (verb: to *mikveh*)

mitzvah (MITS-vah): Any commandment in the Torah. Colloquially, a "good deed." (plural: mitzvot)

nefesh (NEH-fesh): The first or lowest level of the soul, corresponding to the life force of the body.

neshamah (neh-SHAH-mah): Third level of the soul, corresponding to the intellect and also the "immortal soul" which survives death.

Olam Ha-ba (O-LAHM ha-BAH): The "World to Come" or spirit world.

prayer shawl: A ritual garment worn by Jews during the morning prayers. Often white with stripes, it can be any color or design but must have four corners with tassels, called *tzitzit* or "fringes," that are tied in a specific traditional way.

Reb (REB): "Sir" in Yiddish. Term of respect used by Hasidim, often denoting a teacher. In Yiddish it is used with the *first* name but in recent American usage can be used with the surname.

Reb Zalman (ZAHL-man): Rabbi Zalman Schachter-Shalomi. See "B'nai Or."

Rebbe (REB-uh): A Jewish teacher, not necessarily ordained; also, leader of a Hasidic sect, considered an enlightened master.

Rosh Hashanah (ROSH ha-SHAH-nah): The Jewish New Year, which comes near the autumnal equinox. It is a solemn day of judgment and repentance, on which the ram's horn (shofar) is blown.

ruach (ROO-akh): Literally "spirit." Second level of the soul, corresponding to the emotions and conscious ego.

Seder (SAY-der): Literally "order." The ritual meal on the first two nights of Passover. A similar meal on Tu B'Shevat.

Sephardic Jew (seh-FAR-dik): A person who is descended from the Jews who were expelled from Spain by Ferdinand and Isabella in 1492 or in subsequent persecutions.

Shabbat (shah-BAHT): The Jewish Sabbath, beginning before sundown on Friday evening and ending after dark on Saturday night. Celebrated with prayer, song, feasting, study, and story-telling.

Shema prayer: Central prayer of Judaism: "Hear *(shema)*, O Israel, Adonai is our God, Adonai is One." Also said on the deathbed.

sparks, holy: Fragments of Divine Light or consciousness that are trapped or enmeshed in the physical world. "Raising holy sparks" refers to elevating these fragments of Divine Light back to their proper place in the universe, i.e., restoring wholeness.

stetl (SHTET-'l): A small Jewish village in Eastern Europe, such as was portrayed in *Fiddler on the Roof.* Has a nostalgic connotation of "down-homeyness" and Old-World Jewish culture.

streimel (STRAI-mul): A traditional fur hat worn by Hasidic Jews on Sabbaths, festivals, and other special occasions.

Talmud (TALL-mud): A many-volumed compilation of Jewish teachings, both legal and non-legal, spanning 200 B.C.E. to 500 C.E.

tefillin (teh-FILL-in): Small black rawhide boxes with leather straps, containing specific passages of Scripture written on parchment, worn on the head and arm during morning prayer.

Third Destruction: Term used by some Jews for the Holocaust. The First and Second Destructions were of the First Temple in Jerusalem in 586 B.C.E. and the Second Temple in 70 C.E.

tikkun (tee-KUN): "A repairing," a reparation for past actions.

tikkun chatzot (Tee-KUN khat-ZOTE): Midnight prayer focusing on repentance and the coming of the Messianic Age.

tikkun olam (tee-KUN o-LAHM): "To repair the world." New Age equivalent: to clear up bad karma; planetary healing.

Tisha B'Av (tish-a BAHV): The nineth day of the Jewish month of Av, falling in July or August. A fast day, mourning for the destruction of the First and Second Temples, and the exile of the Jews.

Torah (TOE-rah *or* toe-RAH): Specifically, the Five Book of Moses; more broadly, the sum total of all Jewish teachings and commentaries, both written and oral.

tshuvah (CHOO-vah or choo-VAH): Literally "returning" to Jewish observance of *mitzvot*. In a more general sense, repentance. The correct idiom is "to do *tshuvah*."

vision quest: A ritualized retreat into solitude to seek guidance from the Creator. Usually associated with Native American religions. The Jewish equivalent is *hitbadedut*, "to make oneself dwell alone," taught especially by Reb Nachman of Bratzlav.

yahrzeit (YAHR-tsite): Anniversary of a death, usually observed by lighting a candle and making a donation or sponsoring a feast in memory of the deceased.

yarmulke (YAH-muh-kah): A Jewish skullcap. Available in many styles, the colors and designs have no religious significance but may indicate a social connection with a particular Jewish group. Traditional Jews cover their heads to show respect before God.

yechidah (yeh-KHEE-dah): Literally "unity." The highest level of the soul, which is united with the Creation and in touch with God.

YHVH: The unpronounceable Name of God. (Neither "Yahweh" nor "Jehovah" are true pronunciations and are never used by Jews.)

Yiddish (YID-ish): A language spoken by Jews of Eastern European background. Based on medieval German, it includes many words of Hebrew, Aramaic, and Slavic origin. Yiddish is the "mother language" of home and marketplace and is still spoken by many Jews in America and Israel. It is written in the Hebrew alphabet.

Yiddishkeit (YID-ish-KITE): Literally "Jewishness." The life style of traditional Jews including but not limited to observance of the *mitzvot,* holidays, customs, etc. Jewish ambience.

Yom Ha-Shoah (YOME-ha-SHO-ah): Holocaust Remembrance Day, marking the beginning of the Warsaw ghetto uprising, it is observed after Passover each year with memorial services and educational events.

Yom Kippur (yahm-KIH-per *or* yome-kee-POOR):

The Day of Atonement, holiest day on the Jewish calendar. Yom Kippur is a day of fasting, prayer, and repentance.

Zaddik (TSAH-dik): Literally "righteous one." A holy person, saint. Also a Hasidic Rebbe. (plural: Zaddikim)

Zohar (ZO-har): A compilation of Jewish mystical teachings and stories, first published in the thirteenth century, and attributed to the first-century mystic, Shimon bar Yochai.

Index

About the Author

Rabbi Yonassan Gershom was born in Berkeley, California, grew up in the Philadelphia area, and received his ordination from Rabbi Zalman Schachter-Shalomi, internationally known pioneer in Jewish spiritual renewal. Over the past fifteen years, Rabbi Gershom has developed and taught workshops on kabbalah, helping seekers of all spiritual paths to integrate traditional ritual with personalized holistic consciousness. His work has appeared in numerous periodicals and anthologies, and he is the author of *49 Gates of Light: Kabbalistic Meditations for Counting the Omer.*

Rabbi Gershom currently teaches at the Institute of Adult Jewish Studies in Minneapolis and serves as a nursing-home chaplain. His hobbies are gardening, camping, and nature study.

What Is A.R.E.?

The Association for Research and Enlightenment, Inc. (A.R.E.®), is the international headquarters for the work of Edgar Cayce (1877-1945), who is considered the best-documented psychic of the twentieth century. Founded in 1931, the A.R.E. consists of a community of people from all walks of life and spiritual traditions, who have found meaningful and life-transformative insights from the readings of Edgar Cayce.

Although A.R.E. headquarters is located in Virginia Beach, Virginia—where visitors are always welcome—the A.R.E. community is a global network of individuals who offer conferences, educational activities, and fellowship around the world. People of every age are invited to participate in programs that focus on such topics as holistic health, dreams, reincarnation, ESP, the power of the mind, meditation, and personal spirituality.

In addition to study groups and various activities, the A.R.E. offers membership benefits and services, a bimonthly magazine, a newsletter, extracts from the Cayce readings, conferences, international tours, a massage school curriculum, an impressive volunteer network, a retreat-type camp for children and adults, and A.R.E. contacts around the world. A.R.E. also maintains an affiliation with Atlantic University, which offers a master's degree program in Transpersonal Studies.

For additional information about A.R.E. activities hosted near you, please contact:

A.R.E.
67th St. and Atlantic Ave.
P.O. Box 595
Virginia Beach, VA 23451-0595
(804) 428-3588

A.R.E. Press

A.R.E. Press is a publisher and distributor of books, audiotapes, and videos that offer guidance for a more fulfilling life. Our products are based on, or are compatible with, the concepts in the psychic readings of Edgar Cayce.

We especially seek to create products which carry forward the inspirational story of individuals who have made practical application of the Cayce legacy.

For a free catalog, please write to A.R.E. Press at the address below or call toll free 1-800-723-1112. For any other information, please call 804-428-3588, extension 220.

A.R.E. Press
Sixty-Eighth & Atlantic Avenue
P.O. Box 656
Virginia Beach, VA 23451-0656